AMERICAN BREAKDOWN

AMERICAN BREAKDOWN

*Why We No Longer Trust
Our Leaders and Institutions and
How We Can Rebuild Confidence*

GERARD BAKER

TWELVE

NEW YORK   BOSTON

Twelve

Hachette Book Group

1290 Avenue of the Americas, New York, NY 10104

twelvebooks.com

twitter.com/twelvebooks

First Edition: September 2023

Twelve is an imprint of Grand Central Publishing. The Twelve name and logo are trademarks of Hachette Book Group, Inc.

The publisher is not responsible for websites (or their content) that are not owned by the publisher.

The Hachette Speakers Bureau provides a wide range of authors for speaking events. To find out more, go to hachettespeakersbureau.com or email HachetteSpeakers@hbgusa.com.

Twelve books may be purchased in bulk for business, educational, or promotional use. For information, please contact your local bookseller or the Hachette Book Group Special Markets Department at special.markets@hbgusa.com.

Library of Congress Control Number: 2023940235

ISBNs: 978-1-5387-0570-4 (hardcover), 978-1-5387-0571-1 (ebook)

Printed in the United States of America

LSC-C

Printing 1, 2023

For Kitty, Claudia, Eliza, Arabella, and Scarlet

CONTENTS

Introduction: What Went Wrong? ix

CHAPTER 1. The Great Distrust 1

CHAPTER 2. A Vote of No Confidence 28

CHAPTER 3. Selling Out: How Corporate America Forfeited
Trust 53

CHAPTER 4. Bad News 89

CHAPTER 5. Struggle Sessions 115

CHAPTER 6. Subscribe, Follow, Like, Distrust 140

CHAPTER 7. Trust Me, I'm a Doctor 164

CHAPTER 8. Mutual Mistrust 192

CHAPTER 9. Conclusions: Rebuilding Trust 214

Acknowledgments 241
Notes 245
Index 253

INTRODUCTION: WHAT WENT WRONG?

THIS BOOK STARTED out as an attempt to explore what has gone so badly wrong in America in the twenty-first century.

You don't have to be an extravagant pessimist or an America-hater to think that the last twenty years have been among the most dispiriting periods in the relatively short history of the United States.

At home: escalating levels of political strife and division; stagnating economic performance; financial instability; an alarming proliferation in social pathologies like addiction, loneliness, and suicide; a deadly pandemic and a chaotic response to it that has left lasting economic and social scars. Overseas: failure in one American military operation after another; the rise of authoritarian challenges to American influence; and a steadily accelerating decline in America's status as the lone global superpower. Springing from all this, a widening loss of faith—from all political sides—in the very ideas and values that America has stood for.

I'll be the first to acknowledge that attempting a single-volume explanation of all this seems a tall order. But it seemed especially important to me, as an immigrant to this country who has made his home, raised a family, and enjoyed a happy and rewarding career here, to try to understand what could have gone wrong—in such a short period of time—and to offer at least some ideas on how to fix it.

As it happens, this era of American breakdown has largely coincided with my own presence on these shores—I hope the two aren't connected. I came to America near the turn of the last century, when American prestige and power was at its zenith. Like millions of immigrants before me I was drawn by the irresistible allure of a country and a people forged in pursuit of a universal ideal they had succeeded spectacularly in achieving.

Of course America has had deep, scarring flaws from the nation's very founding—and long periods throughout its history in which its virtues sometimes seemed to be less of a match for its challenges. But time and again, it has been the country's demonstrated ability to meet and overcome these challenges, to continually reform and improve itself that actually makes America an even more admirable model.

I came of age in the Cold War, my formative years spent in a Britain in which, for all its own proud history as a democracy and its outsize influence in forging a great civilization, there was much doubt about the future of what we stood for and defended. We were engaged on the side of the United States in another existential struggle for freedom, but there were many in Britain and Europe who were doubtful about whether the American system—which seemed to some like an unappealingly harsh form of freedom, with its taste for untethered capitalism and its apparently extreme elevation of individual rights—was really the best model for human civilization. Perhaps there were virtues in a more collectivist, even socialist approach; certainly, much of the European population seemed to believe so.

It was in the heat of these debates that I first visited the United States as a young man in 1986. As it happens, I had also just recently visited the Soviet Union for the first (and only) time. The effect on me of the contrast between the two experiences was life-altering: it was as though someone had turned on a light bulb in my head. America was vibrant, colorful, diverse, hopeful, and its people were busy creating things; building, moving, arguing, constantly examining their lives, their society, and always coming up with ways to improve it, even beyond the levels of prosperity and freedom already enjoyed.

The USSR by contrast was like a prison; gray, bleak, its people immiserated and incarcerated in a system they had not chosen and could do nothing to change, cowed by years of repression, worn down by economic failure and the fear induced by the totalitarian system.

It was evident to me that America—for all its many faults—was not just a more successful country. It was a morally superior country—its system the closest we had, in many centuries of developing human dignity, to the best model the world had ever come up with.

Ten years later, in 1996, I was happy to call America my home—arriving here to take up a job in journalism, accompanied by my small but growing family.

By then America had if anything reached a new zenith.

As the twentieth century ended, Americans could look back on it and reflect that they had won the Cold War, triumphed in two hot ones, helped liberate half the planet from history's most dehumanizing ideologies, advanced a free market capitalism that had led more humans out of poverty than any economic system ever devised, birthed new waves of technology that were changing the way people lived, worked, and communicated, and given the world the most flourishing bounty of intellectual, cultural, and scientific capital since the Enlightenment.

If you looked closely, sure, you could see the small cracks beginning to open in the edifice of success—rising political polarization;

the steady creep of corrosive ideology through the nation's cultural institutions; a growing hubris about the country's ability to shape the world; but it seemed invincible and secure. Yet even as they acknowledged that their nation was a continuing work in progress, Americans could—and did—look at themselves and the country they had built with satisfaction, honor, and immense pride.

A quarter of a century later the cracks have opened up into vast, corrosive seams, weakening the cohesion of American democracy and society, and threatening to break the nation apart altogether.

Throughout all this I have had an unrivaled opportunity to witness and reflect on this American breakdown—in a succession of roles as reporter, editor, and commentator for several major global news organizations.

As I reflected on the steadily growing rot in the American project, it became clear that a common factor lay behind the national breakdown. Trust, the essential bond that holds any society together, was unraveling. Americans were not simply divided against one another, disappointed in the failures of successive governments and losing faith in the country's ability to meet its challenges. Something much more corrosive was at work. Vast numbers of Americans no longer seemed to have trust in their leaders, in their important social and civil institutions, even in their common values and ideals, or ultimately in one another.

This struck me most clearly in the field of journalism, in which I had spent my career. In my lifetime the news business has gone from being an institution that—for all its many faults—was relied on by most Americans to give them a broadly accurate, fair picture of the news to one that is no longer trusted at all by most people.

No one ever believed everything they read in newspapers or saw on television, but thirty years ago the majority of Americans saw the news for what it was. Journalism was a generally honest effort by imperfect but decent people doing their best to report what was happening in the most accurate and fairest way they could. Their goal was to give citizens the information they needed and wanted about their country, the world, their government, leading companies, and other institutions to help them make informed decisions, based on their own interpretations and opinions.

Thirty years later, the reputation of the news media is so damaged that to hear someone talk about journalism that is generally believed and trusted sounds like something from ancient history.

There are still plenty of honorable people in journalism, committed to reporting and explaining the news in an impartial or, to use a now inexplicably discredited term, objective way. My colleagues at the *Wall Street Journal*, a newspaper that continues to strive to maintain the highest standards, are an example.

But these days so much journalism is practiced by people who do not even strive to achieve this basic objective. Instead they seem to believe they have a superior intellectual and moral understanding and are anointed with a divinely ordained obligation to guide the unseeing masses to a higher truth that has been revealed only to the journalists themselves. This frees them from the cumbersome obligation to be fair or seek objective truth and instead commits them to promoting an ideological perspective, to propagate a particular political and cultural orthodoxy. In almost all traditional and modern media, news is now indistinguishable from opinion, polemic, and propaganda. No wonder surveys tell us that large majorities of Americans don't trust it.

As I saw what had happened to my own trade, I began to understand that the media was not the only institution in America that had forfeited the confidence of large numbers of Americans. In fact this collapse in trust was the common flaw undermining so many institutions in America.

Just as for modern news, there is a widening gulf between the people responsible for it and most of the country; so it is with America's most important political, cultural, and economic institutions.

On the one hand, the elites, the new establishment, expensively educated, versed in all the modern progressive nostrums of the age on American culture, society, and history.

For this group—who comprise much of the nation's political leadership, almost its entire academic establishment, most of the people who control its news and cultural output, and a good deal of its corporate elite, the United States has never escaped its legacy of being an irredeemably malignant force for oppression and privilege. This modern elite rejects the idea that America has been a great force for good. Focusing on the baleful aspects of the nation's history and the continuing challenges the country faces today, it ignores the overwhelming evidence that, compared with most countries in the world, America has been and still is a uniquely benign force for freedom and prosperity.

If the self-image of Americans a generation ago was that of a smiling GI receiving flowers from gratefully liberated peoples, today, for so many of these elites, it's a police boot stamping on a human face.

On the other side, ordinary Americans, who had always believed in their nation's virtues, even as they understood and accepted its many flaws. But they believed that the American values they had inherited were worth preserving, even as they would continue to adapt to changing circumstances and standards. These regular Americans were not inclined to repudiate most of the nation's history, tear down the icons of its creation, and engage in a cultural expurgation of its sins.

It is this growing gulf between powerful elites that more than anything has generated the destabilizing levels of distrust we now see in American institutions and society. This loss of faith and confidence reflects the distance that separated most Americans from their leaders over the last twenty years—in politics, government, the judiciary, education, big business, technology, even science and medicine, trust in which is a bedrock of any society's health and well-being.

Even up to a decade ago, large numbers of Americans largely trusted what they were told by media, corporations, judges, federal agencies, and public health officials. But too many times in the last ten years they have discovered that what they were being told by these organizations and their leaders was not true.

All this has been happening as other factors combined to further erode trust in these institutions. The record and performance of the leadership of public and private sectors in America in the last two decades has sapped the country's confidence in itself and damaged the lives and livelihoods of ordinary Americans.

The rot in our leading institutions through a quarter of a century of intellectual corruption by an ideological elite has matured at a time of broadening public malaise induced by twenty years of American political and economic failure that has undermined faith in the very system that made America great.

Administrations that pursued disastrous foreign policies and failed wars; political leaders and a permanent government that seemed uninterested in the very idea of national borders and the need to protect the country's identity; corporate leaders who pursued self-centered business strategies that led to financial collapse and economic ruin. And even as these actions and decisions were undermining the country, the people responsible seemed subject to no accountability—the burdens of their errors and self-serving decisions were carried mostly by the regular Americans who were not responsible for them. So the cycle of rising distrust, proliferating failure, and rising distrust continued.

At the same time, civic institutions in which Americans once placed their confidence have also seen drastic declines in trust. Trust in churches has been undermined by declining religious observance and shocking clerical scandals; labor unions, in retreat in the private sector but ever more dominant in the public sector, are increasingly seen as pursuing self-serving and politically motivated ends; even voluntary institutions such as community groups, social clubs, and charitable organizations have been abandoned in a country that has become more atomized and its citizens more isolated from one another.

Above all, this broad loss of trust in institutions contributed to sharply declining levels of mutual trust among Americans themselves. The basic faith people have in other citizens to play by the rules, obey the law, and accept their wider social responsibilities is as essential to a nation's success as the human capital of its population and the economic capital of business. But in the last ten years, survey data indicates that millions of Americans have stopped trusting one another.

This pathology of distrust across American society is eating the country away from the inside.

It's unsurprising that members of the elites who bear the primary responsibility for the failures that have created this distrust prefer to attribute the country's problems to other factors—usually to the people whose trust they have forfeited. Journalists, academics, leading members of business, and the permanent bureaucracy are quick to ascribe the collapse in public confidence to the rise of unscrupulous politicians, fomenting an extremist populism. They're right that the popular revolt against American leadership in the last decade or so has produced some ugly spawn. Conspiracy theorizing peddled by right wing figures and violent assaults on political institutions carried out by their followers have surely exacerbated the divisions in the nation and further undermined trust.

But to focus on the most extreme and hateful manifestations of public disillusionment is to miss the underlying cause. It is the misguided leadership of the last twenty years rather than the response to it that explains America's current plight.

This country didn't pass from success to failure in two decades because of the intolerable behavior in the recent past of some angry political extremists. America in fact hasn't failed. Americans have been failed—misled by inept and deceitful political leaders, deserted by predatory and mercenary corporate chiefs, and, above all, betrayed by a cultural elite that has exploited the very freedom this country gave it in order to undermine it.

Throughout its history America has done more for human prosperity and freedom than any other economic or political system devised. If it is failing now, it is because America is losing its soul, its very sense of purpose as a society, its identity as a civilization. The United States is in the grip of a modern ideology that disowns its own genius, denounces its own success, disdains merit, elevates victimhood, embraces societal self-loathing, and enforces it all in a web of exclusionary and authoritarian rules—large and small.

Repairing the shattered trust of this American breakdown will have to start with reviving faith in America itself.

AMERICAN
BREAKDOWN

CHAPTER 1

The Great Distrust

NEXT TIME YOU board an airplane, think—if it doesn't make you too anxious—about the number of different people you trust to get you safely to your destination.

You trust that the aircraft maker built the plane correctly, that its engineers were qualified and completed the job to perfection. You trust that the army of maintenance staff who inspect the plane every day and make the necessary adjustments and repairs also perform to the highest level and did their job thoroughly today. You trust that the airline has employed pilots who are properly qualified and that the airline has trained them to deal with almost any eventuality that can come about when they are in the cockpit.

You trust them not to have employed someone with a suicide wish or terrorist sympathies. You trust the pilots themselves not to have gone on a bender last night, so they're not hung over and liable to make some catastrophic error. You trust law enforcement to ensure that they catch the occasional pilot who might be incapable for whatever reason. You trust that the various regulators, accountants, lawyers, and everyone else whose job it is to ensure that the airline is a fit and proper organization are doing their job—that someone wasn't bribed or tricked into signing off on some corner-cutting exercise.

You trust the pilots and employees of other aircraft and airlines not to do something calamitously stupid that could cause potentially terminal damage to your plane. You trust that the air traffic controllers the government employs are all fully trained, competent, and alert. Maybe you're a nervous flier, but you read in a trusted news outlet that the airline has the best safety record in the aviation business, and you trust the reporters to have got the story right.

We could go on. In short, to take the simple step that tens of millions of humans take every day to be delivered safe and alive to their destination is a decision that rests on a mountain of trust in literally thousands of people—engineers, managers, pilots, accountants, lawyers, journalists, and government regulators—to do their jobs honestly, safely, and effectively.

Trust is the essential feature that allows society to function—and the more modern and complex society grows, the more important trust is. There are so many things we cannot possibly be expected to know that are needed to make that safe journey. When you take a flight you don't peruse the latest maintenance reports out of Boeing or Airbus, or flip through the accounts of those companies; I bet you don't try to look up the precise training qualifications and standards required of air traffic controllers or pilots, to see if they match up to the kinds of demands those jobs will place on them. You don't even know what those demands are. What most of us know about flying a plane and safely landing it somewhere could be written in triplicate on a postcard.

It's the same with everything we do—buying food in a supermarket or eating out in a restaurant; depositing money in a bank; putting our credit card details online so we can buy stuff effortlessly; submitting ourselves to the anesthetist who sends us to sleep before the surgeon we trust performs an operation that could save or end our lives.

"Trust but verify" is an old Russian proverb, but for almost all practical purposes, it's completely impossible. We can't verify that everyone who has to do their job properly for us to live and work and thrive is actually doing their job properly. So we place our trust in others.

Now imagine what happens when trust starts to erode. Maybe someone who works for that airline you were planning to fly has told you some troubling stories about drug-taking among the maintenance staff. You've heard there's been an outbreak of salmonella poisoning at your favorite local restaurant. There are rumors that the bank where you have all your money has made some bad investments and may have difficulty meeting withdrawal demands. There's been a news report of a cyberattack at a big online retail company, and millions of personal details have been acquired by criminals. The hospital we are about to visit for that surgery has, it turns out, recently lost several patients on the operating table.

Without trust we can't work, eat, bank, trade, travel, invest, even play. It defines our relationship with institutions, businesses, and government.

Adam Smith, the great philosopher and economist, noted that a defining characteristic of humanity was the willingness to bargain and trade; without trust that fundamental feature of our lives would be impossible.

"Nobody ever saw a dog make a fair and deliberate exchange of one bone for another with another dog," he wrote in *The Wealth of Nations*.[1]

Trust has evolved over time, of course. Early man trusted only family and his immediate community—and maybe he didn't trust them much farther than he could throw them. Gradually, the growing complexity of societies required increasing levels of trust in people we had never met—and different cultures and nations evolved different levels of trust.

Trust also determines the efficacy of our relationships with each other. Economists call the network of trust we build up in our relationships *social capital*, akin to physical or human capital as a crucial contributor to prosperity, growth, and well-being.

Francis Fukuyama, in his 1996 book, *Trust: The Social Virtues and the Creation of Prosperity*, explains the significance of trust this way:

> Social capital is a capability that arises from the prevalence of trust in a society or certain parts of it. It can be embodied in the smallest and most basic social group, the family, as well as the largest of all groups, the nation, and in all other groups in between. Social capital differs from other forms of human capital insofar as it is usually created and transited through cultural mechanisms like religion, tradition, or historical habit.

On the global spectrum of trust the United States is a relatively low-trust society. In some communities, in many Asian countries for example, a high level of trust is culturally established—meaning that citizens don't need a whole panoply of rules and legal contracts to ensure fair interactions between people. If you accidentally overpay a contractor in Japan, chances are he'll realize your mistake and refund you the difference without the need for you to take him to court. In the United States, it's quite likely that that contractor will be enjoying a luxury vacation or a new car with the excess funds you gave him, and you'll have to sue him to get your money back.

So in America we have legal procedures, regulatory structures, enforceable contracts to ensure that, when direct, interpersonal trust can't be relied on, we can all continue to live and work according to a basic understanding of fairness.

But, crucially, that system still depends on trust. It relies on trust in the institutions that we have created to facilitate, police, and enforce the rules of engagement and exchange. We trust the government to make and execute the laws. We trust the judiciary to interpret and implement the law impartially; we trust companies to make goods and services we need and want and make profits for their owners; we trust news media and cultural institutions to give us the knowledge that we need to make informed decisions. We trust professionals—accountants, architects, lawyers—to provide us with their services that make our lives easier. We trust scientists and the medical profession to act in our best interests so we can be healthy and happy.

These are the basic building blocks of our functioning society and have been for more than two centuries. But if trust is eroded, society's cohesion crumbles; the relationships that power an economy falter, and the effectiveness of governing institutions is weakened.

In America today this erosion has been under way for a couple of decades and has now reached a critical point. Trust in all of these institutions, all the pillars that hold up the edifice of American democracy and society, is crumbling.

The Gallup organization has been measuring trust among the public in the most important American institutions—from the presidency to the Supreme Court to big business, science, and the media—for fifty years.

In the summer of 2022, Gallup found that across fourteen key institutions, the average proportion of Americans who said they had "a great deal or quite a lot of confidence" in them was 27 percent. That was the lowest number ever recorded; in the 1970s, when Gallup started measuring the number, it was close to 50 percent.

"Average confidence was at least 40% from 1979 to 1990 and from 1998 to 2004," Gallup says, but now, "most of the institutions Gallup tracks are at historic lows, and average confidence across all institutions is now four points lower than the prior low (in 2014)."

Of the institutions Gallup has tracked consistently, only the military and small business have held on to the level of public trust they enjoyed fifty years ago. The rest—government institutions as well as big business, the media, public education, the medical profession, science, and technology—have seen the trust placed in them collapse.

Other surveys match these findings. The Pew Research Center has conducted similar surveys for thirty years, and it finds that the public's trust in most of the cornerstone American institutions has dropped sharply. The General Social Survey conducted by NORC (formerly the National Opinion Research Center) at the University of Chicago and the American National Election Studies at Michigan and Stanford have found the same broad decline in levels of trust Americans have in their institutions.[2]

Perhaps more alarming still is the decline in levels of trust Americans have toward one another. When asked, in the words of the General Social Survey, "generally speaking, would you say that most people can be trusted or that you can't be too careful in dealing with people?" the proportion of those saying people can be trusted has dropped from about half to less than a third in the last fifty years. This plummeting social trust is dramatically weakening the bonds that tie Americans together.

America finds itself then, at the end of the first quarter of the twenty-first century, a country fundamentally ill at ease with itself; a nation in which large numbers of its citizens profoundly mistrust the leaders and institutions that govern them, the businesses that supply them with their needs, the people who educate and inform them, and, increasingly one another.

How did this happen? How much further can it go? What will it mean for the unity or even the very continued existence of the United States? And how can we start reversing this long and threatening decline?

These are the questions I attempt to answer in this book. I'll examine the causes of the collapse of trust in all the important institutions of American life and of the trust Americans have in one another. The decline is long established and broad-based. Its causes are multiple and complex, and reversing the slide will be equally long and complex, but I believe there are ways in which both the institutions themselves and American citizens—who have demonstrated a remarkable capacity to overcome the greatest challenges in the past—can begin to restore confidence.

This is not intended as a politically partisan book. It's true that I approach the subject as a conservative, and a large part of my diagnosis of the trust crisis is rooted in what I perceive as the rapid advance of progressive ideologies in American institutions in the last thirty years or so. But there is plenty of blame to go around—politicians on both sides of the political divide have forfeited trust with their words and their behavior, and the loss of trust has been so large and so widespread that a simple one-sided political narrative would be insufficient.

First, an important word about the terminology.

When trust evaporates it can be replaced with either mistrust or distrust. While the two terms are often used interchangeably, there is a narrow distinction. Mistrust means simply the absence of trust—a kind of neutral condition that implies wariness more than outright hostility. You may mistrust someone you've never met before who's offering to sell you something, but you might be interested and want to investigate further.

Distrust is much more active and antagonistic. Distrust is what

7

you feel when someone you know and perhaps once trusted has let you down before. You aren't uncertain whether to trust them. You're certain you shouldn't trust them.

Unfortunately in America, mistrust—which can be healthy, a reasonable skepticism about whether to place your confidence in people or institutions—has given way over the years to active distrust—the belief among many American that, because of what they have seen and heard with their own eyes and ears, the institutions that compel their trust have actively forfeited it.

This underscores another important dimension to the notion of trust. In many ways the problem we face in America today is not a lack of trust but a lack of trustworthiness. It's not that Americans have suddenly, for no reason, started distrusting institutions that merit their trust, it is that the institutions themselves have become untrustworthy. As we shall see this forfeiture of trust by leading institutions is echoed in a perception of declining trustworthiness among many Americans themselves. In all kinds of ways, we have learned not to trust one another because we have done things that make us untrustworthy.

As Robert Putnam, a political scientist, said in a 2022 interview with NPR,[3] in "Trusting somebody who is not trustworthy is not a virtue. That's gullibility."

Think about that airplane analogy and the bad things that must happen for you to actively distrust the airline, and then think about the things that have happened in the first couple of decades of the twenty-first century and understand why distrust is now so widespread. Time and again institutions that had enjoyed high levels of trust in the past have betrayed that trust and in the process made themselves untrustworthy:

- A trusted government told Americans in 2003 that an enemy had weapons of mass destruction and was poised to deploy them against the United States, in an even more devastating attack than had happened on September 11, 2001, and that a war to disarm the country would be easy for the US military, who would be greeted with sweets and flowers as liberators.

- Trusted bankers and regulators told Americans in 2008 that the financial system was sound, that their money was safe, and when that turned out to be false, people discovered that it was ordinary Americans who would bear most of the cost in lost jobs and homes while those who had caused the crisis were bailed out by the government.

- Trusted technology companies told Americans the personal data they handed over was secure and that the new apps and platforms they were using were good for them even as these tech giants knew that neither was true.

- Trusted big businesses told Americans that the companies' pursuit of global markets would be good for the economy, create jobs, and lower prices. And when this turned out to be less than half true, these businesses turned themselves into propagandists of an ideology most Americans did not espouse.

- Successive trusted administrations and congresses insisted they were controlling illegal immigration across the southern border, even as the numbers illegally streaming across grew year after year.

- Trusted news organizations and commentators told Americans that the winning candidate in the 2016 presidential election worked with the Russian government to secure his election, a claim that was false.

- The incumbent president—trusted by his supporters, at least—told Americans that the 2020 election was stolen by his opponent and some combination of dead Venezuelan presidents and crooked local election officials in the United States.

- Trusted public health officials ordered Americans to stay home during a pandemic, insisting that they were following the "science." But over the next three years the "science" seemed to shift depending on those officials' objectives: on lockdowns, mask-wearing, and vaccine efficacy.

These episodes, coming especially after a time when Americans had so much reason to have trust in their system—the end of the Cold War and what seemed like the triumph of American-style liberal democratic capitalism—fed the distrust that now defines American politics and culture.

What happens to a society when trust collapses? Rising distrust is devastating to a nation's cohesion and sense of purpose, and in the United States today we are already seeing signs of the advanced progress of the pathology.

First, social and political disintegration.

Distrust is a primary source of conflict—in personal relationships, in international affairs, and in domestic conditions.

When one state doesn't trust another state's communications and fears its intentions, the risk of conflict is dramatically increased. It becomes necessary to protect against the possibility that the other side is planning something malevolent by preemptively striking. The nearest the world has come to nuclear holocaust arose over the Cuban Missile Crisis precisely because of this mutual distrust between the United States and the Soviet Union.

Domestically, our current climate in this country resembles mutually distrusting armed camps ready to do whatever is necessary to protect themselves and their values. In the last few years the level of domestic tension has engendered rising fears of a second Civil War, or at best, a formal national "divorce" and possible division of the once United States.

The events of January 6, 2021, were an alarming foretaste of this and happened precisely because of the kind of distrust that can undo a nation's bonds. Supporters of Donald Trump believed his claims that the election had been stolen—because they had ceased to trust not just their political opponents (including many members of the Republican party of which Trump was nominally the leader). They also distrusted the media's coverage of the election results, the words of experts who had validated the election, and even judges who had refused to uphold Trump's bogus claims. This level and breadth of distrust prompted them to believe their country was being "stolen." Their distrust was fueled of course by falsehoods told by the president and his supporters. But it stemmed from a much deeper loss of faith in America's political and cultural leaders.

Even if we stop short of this kind of violent expression of mutual hostility, rising levels of distrust can make political and social cohesion impossible. A Cold Civil War in America is making the nation harder to govern as differing political factions challenge the legitimacy of democratic authority. This is a phenomenon of both the left and the right in America. The right may believe in fictions of a "stolen election" and a "rigged system," but the left believes in a nation that is "systemically unjust" and "structurally racist." When the most vocal and dynamic forces in both main political parties reject not just each other's ideas but the very foundations of US democracy, the prospect of any progress in addressing the nation's problems are dim.

Beyond political conflict, rising distrust is tearing apart the fabric of a diverse society. America is among the most diverse countries on earth—full of people from different ethnicities, religions, and educational backgrounds, a country defined by the astonishing range of experiences of its people. For that extraordinary breadth of differences to cohere requires a minimum level of mutual trust. It demands at base an agreed-upon set of values and principles—or at least facts.

But the collapse in the faith people have in the biggest institutions of American life is having the opposite effect—driving them into their own narrowing fields of experience, and this in turn is not only leading to sharp divergence in the values that people hold—it is even cheating a divergence in the perceived facts that shape their world.

We live in what has been called a post-truth era. The lack of trust Americans have toward traditional institutions of authoritative information, such as government or the media, leads them to find their own sources of information—data, facts, evidence that suit their own views while excluding anything that might challenge them.

"You're entitled to our own opinion but you're not entitled to your own facts," quipped Senator Daniel Patrick Moynihan in the 1960s. How old-fashioned that seems now. Of course we choose our own facts and dismiss inconvenient ones.

When you do this, you open the floodgates to all kinds of falsity dressed up as truth. Conspiracy theories have always played a part in American culture and politics, but today they can hardly be labeled conspiracy theories as such because large numbers of Americans take them as truth. Again, this is a phenomenon common to left and right— whether it involves believing the country is run by a cabal of pedophile politicians who drink the blood of children, or whether some shadowy group controls the process by which federal judges are appointed.

The risk is that as distrust rises, more Americans choose to believe what suits them, and the very idea of consensually agreed empirical facts dissolves.

A third consequence of rising distrust is that it renders institutions ineffective at what they are supposed to do.

A loss of trust in government weakens the ability of government to do its job. We have seen this most powerfully in the uncertainty and caution that has characterized US foreign policy in the last ten years. The distrust engendered by the failures of the wars in Iraq and Afghanistan has made Americans deeply skeptical about further foreign entanglements. That in turn is reflected in critical national security decisions taken by successive administrations in the last decade—with potentially catastrophic results for the United States in a world in which its power is increasingly challenged by a foreign rival.

Rising distrust of science and medicine will make Americans sicker and less able to take advantage of discoveries and advances that will improve the quality of their lives. Distrust of educational institutions weakens one of the most critical pillars in building the human capital needed for a successful economy and creative culture.

Distrust of the news media undermines a fundamental principle of democracy—the accountability of powerful people and institutions by scrutiny and exposure. Distrust of big business reduces the effectiveness of American capitalism, creating tensions between managers, customers, workers, and shareholders. Distrust of technology dilutes the ability of Americans to gain from rapid technological changes and improving efficiency and productivity.

Voluminous research from the United States and other countries shows that widespread distrust also has a negative effect on civic engagement and even civil obedience and law enforcement.

In a 2000 paper, "Political Trust and Trustworthiness," Margaret Levi and Laura Stoker found that in communities where people had a high level of trust in leaders they were much more likely to obey the law and accept as legitimate the dictates of authorities, even if the rules contradicted their personal interest in the short term.[4]

Whether citizens judge politicians or government trustworthy influences whether they become politically active, how they vote, whether they favor policy or institutional reforms, whether they comply with the political authorities and whether they trust one another.

Conversely, when citizens have low levels of trust, they not only become less engaged in civic activities, they start doubting the legitimacy of the legal structures and processes they face. Low-trust societies, such as many countries in Latin America, are characterized by chronic lawlessness and declining incentives for rigorous law enforcement. High-trust societies, common in Asia, are the polar opposites—with strong respect for the law and low levels of criminality.

There is also growing evidence that widespread distrust has a negative effect on economic performance.

In a 2022 paper for the Inter-American Development Bank, economists Philip Keefer and Carlos Scartascini examined the relationship between trust and economic outcomes in countries in Latin America and the Caribbean.[5] Their conclusion was that distrust directly undermined prosperity:

> It suppresses growth and innovation; investment, entrepreneurship, and employment all flourish when firms and government, workers and employers, banks and borrowers, and consumers and producers trust each other.

As trust declines, inefficiencies in the system multiply. Distrust means that "others will act opportunistically. They will make promises they can't keep, renege on promises they can keep, and violate norms to take advantage of other people who adhere to them. In short, trust is faith in others—in their honesty, dependability and good will."

Low-trust societies are characterized by high levels of tax evasion because citizens believe the money will be wasted or spent corruptly; loose compliance with laws and regulations; a lack of trust in customers and business partners; and a large informal economy with all the insecurities it produces.

A final impact of collapsing trust is on the health of society itself—the mental health of individuals, the value of relationships, and the sense of community that is vital for well-being.

In 2021, researchers Jan-Willem van Prooijen, Giuliana Spadaro, and Haiyan Wang examined the relationship between the perceived qualities of a nation's institutions and the social relationships within society.[6]

> Suspicion of institutions reduces trust between strangers, within-group cooperation, commitment and pro-social behavior, and increases prejudice, intergroup conflict, polarization and extremism. We conclude that institutional distrust and conspiracy theories erode the fabric of society.

What's more Americans are acutely aware of the damage all this rising distrust is doing to the nation's social cohesion. A Pew Research survey in 2022 found large numbers of respondents citing distrust specifically as being among the most serious challenges facing the country.[7]

"Some see fading trust as a sign of cultural sickness and national decline," Pew's researchers said. "Some also tie it to what they perceive to be increased loneliness and excessive individualism. About half of Americans (49 percent) link the decline in interpersonal trust to a belief that people are not as reliable as they used to be."

The scale of the damage that distrust is doing to America—politically, culturally, economically, psychologically—is crystal clear. So is the evident probability that all these pathologies will get worse unless something changes—urgently and radically.

To begin to understand what can be done it's necessary to ask: what has gone wrong?

Like Leo Tolstoy's unhappy families, each institution examined in this book has lost the trust of people in its own way and for different reasons, but there are some common factors that explain the wide collapse in confidence I set out.

To many of our political and media leaders, the primary source of the problem is simple: the arrival on the scene in 2015 of Donald Trump, a shock to America's politics and culture that has upended the established norms by which modern America has functioned for decades.

It's a comforting idea, and it's understandable why so many people favor it. Trump is a human wrecking ball whose behavior, manners, and rhetoric are explosive and frequently destructive. It's certainly true that he made a full-frontal assault on the biggest cultural and political institutions in America the centerpiece of his run for the presidency in 2016. It's also true that his own apparently uncontrollable tendency to tell untruths has done astonishing violence to any lingering idea that politicians can be trusted to be honest.

It's no accident that if you asked the leaders of the institutions that have seen the greatest declines in trust over the last fifty years—government, media, universities, big business—some version of "Trump's to blame" is probably the answer they would give to the question of why trust has declined. It's not their fault. It's all the fault of some malevolent lying narcissist, some serpent-like creature who corrupted America's Garden of Eden.

But the temptation to blame him for singlehandedly causing the collapse in trust in American institutions won't work.

To claim that things in twenty-first-century America were basically fine until an aging real estate mogul and reality TV star came along and destroyed trust in our institutions is an act of willful blindness. Trump didn't invent the mistrust and discontent that existed in America in 2016. He articulated it and exploited it with unusual skill, but to suggest that he is the architect of collapsing faith in America would be to assign him the kind of power and influence only he thinks he really wields. In any case, as I shall show in this book, the decline in trust measured by surveys and other metrics had been going on even before Trump was telling people "You're fired" on *The Apprentice*.

A more plausible version of this claim is the acknowledgment that large numbers of Americans had lost confidence in US institutions by 2015, but to attribute that to the behavior and rhetoric of conservatives over a longer period.

This idea states that, with its anti-government agenda, the far right, through its growing influence and ultimate takeover of the Republican Party, has been steadily seeding the idea in people's minds that American institutions can't be trusted over decades.

"Anti-government rhetoric has been the central strategy of the contemporary Republican party and the glue that most reliably bound together its coalition dating back to Barry Goldwater and the rise of the conservative movement within the GOP," wrote Amy Fried and Douglas Harris, two professors of political science in the *Washington Post* in 2021.[8] "This strategy has proved powerful in winning elections, undermining faith in institutions controlled by Democrats and waging successful issue fights without having to engage on policy substance."

It's a neat explanation that doesn't withstand much scrutiny. For one thing, trust in government was at consistently high levels in the

1980s, when Reagan and the supposedly corrosive Republican Party he led were in power. Back then it was, if anyone, Democrats who thought government was not delivering on its promises. It is also missing any acknowledgment of the possibility that many people are dissatisfied with government not because they have been brainwashed by conservative politics and media, but because, well, government hasn't done much that they approve of in the last twenty years.

In fact as an explanation, it's unintentionally revealing. Members of the academic elite casting blame elsewhere for the decline in trust in elites implicitly capture the problem itself.

This argument conveys the kind of self-awareness that someone might betray when they say, "People don't trust me anymore, and it's all their fault." In its arrogance it suggests that virtue is on the side of the establishment and that somehow others are responsible for vice in society.

It's reminiscent of the old Bertolt Brecht line about East Germany under Communist rule:

> Some party hack decreed that the people had lost the government's confidence and could only regain it with redoubled effort. If that is the case, would it not be simpler if the government simply dissolved the people and elected another?

The leaders of the elite institutions would probably like to do exactly that—swap the current ungrateful population of much of America for some properly grateful citizens who more fully appreciate the great work these institutions have performed.[9]

As Robert Putnam puts it, "We have been experiencing declining economic equality, the deterioration of compromise in the public square, a fraying social fabric, and a descent into cultural narcissism"—four horsemen stalking America.

What's especially galling about the attempt by the leadership of the institutions that have seen such a precipitous fall in trust to blame that decline on the people whose trust they have lost is that it fails to acknowledge perhaps the most important reason for the slump in confidence.

A proper attempt to understand what's gone wrong would explore the reasons for the vast gulf that has opened up in the last thirty years between those elites and the rest of the country. This divide takes many forms—economic; cultural; social; political. It can be recorded in widely different political outlooks and measured in disparities not only in income and wealth but also in social conditions such as levels of educational attainment. It is a gulf that is geographic as well as social and economic—with like-minded, highly educated folk clustering in the big metropolitan areas on both coasts and the less empowered citizens in smaller towns, suburbs, and rural communities in the middle of the country.

This divide is itself the result of a number of profound changes in the last thirty years, the most important of which is globalization. This is much more than the economic phenomenon of increased global integration that followed the end of the Cold War, whose consequences we have become familiar with. It is a much more far-reaching development that has played a key role in dividing Americans into two broad camps: those who see themselves increasingly as members of a global community and take on increasingly borderless ideas and values, and those whose beliefs and culture remain rooted in the United States.

The globally minded crowd represents a kind of overclass that has more in common with its counterparts in London, Paris, or Singapore than it does with its compatriots in Louisville, Peoria, or Scranton. Unsurprisingly, they are largely skeptical about or even hostile to restrictions on immigration and free trade. They turn their backs on and deride the very idea of national identity and distinctive American culture, and they prioritize planetary concerns—climate change, migration, shared ideological values—over the interests of domestically rooted Americans.

This overclass represents a new establishment that has occupied the commanding heights of almost all the major economic, cultural, and political institutions in the United States in the last thirty years. It is much more than the plutocratic business leadership that hops back and forth to Davos every year, and includes academics, journalists, entertainers, professionals, government bureaucrats, even teachers.

The development of this highly educated and powerful elite has resulted in a radical realignment of American political and cultural ideology. In part because it espouses a view of the world that emphasizes global connectedness and de-emphasizes national identity, the overclass has developed a relatively new belief system that has more or less displaced traditional religion as the cornerstone of a set of philosophical ideals and a creed for living. The rest of the populace, less influenced by these globalist ideals, remain mostly committed to traditional American values—as well as to religious beliefs. In the famous words of Barack Obama, uttered in an unguarded moment when he first ran for president, these benighted working-class types "get bitter. They cling to their guns or to religion or antipathy to people who aren't like them or anti-immigrant sentiment as a way to explain their frustrations."

But something else defined this new alignment. The self-imagined enlightened, globally conscious classes rose to economic, political, and cultural pre-eminence at just about the same time as a radical new ideology was progressing through the nation's universities and colleges and into the workplace. Variously called critical race theory, identitarianism, and other neologisms, the ideology placed an individual's race, gender, or sexual orientation at the core of their existence. It stemmed from the proposition that western society, but especially America, is historically dominated by privileged white, heterosexual, cisgendered males, and that that dominion has exerted itself in every aspect of life—from government and business to sport and language. The white supremacy of the patriarchy was so embedded that it could not be redressed by quaint ideas such as equality before the law or laws against discrimination. It required the acknowledgment that racism, sexism, and bigotry inhered in all aspects of life and society. The way to reverse these injustices was to elevate minorities above the historical oppressor class of white Americans. Among other things this meant that traditional ideas of merit, talent, and hard work as key drivers of advancement should be replaced by identity.

This was a powerful combination. A new ideology began shaping the minds of similarly educated young Americans just as American elites were shifting their focus from domestic needs and demands to more global, supranational ideals. There was no immediate, obvious convergence but there was considerable overlap between these two trends. On issues such as immigration, the elites who favored open borders overlapped with the ideologues who believed that since America was irredeemably racist, it had no right to stop people coming to its shores. On climate change, the globalists bought the arguments of climate alarmists that only planetary cooperation could save the Earth, and the ideologues attributed global warming to the colonial rapacity of white American capitalists.

The adherents to these ideologies became steadily dominant in American society over the last three decades and used their control of the key institutions to realize their goals. What they had in common, of course, was contempt for most ordinary Americans who shared neither the idea that the nation state was an irrelevance nor the claim that America was inherently evil.

The dominant position occupied by these people in the most powerful positions in government, the media, academia, big business, technology companies, entertainment, and elsewhere has—more than anything else—driven the wedge of distrust between the bulk of Americans and their leadership. The elevation of ideology and identity over the virtues of merit and hard work has been crucial in eroding the trust that ordinary Americans have in their leading political, economic, and cultural institutions.

But this progressive revolution at the top of American society is not the only factor undermining trust between regular Americans and their leaders.

The growth of economic inequality has played a key role too.

I explore the phenomenon in more detail in Chapter 3 within the context of declining trust in big business. But the effects of inequality are so pervasive that they need to be understood as an important driver of mistrust across the whole of American society.

A few statistics illustrate the scale of the gap that has opened up among the different classes of Americans. The shares of income and wealth of the top 1 percent and top 5 percent have grown dramatically over the last fifty years.[10] The Federal Reserve estimates that in 2017 the richest 1 percent owned 38.5 percent of the total wealth of the United States. The bottom 80 percent of the population owned about 15 percent. In 1965 the average chief executive of one of the top 350 companies in America was paid about twenty times the wages of his average employee. In 1989 that ratio was 59 to 1. By 2021 it was 399 to 1.

Not only have the wealthiest done spectacularly better than average workers but the prevalence of extreme deprivation has also shot up.

In many communities in the country, income levels among the poorest Americans are flat or declining in real terms. On top of that, the least advantaged are actually getting sicker and living less long than they used to, with life expectancy for white working-class men in the country actually declining for the first time in generations.

A clear majority of Americans have told pollsters consistently for more than twenty years that the country is on the wrong track, and similar majorities are deeply pessimistic. A survey by the *Wall Street Journal*/NORC in March 2023 found that almost 80 percent of Americans are not confident that life for their children's generation will be better than their own. The same poll found that almost half of Americans say their finances are in worse shape than they expected for their current stage of life.[11]

Almost all studies of trust indicate that widening inequality is a reliable predictor of declining trust as those left behind come to see the system as unfair, believing that those who have done vastly better did not achieve their success on merit, but because of unjust advantages.

Two other phenomena of the last thirty years have played a role in intensifying Americans' distrust for institutions and one another.

The first is the problem of sheer size. Economic trends such as globalization, industrial concentration, and rising numbers of mergers and acquisitions have created huge companies that are increasingly remote from customers.

Many sectors are now dominated by a handful of companies. The biggest companies in America have grown even bigger in the last twenty years. Walmart now employs more than two million people—almost doubling in size in the last twenty years. J. P. Morgan's total assets have likewise almost doubled since the financial crisis in 2008.

To be sure these are efficient, successful companies that have in large part grown by offering better services than the competition. But people find it much harder to trust big business over small businesses, and the sheer scale of these institutions leaves regular Americans with a growing sense of powerlessness.

As big businesses have gotten bigger, smaller businesses have disappeared. The rate of start-up growth in the United States has declined sharply in the last twenty years. The Kauffman Foundation, using its own research and US census data, found that the number of companies less than a year old declined as a share of all businesses by 44 percent between 1978 and 2012.

In recent years there has been a small reacceleration in the number of new businesses, but overall growth remains historically sluggish.[12]

According to the Congressional Budget Office, the rate at which firms were created declined from 10 percent of all new businesses in 1982 to 8 percent in 2018, and the share of employment at new firms (less than five years old) fell from 14 percent to 9 percent over the same period.[13]

As we shall see in Chapter 3, American trust in big business has dropped sharply in the last two decades, but the broader implications for trust are significant.

The size problem is manifest in other areas too—notably government.

In the 1970s federal government spending was somewhat below 30 percent of gross domestic product. In the last ten years—even taking out the extreme effect of the pandemic year in 2020—spending has averaged over 35 percent, and it is still rising.

Schools have grown exponentially. Undergraduate enrollment at the University of Michigan is 2.5 times today what it was in 1960. At Yale the number of undergraduates has increased by more than 20 percent in the last fifteen years. The picture is repeated across higher education.

The vast scale of the institutions may be justified in terms of economies of scale, or by the larger purpose they are serving, but dealing with these Brobdingnagian entities induces a sense of smallness in us. We feel overwhelmed and beaten down by the bureaucracy. The task of holding massive institutions to account is as difficult these days as summoning a customer service representative on the phone.

In his 2015 book, *More Human*, Steve Hilton, a former adviser to the British prime minister, now an entrepreneur and TV host, identified the problems for society as institutions get larger, more remote, and less accessible.

Summarizing the problem of scale and remoteness, he explained that businesses, government, and other institutions had become "too bureaucratic, too removed from the human scale. What we need to do if we really want to deal with the frustrations [people] have with the things going on in their lives is not to do with changing the policies or changing the government. It's about taking a deep look at the structural issues, the causes of some of these problems. We've got to do so in ways that are more human."

One final contributor to declining levels of trust should be mentioned here. It demonstrates how a higher level of mistrust—as distinct from distrust—can be beneficial as well as detrimental to society.

The explosive growth and ubiquity of information technology in our lives in the last thirty years has transformed them in multiple ways.

I explore this—and especially the impact of social media and big tech companies—in Chapter 6. But the advent of the internet, the digital accessibility provided by the smartphone, and the vast network of connections they have opened up have played a huge role in weakening confidence in almost all major institutions.

Too much has probably been made of the growth of "fake news" and misinformation on the internet in the last decade or so and its impact on decision-making. The evidence that factually false information and contrived fictions have changed the views of voters is thin. It seems in fact that they mostly have the effect of simply affirming views already held, rather than changing minds.

But there can be little doubt that personal technology and the access it offers to unlimited quantities of information has changed the way citizens behave in virtually all aspects of their lives.

In democratizing knowledge, enabling everyone on the planet to access data and sources that in the past were available only to a select class of gatekeepers, often qualified professionals, officials or researchers, the internet has empowered individuals at the expense of traditional authority.

This has clearly had benefits. People are no longer wholly dependent on mainstream news organizations for reports on and interpretations of events of significance. They can verify at least some of the information themselves—reading the whole of a government report, say, rather than an edited version, or watching the full video of a speech or protest rather than excerpts. In the past, news organizations, reporters, and editors with a conscious or unconscious ideological bias were able to convey what they wanted, with little accountability. Now anyone with a laptop or a smartphone and an internet connection can be a fact-checker, comparing one source of information with others. This has surely led to an increase in mistrust of the information coming out of traditionally powerful institutions, but it may be seen by many as an improvement on the past.

Yet in small and large ways this democratization of information has significantly helped undermine trust in other, less beneficial ways. Certain authorities—medical professionals, for example, scientists, and others with deep specialist knowledge—are uniquely equipped to analyze and interpret information and data. An untrained amateur, simply googling articles about these subjects, may well come across information that seems to contradict the authorities' account. But without the education or experience necessary to properly understand the data, the amateur's judgment cannot be set alongside that of the professional. Every doctor can tell stories about patients who have thoroughly investigated their own symptoms and challenges the doctor's diagnosis and prescription. Sometimes the accountability that offers can be a good thing. More often it isn't.

Anyone who's lost money to a fraudster, believed the lies of an unfaithful lover, or wasted an afternoon waiting for the repairman who swore he'd show up has learned the hard way that trust can be a two-edged sword. We have all learned the validity of the old saying, "Fool me once, shame on you. Fool me twice, shame on me."

A healthy skepticism and awareness that misplaced trust can be ruinous to prosperity, love, and life itself is an essential tool for surviving the vagaries of human unreliability. So too with our interactions with the institutions that dominate our society. No government, news organization, company, doctor, teacher, or scientist has ever or will ever demand our unquestioning trust.

But a high level of trust in these institutions remains indispensable for us to be able to function as members of a fair society, an efficient economy, and a successful democracy. The loss of trust among so many Americans in so many of these institutions in the last thirty years is having increasingly evident and devastating effects on America as a society and its prospects as a thriving country. Restoring that trust is a task for everyone and will demand effort and sacrifice, but it begins with the leaders of those institutions themselves.[14]

CHAPTER 2

A Vote of No Confidence

D ISTRUST OF GOVERNMENT is an American virtue. The nation was founded because the government that ran it ceased to be trusted by the people it ruled to pursue the general good.

The canons of the founding fathers, from the Declaration of Independence to the Federalist Papers, are disquisitions on the essential untrustworthiness of rulers, litanies of the many abuses government is prone to, and prescriptions for how to constrain the inevitable tendency of government to destroy liberty and ruin lives.

In just the second paragraph of "Common Sense," Thomas Paine's great revolutionary tract, the author succinctly makes the case that government itself—not just the tyrannical British monarch over the water—is inherently untrustworthy.

> Society in every state is a blessing, but Government, even in its best state, is but a necessary evil; in its worst state an intolerable one.

The Constitution itself, of course, was intended to ensure that the necessary evil was constrained as much as possible to avoid the intolerable one and still produce a government consistent with efficient rule. Its delegation of authority to the states, its elaborately constructed separation of federal powers, and its long list of individual freedoms protecting speech, the press, assembly, religion, the right to own guns, along with various rules to ensure due process at law, all proceeded from the fundamental American assumption that government could not be trusted and that without the protection of an independent judiciary, citizens would be oppressed.

It's no wonder, given the country's origins, and the controlling authority of a document rooted in such profound distrust of rulers, that throughout American history, this animus toward central government—and the struggle to manage it—has driven the nation's politics. From the founders' disputes about federalism, to increasingly contentious early debates about states' rights, to the Civil War—presented, if only speciously, by the Confederates as a battle to reign in an overpowerful national government—to waves of populist political movements in the nineteenth and twentieth centuries, to political and judicial battles over the New Deal, to the Reagan Revolution, the intrinsically American instinct to fear and distrust the power of government has loomed large and always received powerful political expression.

"There is danger from all men," John Adams said. "The only maxim of a free government ought to be to trust no man living with the power to endanger the public liberty."

No other major democracy in the world has had this thread of deep mistrust running through its history.

And yet, for all this long legacy of established mistrust, there is something especially perilous about the situation the United States finds itself in today. To some, perhaps, who take the long view, a lack of faith in Washington might be construed as not merely a historical continuation of a profoundly American trait, but even perhaps an affirmation of a great American good.

But this is too sanguine.

The distrust Americans have built up toward their government in the last twenty years not only runs wider and deeper than has ever been recorded by regular polling. It is also more intense, more destabilizing, and increasingly manifests itself in more disruptive and even violent ways.

The Pew Research Center, which conducts large annual surveys of Americans on a range of topics, has been measuring the level of trust in the institutions of US government since the 1950s.

Not surprisingly, since the 1950s and early 1960s are generally viewed by historians as among the most successful and harmonious in US history, in the early years after the Second World War, trust in the federal government was high.

In 1964, according to Pew, almost three quarters of Americans said they "trusted the government to do what is right just about always/most of the time." As the turbulent years of the 1960s and 1970s unfolded, that number dropped sharply, and by 1980, barely a quarter of respondents expressed that level of trust. But over the next twenty years, Americans' confidence recovered, and, after a short dip amid recession and political uncertainty in the early 1990s, by 2000, more than 40 percent of Americans were expressing faith in their government.[1]

But in the past two decades trust has collapsed again. In the last few years only one in five Americans expressed a high level of confidence that government will do the right thing.

Part of this decline reflects hyperpartisanship—a topic we'll review in detail in this book. During Republican presidencies, higher numbers of Republicans trust government; when a Democrat is in the White House, more Democrats express trust. But, strikingly, supporters of both parties have much less faith than they used to—even when their own guy is in power. When Ronald Reagan was president, at one point two-thirds of Republicans said they trusted the government. But when Donald Trump was in office, the highest trust number reported among GOP supporters was 36 percent. In 2000, under Bill Clinton, half of Democratic voters trusted the government. In the eight years of Barack Obama's presidency, the highest number was 37 percent.

The decline in confidence is not only broad and bipartisan, it is increasing in intensity. The proportion of Americans who describe themselves as "angry" with the federal government has almost doubled since 2000. Underlying this rising ire is that more and more Americans seem to believe that just about the entire political structure is illegitimate.[2]

The most dramatic illustration of both the power of this distrust and the danger it poses was demonstrated in the riot on Capitol Hill on January 6, 2021, when a large mob of angry supporters of Donald Trump stormed a session of Congress in an effort to prevent the formal certification of the election of his opponent, Joe Biden.

Although some Republicans and supporters of Trump have sought to downplay the seriousness of the episode, suggesting it was merely an outburst of "mostly peaceful chaos," that somehow mingled with a sudden influx of overexcited sightseers to the Capitol, the violence that day posed a serious threat to the orderly transfer of political power—perhaps the most important process any government performs. It—and the reaction to it by many Republicans who expressed support for it—revealed how fragile faith in the most basic institutions of government has become. It stemmed from false claims by Trump and his supporters that Biden had been illegitimately elected, propelled to a fake victory by some combination of nefarious actors involving dead Venezuelan dictators and live fraudulent voting machines.

But while the January 6 attack was easily the most egregious assault on the federal government in decades, it should be remembered that a refusal to accept the outcome of elections—a sentiment that strikes at the very heart of trust in government—has bipartisan roots going back decades.

In 2000, a near dead heat in the presidential election between George W. Bush and Al Gore had to be resolved by a Supreme Court decision. While Gore, the Democrat, accepted the final ruling, many Democrats did not, and claimed for years afterward that the election had been "stolen."

Again in 2004, when Bush won by a wider margin, many Democrats—in a curious foretaste of Trump supporters' fictions sixteen years later—alleged falsely that crooked voting machines in Ohio had flipped the state to the Republican. In the congressional vote to formally certify the election results thirty-one House Democrats and one Senate Democrat voted not to accept Ohio's count. That too was a preview of the more explosive action in Congress in 2021. In 2016 Hillary Clinton, the Democratic candidate, formally conceded defeat to Trump, but spent the next four years insisting the election was illegitimate, fueling outrage among many Democrats and widespread questioning of the authority of the Trump presidency, which was further inflamed by an extended period in which Democrats and much of the media claimed Trump had won thanks to claims of collusion with Russia that were proven false.

We could add to these fabricated allegations of illegitimacy the fraudulent claims by many Republicans after 2008 that Barack Obama had been born in Kenya and was therefore ineligible to be president, or that Democrats routinely voice distrust in a constitutionally established Electoral College that has resulted in a Republican winning the White House despite losing the popular vote twice in sixteen years.

But the larger point is that a hallmark of American politics for the last twenty years has been a growing refusal to acknowledge the basic legitimacy of election results.

The other branches of the federal government have also been the subject of claims of illegitimacy.

The US Senate, whose composition was carefully chosen by the Constitution-writers to give additional protection to the rights of states against a powerful federal government and a House that was more responsive to populist sensibilities, has been increasingly challenged by Democrats. They claim that the arithmetic that allows for two senators for each state produces an unrepresentative outcome, since states with small populations, more of which happen to be Republican, are disproportionately represented.

With similar logic, the Supreme Court's legitimacy has been under increasing challenge. Now that six justices on the court were nominated by Republican presidents and confirmed by a Republican-controlled Senate composed under these rules, a growing number of Democrats question the legitimacy of the court itself and want to radically change its composition.

When this court in 2022 voted to overturn the landmark 1973 *Roe v. Wade* decision that found a Constitutional right to an abortion, large numbers of Americans said they no longer trusted it. A Gallup poll in September 2022 found that the proportion of voters that held a "great deal of trust and confidence in the judicial branch headed by the US Supreme Court" had dropped to a record low—47 percent.[3]

Beyond this rising mistrust of government in the executive, legislative, and judicial branches is a deepening suspicion of the bureaucracy of the federal government. Institutions like the Federal Bureau of Investigation and the Central Intelligence Agency have always aroused significant unease among some Americans. Repeated scandals and evidence of abuses of power by federal law enforcement and intelligence agencies have been a recurrent feature of American government, especially since the Second World War.

But in the last few years public attitudes toward these institutions soured noticeably. This seems to have been in large part the result of rising mistrust among Republicans after revelations about the agencies' role in investigating mainly false allegations of collusion between Donald Trump and Russia. But there has also been evidence of a wider fear that the permanent government has become increasingly politicized.

The performance of institutions once held in reasonably high esteem has further eroded public trust. The activities of the Centers for Disease Control and Prevention and its leaders during the COVID-19 pandemic—demonstrating by turns desultory uncertainty and over-confident authoritarianism—weakened confidence in an agency that claims science as its guide.

The term "deep state," a phrase once associated with plots from thriller novels about nefarious agents pursuing conspiracies inside government, has entered the political mainstream.

Donald Trump—once again—has been the leading proponent of the claim that politically motivated officials in the bureaucracy used institutional chicanery, media leaks, and outright obstruction to thwart his aims and even bring down his presidency. Some of this can surely be ascribed to performative paranoia on the former president's part, and his appeal to the conspiracy theorizing that holds some Americans in its grip.

But some of it undoubtedly reflects a reality about a significant part of the Washington bureaucracy wedded to its own interests and objectives, irrespective of the outcome of elections.

It was Chuck Schumer, after all, the leading Senate Democrat, who actually cited approvingly the possibility that intelligence officials might seek to destabilize Trump if he challenged them.

"Let me tell you, you take on the intelligence community, they have six ways from Sunday at getting back at you," he said in an MSNBC interview early in Trump's presidency.

Other commentators, with no taste for Trump or right-wing conspiracy theories, have pointed out that the dramatic expansion of the security apparatus of the US government in the years following the 9/11 terrorist attacks had created its own state within a state with power that has not always been successfully checked by political oversight or control.

Alfred W. McCoy, professor of history at the University of Wisconsin–Madison, has written in his book *In The Shadows of the American Century: The Rise and Decline of US Global Power* of the emergence of a "fourth branch" of the federal government.

"Over the longer term it could be seen as a threat to democracy, creating a bureaucratic apparatus that's autonomous, even independent from both the executive and legislative branch," he said in a 2017 interview with The Intercept.[4]

The most troubling manifestation of rising distrust of the leaders, institutions, and officials of government is the steady rise in political violence in the last decade.

The Capitol Hill riot of 2021 is, as we have discussed, the most extreme example, as much for its goals—the overthrow of a constitutional process—as for the mayhem that unfolded that day. But there had been plenty of indications that escalating hostility toward representatives of the federal government was leading to acts of violence. In 2017, an angry Bernie Sanders supporter who had published online anti-Trump and anti-Republican screeds shot several members of Congress, including Steve Scalise, the third-ranking leader of the

GOP in the House of Representatives, at a congressional baseball game. In 2022, an armed man traveled from California to the Washington, DC, area home of Supreme Court justice Brett Kavanaugh, planning to assassinate him over his judicial views on abortion, before giving himself up to police.

The United States has experienced political violence before, of course, most recently in the 1960s, and the level of violent political activity in the last few years is still mercifully well below what it was then. That wave of violence stemmed from a similar loss of faith in governing institutions over a range of policy and cultural shifts. The civil rights movement and an angry backlash to the radical changes it brought in American society from some white supremacists was one important source of distrust and violence. US casualties in the Vietnam War and the impact of the draft on young Americans and their families was another factor that produced disaffection and radicalism. Extreme ideological movements of the era, particularly on the left, also encouraged a rejection of American government and institutions and sometimes the resort to violence that followed.

While the recent examples of violent extremism have been more isolated and sporadic than those of a half century ago, the disaffection and hostility to government seems broader-based and more inchoate this time, less focused on particular policies, but more on a wider sense of mistrust that is perhaps more menacing as a result.

In attempting to explain the decline in confidence in government, much attention, especially in the media, has focused on the turbulent years in which Donald Trump has dominated the political scene. Responsibility is usually laid at his door and that of a large swath of Republican politicians and supporters. It's certainly true that the former president's tenuous relationship with the truth, the ugly rhetoric he has deployed, and the borderline-insane conspiracy theories often believed by his supporters have played a part in undermining faith in political authority.

But the loss of trust has much deeper roots than Trumpian rhetoric and behavior. Indeed, Trump emerged on the political scene in significant part because of the deepening mistrust many Americans felt with the system.

What we have seen in the last few years is merely the extreme culmination of a trend that began two decades ago and is the product of several developments.

Three main factors have created the current conditions of widespread mistrust in the institutions of federal government: political performance, hyperpartisanship, and technocratic failure.

*   *   *

Trust in government is in part a function of the perceived performance by its citizens of the country it governs, and the simplest explanation for the loss of confidence in Washington over the last twenty years is also the most persuasive one: two decades of failure by political leadership.

There have in fact been few more demoralizing eras for the United States since its founding than the twenty-first century so far.

It has been marked by economic stagnation, financial crisis, foreign policy failure, declining American global power, and the loss of more than a million lives in a pandemic.

This record seems especially disappointing when compared with what came before. In the last decade of the twentieth century the United States had experienced a period of rapid growth and advancing productivity, won one cold war and a couple of hot ones, and was widely perceived to be the unchallenged superpower in what was memorably termed in two seminal essays at the time, as the End of History or the Unipolar Moment.[5]

Since we know triumph and disaster are both famously imposters, the scale of US failure in the last twenty years can be overstated. The euphoria that attended much of the commentary on America's standing in the 1990s was as overdone as are the lamentations about it now. In many ways America's recent travails reflect less on the performance of leaders in Washington and more on historic shifts around the world—the rise of China, and new economic powers in India and elsewhere, the challenges that globalization has surfaced, the devastating reality of a pandemic that was global. To that we can add a wider decline in the economic and cultural weight of traditional US allies—"the west"—in Europe and elsewhere.

But even taking a rounded, more global view of what has happened in the last twenty years, it's difficult to find much to celebrate in the achievements of America's political leadership, and given that at least some of the most important woes can be ascribed to specific decision-making failures in Washington, it's understandable that they have eroded public confidence.

The terrorist attacks of September 11, 2001, baptized the new century in an unexpected and horrifying way. On the one hand they represented an unprecedented body blow to American self-confidence. But they came at the end of that decade of post–Cold War exuberance, bordering on hubris, that tricked America's political leaders into overestimating the solitary superpower's real strength.

The immediate expression of national unity and widespread popular goodwill toward the administration of George W. Bush initially provided an opportunity to exact justice for the heinous act of terror and quickly restore American self-esteem and a reminder of its unique global reach.

The war in Afghanistan at first appeared to reaffirm the nation's strength. The toppling of the Taliban government that had provided safe harbor for the authors of the 9/11 attacks—achieved in that so-called "graveyard of empires" in the space of just a couple of months—avenged America's humiliation and suggested the United States could not only restore its preeminence, but use the quick victory to exploit it.

Wiser political leadership at the time might have built on the immediate success in Afghanistan to bend the new strategic realities to America's advantage. But the administration of George W. Bush instead made the fateful decision to press that advantage by invading Iraq, a decision that must rank as one of the worst foreign policy mistakes in US history.

Both the decision to invade and the communication of the rationale for it to the public had ultimately disastrous effects on public trust. Despite the arguments of some critics, the Bush administration did not willfully lie about Saddam Hussein's weapons of mass destruction, but it did mislead.

As Robert Draper captures in his book *To Start a War*, the case for the invasion was made by carefully selecting intelligence that supported a decision that had already been made for larger strategic reasons, and deliberately ignoring evidence that contradicted it.

Quoting Goethe, Draper's epitaph—"a man is not deceived by others. He deceives himself"—defines the Iraq tragedy.

The misdirection of the American people over the real threat from Iraq might have mattered less if the war had gone as smoothly as Bush and his top officials led them to believe it would.

"They promised us a war that would be quick, easy and cheap," a

European defense minister who supported the war ruefully noted in a conversation with me shortly after. "It turned out to be none of those things."

The failure to commit enough forces for the task or to have any kind of feasible plan for handling the post-invasion were catastrophic errors.

While many hundreds of thousands of Iraqis died, the human cost to the United States was, in comparison with, say, Vietnam or Korea, relatively small—4,400 lives lost and 30,000 wounded. But the strategic cost—to America's reputation and its influence in the region, to the credibility of its intelligence capabilities—was enormous.

Perhaps most damaging of all was the loss of confidence Americans had in their government—a loss that has sharply diminished Americans' appetite for future military engagement, undermining the nation's ability to project strength around the world. The costs of this caution have been felt too—with half-hearted military interventions in Syria and Libya under Barack Obama leaving the United States in an even weaker strategic condition in the Middle East.

Afghanistan was always deemed the "good war"—even by many critics of the Iraq conflict—but after the initial success, the United States became mired there too in a long and messy struggle to impose order and some kind of democratic rule. In 2021, after twenty years, more than 2,000 US military deaths, and 20,000 wounded, American forces staged a chaotic withdrawal as the Taliban resumed control of the country.

If these military and diplomatic disasters had occurred at a time of domestic economic success, the impact on Americans' relationship with their government might have been dimmed.

But the last twenty years have also been marked by economic stagnation, financial crisis, and deepening social dysphoria.

In the 1980s and 1990s the US economy grew at an average annual rate of 3.2 percent. In the first decade of the 2000s, the rate dropped to 1.9 percent. Between 2010 and 2019 it edged up to 2.3 percent, still well below the historic average.

The reasons for this stagnation are manifold, but two key factors stand out. Demographics have played a role: as the population ages, and now that most women have entered the workforce, growth in the labor supply is shrinking. Declining productivity growth has almost certainly played an even more important role. Since 2005, labor productivity has slumped—growing at an annual average rate of 1.3 percent, barely a third the average rate of 3.3 percent of the previous decade.[6]

Not all—or even much—of this stagnation can be ascribed to failures by politicians in Washington, of course. But failure to redress long-term economic weakness is obviously the responsibility at least in part of government. Leading left-leaning economists like Lawrence Summers, the former treasury secretary under Bill Clinton, have argued that the United States has been in a period of "secular stagnation," with weak demand. Conservative economists believe the slowdown is more to do with a larger state crowding out the private sector.

Whatever the diagnosis, the inability of government to come up with a prescription in the face of continuing structural weakness has undermined Americans' faith in Washington.

This chronic economic debility has played a central role in one of the most dismaying features of American society in the last twenty years. Social alienation, increasing drug and alcohol dependency, and family breakdowns, especially among certain demographic groups have become distressingly commonplace.

In their 2020 book *Deaths of Despair and the Future of Capitalism*, Anne Case and Angus Deaton, two professors at Princeton, chronicle the desperate condition of many white working-class Americans. The authors discovered that between 1999 and 2013, the fastest growing causes of death among middle-aged white Americans with relatively low levels of educational attainment were from drug overdoses, suicide, and alcoholic liver disease. The problem was so serious that for this demographic group overall death rates per capita actually increased over the period while for all other groups they continued their long-term decline.

As the authors said, "Those currently in midlife may be a 'lost generation' whose future is less bright than those who preceded them."[7]

No single event in the last few decades has weakened the bond between Americans and their government as much as the 2008 financial crisis and the Great Recession that followed.

It was not simply the scale of the crisis itself, though this was historic. For months in late 2008, financial markets were in freefall, with banks collapsing it seemed almost every week, and wider turmoil roiling the economy. The housing collapse that preceded the banking crisis was the worst the United States has ever recorded, with prices of some homes falling by more than 50 percent over two years.

The combination produced a financial insecurity that almost no living American had experienced. The average net worth of the typical middle-class American household halved from $107,000 to $57,800 in a year.

And then recession hit. The slump that accompanied the financial crisis was the deepest the United States had experienced since the 1930s. More than seven million jobs were lost in two years.

Yet perhaps most damaging to public trust in policymakers through this process was a gathering sense of injustice and anger.

Though the financial crisis hit Wall Street hard, Federal Reserve and government bailouts for many banks were seen by many Americans as favoring affluent Americans who had actually helped produce the crisis in the first place.

As millions of Americans lost their jobs and their homes, the leaders of most of the major banks stayed in place. Only a handful of executives faced criminal prosecution for their role in the crisis. The overall picture was of Wall Street plutocrats cozying up to their friends in Washington to bail them out from the consequences of their behavior while ordinary Americans suffered.

The sense of injustice was heightened by the uneven distribution of support for those affected by the crisis. Anger that some people who had borrowed extravagantly to finance big investments in real estate were able to walk away from their mortgages without cost was the initial spark for the Tea Party protests and political movement that began in 2010.

In his book *Crashed, How a Decade of Financial Crises Changed the World*, Adam Tooze, a financial historian, argues that, especially after the Iraq war catastrophe, the financial turmoil and great recession simply delegitimized the nation's leadership in the eyes of many Americans.

> The financial crisis clinched the impression of disaster. It was a stark historical denouement. In the space of only five years, both the foreign policy and the economic policy elite of the United States, the most powerful state on earth, had suffered humiliating failure.

There were other failures in the last twenty years that destroyed the confidence many people once had—not just in the administration or

Congress of the day—but in the wider political establishment; bipartisan failures that suggested there was something rotten, not merely with one political party, but with the whole governing structure.

High and persistent levels of illegal immigration seemed to draw little effort by politicians of either party to rein it in. Indeed "comprehensive immigration reform" backed by Republicans as well as Democrats looked like merely legitimization of the huge inflows of migrants over the last generation.

The official response to the COVID pandemic—first under Trump and then under Joe Biden—inspired little confidence in the nation's political or administrative leadership. First the Trump administration appeared not to take the threat seriously. Then, long after the virus had ceased to be a serious threat to the vast majority of Americans, the Biden administration insisted on keeping in place many of the irksome restrictions under which people chafed.

*   *   *

Declining trust in the efficacy and reliability of government has been, as we have seen, a bipartisan affair, with supporters and critics of both main political parties expressing growing distrust.

But the sharp rise in partisan sentiment that has been such a powerful feature of American politics in the last thirty years has clearly also played a role in diminishing confidence in the institutions of government.

The race away from the middle in American politics has been well documented. Pew survey data has shown a widening ideological gap between Democrats and Republicans. In 1994 there was a significant overlap between the two sides when voters were polled on a range of ten political values. But by 2014 the overlap had narrowed dramatically.

As Pew explains it: "Twenty years ago the median Democrat was to the left of 64 percent of Republicans, while the median Republican was to the right of 70 percent of Democrats. Put differently, in 1994, 23 percent of Republicans were more liberal than the media Democrat, while 17 percent of Democrats were more conservative than the median Republican. Today those numbers are just 4 and 5 percent respectively."[8]

This polarization diminishes trust in government, because the further apart the two sides are, the bigger the threat they see in the other to their values and even to the nation itself. If there is considerable overlap between left and right, and your side loses an election, you may not be happy about it, but you don't think you're going to lose your country. But when you have so little in common, each election represents an existential threat—a "Flight 93" election, as one writer described the 2016 contest, invoking the heroism of the passengers on the doomed flight on 9/11—the last chance to save America from collapse or tyranny.[9]

That attitude breeds enormous distrust of whatever it is the other side does when it is in government.

The problem is especially acute in the United States today because, by an almost freakish twist of fate, the country is not just divided into two hostile camps. It is divided almost right down the middle, with election after election determined by knife-edge margins.

Since George H. W. Bush was elected president in 1988, there have been eight presidential elections. In none of those contests has any candidate gained more than 53 percent of the vote. Barack Obama came closest in 2008 with 52.9 percent.

In the eight preceding elections, from John F. Kennedy in 1960 to Bush in 1988, on four occasions, a candidate received more than 53 percent: Lyndon B. Johnson in 1964, Richard Nixon in 1972, Ronald Reagan in 1984, and Bush. On three of those occasions the winning candidate got more than 60 percent of the vote.

America has become an entrenched fifty-fifty nation. Landslides were routine before the 1990s but are almost unachievable now. Obama's eight-point advantage over John McCain in 2008 is regarded as a crushing win. It wouldn't have ranked in the top eight margins of victory of the twentieth century.

The reason this poses such a particular problem for trust is that it makes the partisanship self-reinforcing.

For one thing, it makes it much easier for a candidate to claim fraud cost him the election. When you lose an election by 18 million votes, as George McGovern did to Richard Nixon in 1972, it makes no difference if a small number of votes were fraudulently cast. But if you lost by a combined 44,000 in three swing states, as Trump did to Biden in 2020, people can be persuaded that fraud changed the outcome.

But the narrowness of the margins of modern elections also changes the way the losing side thinks about itself and its ideological direction.

When it loses in a landslide, it knows it needs to revisit its platform and indeed its whole program for governing.

The Republicans after 1964 were forced to regroup and rethink, and repudiate much of Barry Goldwater's agenda. After the Reagan and Bush landslides of the late 1980s, Democrats did much soul-searching, ditched the tax-and-spend liberalism of Walter Mondale and Michael Dukakis, and embraced the "New Democrat" centrism of Clinton.

This is how healthy democracies work. Voters choose one party and reject the other. The rejected ones accept the results, jettison the parts of their program that were deemed unpopular, and try again.

But that doesn't work in a fifty-fifty nation.

No side ever really loses. A few points here, a few votes there and they would have won, so they convince themselves nothing really needs to change. In recent years they don't even have to acknowledge defeat but just claim the other side cheated.

The process is magnified by midterm elections. Two years after a party has lost a presidential election it gets a chance to undo part of that result in midterms.

In the last thirty years, of the five times when a new president was elected, on four occasions his party lost seats at the first midterms two years later. The exception was George W. Bush in the special circumstances of the fall of 2002, a year after the 9/11 attacks. That further helps create the impression that the party that "lost" the presidential election didn't really lose on the issues or the merits. Just wait a couple of years, and the pendulum swings your way. What's more, when that happens, both parties then have reason not to trust the government—since half of the elected branch isn't in their control.

*   *   *

One other factor that has diminished confidence in government in the last two decades concerns not elected politicians and lawmakers, but the record of some of the most prominent government agencies and their top figures.

In the 1990s, as politics briefly appeared to be converging on a post–Cold War consensus in which major policy differences over the economy, the size of the state, and strategic priorities would be narrowed, a new breed of technocratic managers emerged, experts in their fields who established reputations for superhuman levels of competence.

The personification of this technocratic elite was Alan Greenspan, the chairman of the Federal Reserve from 1987 to 2006.

Greenspan fit the part of this modern technocratic genius perfectly. He was a PhD economist who had run his own economics consultancy. He was initially chosen to lead the Fed by Ronald Reagan in part because of his reliable Republican credentials—he had served in the White House under Richard Nixon. But he quickly established a reputation for expertise above and beyond partisan politics.

Greenspan's pointy-head status was confirmed by all the usual physical qualities: his appearance—owlish, with over-large glasses framing a featureless face—and his manner—a lugubrious speaking style that included a tendency to speak in the driest of economic abstractions (he once told a puzzled interlocutor in a congressional hearing: "If you think you've understood what I'm saying you probably didn't hear me correctly").

Yet there was also some unexpected color to the grayness. As every profile of him ever written noted, he had played the saxophone professionally when much younger, and while he spoke apparently only the language of academic and market economics, it didn't stop him from enjoying a lively social life. He was a regular on the Washington party scene in the company of his second wife, the more animated and decorous Andrea Mitchell, a television correspondent for NBC News.

His early years at the Fed were rocky—punctuated by the stock market crash of October 1987 when he was just two months into the job. And his determination to signal a tough anti-inflationary approach in the runup to the 1992 election was seen by some close to George H. W. Bush as costing the president's reelection.

But it was in the 1990s that his apotheosis into the Most Trusted Authority in America developed. First, when inflation threatened to take off again in 1994, he persuaded his colleagues to head it off aggressively with interest rate increases. More remarkably, in the second half of the decade, he seemed to understand what no one else did—that the US economy was undergoing a technology-driven productivity miracle. So instead of raising rates again as the economy grew rapidly, in the normal way of central bankers, he allowed the economy to expand, unhindered by aggressive monetary policy.

It seemed to work. Between 1996 and 2000, the United States enjoyed its best sustained period of growth in twenty years, with little or no inflation.

Greenspan had become much more than a central banker. He had become an avatar of technocratic genius.

In 2000 Bob Woodward, unofficial chronicler of the history of contemporary American government, published a biography. The title, *Maestro*, said it all. It was hagiography—the story of how the greatest bureaucrat in history had revived the American economy. That same year, John McCain, running for the Republican presidential nomination, liked to joke that the most important thing he would do if he were president would be to renominate Greenspan for a record fourth term. He was so crucial to US economic success, McCain said, that if by some misfortune the septuagenarian economist should die in office, he would "prop him up, stick a pair of sunglasses on him and have him carry on as normal, like that guy in *Weekend at Bernie's*."

Few humans can expect that they will still be running things even when they're dead, and sure enough, Greenspan's days were numbered. In the next few years, the seeds of the 2008 financial crisis were sown, with massive subprime mortgage lending and an explosion of increasingly complex and risky financial products derived from them and other assets. The Fed, under Greenspan, was not only the intendant of the economy but had responsibility for the health of the financial system. But the Maestro never saw it coming.

As late as the end of 2005, just as housing prices were about to embark on the biggest decline in their history, he told members of Congress there was "no evidence" that prices would fall.

Greenspan, of course, wasn't alone in failing to see the crisis coming. Most central bankers and most economists in fact vastly underestimated the scale of the troubles in the system.

But after he had stepped down from the Fed in January 2006, just before the deluge began, it was inevitable that his failure to see the storm coming just months before the largest financial crisis in seventy-five years tarnished a reputation that had been golden for almost two decades.

It did more than that. It crushed the faith that many people had placed in the idea that there were skilled experts who should be entrusted with handling the most difficult tasks facing a nation. The spectacular failure of the Fed, central banks, and even economics as a discipline shattered the confidence built over the previous decade.

Greenspan was not by any means the only one whose technical expertise was supposed to steer the country through challenges over the last twenty years and who failed. Five-star generals failed to understand the task of dealing with an insurgency in Iraq for years before the United States was finally able to pacify the country. Top public health officials with impeccable credentials in fighting infectious disease floundered during the worst pandemic the United States has faced in more than a century.

The point is not that these officials were incompetent or especially blameworthy. They are human after all. It is that their failures undermined in a much wider way trust in the idea of an expert. If these great men and women with the deepest experience and knowledge could screw up so badly, why should we trust any so-called expert? That was a question that fed the rapid rise in mistrust in the last twenty years—and with it the ascent of populist politics, as voters began to resent being told by this same class of people that they, regular Americans, didn't understand the complexities of a modern economy and society.

We noted at the beginning of this chapter that distrust in a powerful government is a longstanding American virtue. It is a paradox of American history, that, despite that long continuous strand of skepticism about government since the nation's founding, government has in fact got steadily larger and more powerful.

It's true that by European standards the US central government remains quite small—and the relative power that resides in the states still larger than in a unitary system of government.

But the reach and heft of the federal government is steadily expanding.

At the end of the Second World War, US federal spending as a percentage of gross domestic product was below 20 percent. By 1980 it was almost 30 percent, and in the next few years it will approach 40 percent.

Successive government programs, so-called entitlements like Social Security and Medicare, are eating up a larger and larger share of the nation's output, but new programs too, such as Obamacare, have added to the scale of federal outlays.

Is this continuous growth of the state likely to make Americans, long suspicious of big government, more trusting of government? In the minds of progressives who keep expanding the scope of the executive, perhaps making the United States more like Europe will mean the answer may be positive. In Europe, with much larger welfare states, there has never been the deep-seated suspicion of government that exists in the United States, and certainly many Americans benefit from expanded government programs.

But there's another, more likely, possibility in America—that the burden of paying for bigger government is falling disproportionately on the most engaged and motivated in politics. In 2020 the top 5 percent of earners reported 38 percent of total aggregate income in the economy but paid 63 percent of taxes. The bottom 50 percent reported 10 percent of income but paid just over 2.3 percent of the taxes.

As they see more of their income taken by a federal government and they reap fewer of the benefits, their faith in what the government does may erode further.

As if we needed any more reasons for strife, this is likely to be an additional source of partisan tension in the years to come. Strong trust in government has never been a hallmark of the American political mind—for understandable reasons. It seems highly likely that as government grows ever larger, most Americans' trust in it will decline further.

CHAPTER 3

Selling Out: How Corporate America Forfeited Trust

P RESIDENT BARACK OBAMA had rolled out the red carpet in style, and red was the operative word. It was September 2015, and the president was hosting the first state visit by Xi Jinping, the recently installed Chinese communist leader, to the United States. The formal dinner at the White House that evening was a customarily glittering affair. Aside from the usual top ranks of leading politicians and policymakers and a scattering of prominent Chinese Americans, the guest list was dominated by figures from the business world, all eager to be in close proximity to the head of the world's second largest economy, the man who held the golden key to a market of one and a half billion consumers.

When China first began liberalizing its economy under Deng Xiaoping in the late 1970s, following the long dark night of autocratic misrule by Mao Zedong, American capitalists had coveted the opportunities the vast Middle Kingdom seemed to offer.

As the country's economy grew rapidly in the 1980s and 1990s, China promised to be an Asiatic El Dorado for US businesses, constrained by the limits of growth and the high cost of relatively well-paid American workers back home. Who cared about the human rights abuses—the massacre of students in Tiananmen Square in 1989, the genocide of the Muslim population in Xinjiang province, or the constant abuses and threats hurled at the free peoples of Taiwan or Hong Kong—when a billion or more Chinese were yearning to buy smartphones, watch Hollywood movies, access Wall Street financial services, or become fans of National Basketball Association franchises? Why worry about how a country that was becoming the United States' most menacing strategic adversary might use for its own purposes American know-how and technology when hundreds of millions of Chinese workers were available to produce goods and services for a fraction of what their US counterparts were paid? The ambitious American capitalist could always salve his troubled conscience—if he had one—by telling himself the comforting fable that, as China became more capitalist, its people would become more free, and the world would enjoy unprecedented peace, harmony, and prosperity.

The guests in the East Room that night dined on a culturally harmonized menu prepared by celebrity chef (and first-generation Chinese American) Anita Lo—consommé of locally grown mushrooms hinted with black truffles and accompanied by Shaoxing wine, butter-poached Maine lobster with traditional spring rolls, and a dessert display described as a "tribute to the beauty of gardens," complete with a chocolate pavilion and bridge and pulled sugar roses and lotus flowers. As they supped, the alpha-male chief executives of some of the biggest companies in the United States jostled for the attention of the Chinese leader.

The top table was a tapestry of the modern hierarchy of corporate America. Seated either side of the president and first lady and Xi and his wife, Peng Liyuan, were titans of Silicon Valley and Hollywood: most prominent among them chief executives Tim Cook of Apple,

Mark Zuckerberg of Facebook (with his Chinese American wife Priscilla Chan), and Bob Iger of Disney.

Each CEO got a few precious minutes face-to-face with the Chinese leader and used the opportunity to plead with the communist emperor for some special treatment for their business. One of the CEOs who was there described to me the scene that unfolded.

Zuckerberg told Xi that his wife was soon expecting their first child. He wondered if the Chinese president might like to suggest a Chinese name for them to bestow on the firstborn.

"No," he replied coldly, a little puzzled.

Iger told Xi that Disney would be launching its latest theme park in Shanghai soon and beseeched the Chinese leader to come and take part in the opening festivities.

"No," said Xi.

Cook noted that Apple now had hundreds of stores across China and hoped that one of them might soon be graced by a visit from the successor to the Mandate of Heaven.

"No."

The Three Nos, as some future Chinese chronicler may one day label the episode, must have created an atmosphere of excruciating awkwardness, though perhaps not as awkward as the scene at the after-dinner entertainment. For some reason the Obamas had decided that this party so carefully choreographed to emphasize the commonalities between the two countries should conclude with a set by the African American R&B singer Ne-Yo. The star performed his hits with commendable gusto in front of an evidently nonplussed Chinese leader and his wife. While the Obamas leaped out of their seats and gyrated enthusiastically, followed with varying degrees of energy by most of the American guests, Mr. and Mrs. Xi—herself a famed singer of a somewhat different genre—remained rooted to their front-row seats like stone statues in a Beijing flower garden. The dutiful Chinese official delegation, following their boss's lead, remained seated too, lending the entire proceeding an air of cultural dissonance that perhaps symbolically presaged the widening US–China rift to come.

But it was the craven importuning of the most powerful authoritarian on the planet by the leaders of some of America's—and the world's—biggest companies that told its own story about what had become of the United States in the twenty-first century.

Just as the bonds of trust between regular Americans and their political, cultural, and legal institutions have dissolved over the last twenty years, so the faith Americans once placed in the leadership of the companies that supply the goods and services to the nation has dried up.

The little vignette that played out at the White House that night—of wealthy and successful Americans cozying up to the communist leader of America's biggest rival power—vividly illustrates one of the main reasons for the erosion in that trust. US companies have energetically embraced globalization in the twenty-first century, and with it the logic of borderless markets, international trade and capital flows, and low-cost labor. In the process they have ceased to be, in a profound sense, American companies at all. The impact on their fellow citizens is familiar—the offshoring of high-paying jobs, the devastation of once vibrant communities, and the tsunami of social, public health, and economic crises that have followed. No wonder a vast number of Americans today view the nation's leading businesses with distrust.

But the globalization and the elevation of foreign opportunity over American needs that has been so eagerly pursued by chief executives is only one factor that has brought about a precipitous decline in the standing of corporations among the American public. Through their behavior, their public posturing, America's corporate leaders have forfeited the trust and played a critical role in weakening the ties of solidarity that are essential to the cohesion and functioning of a nation.

Of course, there never was some golden age of American capitalism, when grateful consumers enjoyed the finest products and services delivered by corporations committed to the highest standards of excellence in the pursuit of delivering maximum returns for their shareholders while treating their employees with dignity and respect.

We can look back on those gauzy advertising images of happy smiling families seeing the USA in their Chevrolet or enjoying the Breakfast of Champions and be tricked by nostalgia into thinking that there was once a time when the bonds of trust between regular Americans and the corporations that fed, sheltered, financed, and supplied them were always tight, sealing the success of free American markets and ensuring the prosperity of the whole nation.

There have been too many robber barons, too much corporate skullduggery and fraud, too frequent product recalls, company scandals, and financial crises throughout American history for that capitalist nirvana ever to have existed. From the Wall Street Crash to "Unsafe at Any Speed," the history of American companies has been a history of periodic excess, greed, and exploitation.

But for all those missteps, there was no sustained, widespread loss of faith in American business as a whole. Suspicion of big business, of unscrupulous corporate executives ruthlessly pursuing profit at the expense of customers and employees, has always been a feature of economic life. But, used car dealers, door-to-door salesmen, and a few other dubious sorts aside, Americans generally trusted business.

This faith has been one of the most important distinguishing features of American capitalism and politics. While in Europe, mistrust in business leaders and the corporate classes has long been endemic and has helped shape political conditions in those countries—fostering socialist movements and parties that dominated the left side of the political spectrum—in the United States, there was never a strong base of socialist sentiment calling for a wholesale replacement of capitalism. Americans may not have loved all their corporate leaders, but they understood the virtue of the market and the companies that operated in it.

This was in part a reflection of the genius of American capitalism. Americans largely believed in and trusted business leaders because they shared a sense of solidarity with them—if only because Americans believed they could, with talent, hard work, and a little luck, become one of them themselves. For most of the twentieth century, the American Dream seemed at least a plausibly attainable goal for most Americans. Not that many would become billionaires. But there was a high level of trust that the US economy operated on a broadly level playing field. It was affirmed by the fact that many of the business leaders who had achieved unparalleled success had started out with little or nothing.

There were entrepreneurial icons like Henry Ford or Ray Kroc, immigrants like Andrew Carnegie and Levi Strauss, and more recently men like Warren Buffett and Steve Jobs. Their stories not only inspired admiration; they seemed to confirm that America was a place of equality of opportunity. And that deepened the trust Americans had in business.

No longer. In the first decades of the twenty-first century something radical has happened: a startling, widespread, and pervasive collapse of trust in American capitalism. There may still be extraordinary icons of business success, but the pervasive sense is that the system itself is rigged against ordinary people.

In its regular poll of American voters Gallup has been asking people since the 1970s how much trust they have in big business.

In 1999, 30 percent of Americans said they had "a great deal" or "quite a lot" of trust. Only 25 percent said they had "very little" or "none."[1]

By the summer of 2022, those numbers had changed radically.

Today, only 14 percent of Americans say they have a great deal or quite a lot of trust in big business, the lowest number ever recorded. Forty-one percent say they have little or no trust.[2]

In less than a quarter of a century, the leaders of the companies that dominate our economy are regarded with doubt and suspicion by tens of millions of Americans.

Just as with our major political, academic, media, cultural, scientific, and social institutions, so with the organizations that create the wealth of the American economy. Americans no longer trust them.

And just as with those institutions, this pervasive mistrust is not the result of some devious campaign by unscrupulous politicians, wild-eyed conspiracy theorists, or the spread of misinformation on social media.

It's rooted in a simple reality: those corporate leaders themselves have forfeited that trust.

The loss of faith in leadership matters. If people don't trust business leaders to make honest, fair decisions, the success of the entire American capitalist system is at risk. Voters will demand much greater control and regulation of companies, which will stifle innovation and crimp investment—the lifeblood of economic growth. Mistrust between management and workers results in undermotivated employees, industrial strife, higher costs, and lower productivity. But above all, the fraying of mutual trust represents an erosion of the fabric of society itself, another line of cleavage in a country that feels increasingly at odds with itself.

Why have people lost faith in US corporations and the men and women who own and run them?

Multiple factors are at work.

The first is simply the increasing frequency of episodes of company men (and a few women) behaving badly—a string of notorious financial and corporate scandals. In the last twenty years the news headlines have been filled with a run of major corporate collapses, bankruptcies, and frauds. The scale and number of these scandals speaks to something quite rotten in the system of corporate governance, the various interlocking mechanisms designed to ensure the smooth, honest, and efficient functioning of American capitalism.

A second reason has been even more pervasive. Even when they aren't going bust, misleading investors, employees, and customers, or winding up in federal prison, American corporate leaders have lost trust by seeming to pursue agendas that suggest a lack of commitment to Americans and the values they have traditionally held. The pursuit of globalization places American capitalists directly at odds with millions of Americans. Shipping jobs overseas in a never-ending search for cheap labor prioritized their profits over the interests of the country.

The explosive growth of economic inequality has further undermined trust. The levels of wealth and income enjoyed by corporate executives relative to the pay of average worker have reached historically high levels. Americans have historically been almost unique in the west in refusing to submit to envy. Part of the historic success of the US economy rests in the fact that Americans have tolerated and even welcomed phenomenal wealth as a reward for success. But we have reached levels of inequality now that can hardly be justified by relative performance, and large numbers of Americans are starting to suspect that the system is rigged against them.[3]

This shift in wealth and income to the owners of capital and their managers is due in part to the relentless pursuit of scale by corporations in the last twenty years, which has resulted in a startling reduction in competition in most of the major sectors of the economy. Not only does this concentration raise prices and limit choices for consumers; it creates a growing sense of distance between individual Americans and the companies that serve them.

Furthermore, in a pure example of a vicious circle at work, companies have translated their unprecedented scale and economic power into political power, buying influence in Washington and state capitals. Their lobbying efforts there then produce legislation and regulation that tilts the playing field in their direction and further strengthens their economic might.

To all this we can add a relatively recent and highly pernicious phenomenon: as "culture wars" rage over issues such as race, gender, and sexuality and climate change extremism, corporate leaders have increasingly embraced the dominant nostrums of the modern progressive ideology.

By elevating environmental, social, and governance (the notorious "ESG" investing principles) goals, many business leaders have opened an even wider gulf between them and millions of ordinary Americans.

* * *

Corporate and financial scandals have always been a feature of American capitalism. Every now and then someone would be caught with their hands in the proverbial register. But in recent years they have become something of an epidemic.

In the first twenty years of the twenty-first century, the list of companies that have crashed or been discovered to be run by liars, crooks, cheats, or complete fools is long and familiar. Almost all of them had been widely hailed—in the press, among their corporate peers, by politicians whose largesse they enjoyed—as stellar models of American economic success, avatars of dynamism and entrepreneurialism.

Enron, Tyco, Worldcom, Bear Stearns, Lehman Brothers, Bernie Madoff, Theranos, FTX. The names read like a litany of greed, fraud, and the willing credulity of those who are supposed to hold them accountable.

It is particularly striking that these companies represent a range of sectors of the economy—energy; electronics and manufacturing; telecommunications; finance; technology—a scope that suggests the rot in American capitalism may not be especially deep, but it is broad.

The people who ran Enron, which went bankrupt in December 2001, were famously *The Smartest Guys in the Room*, the title of the definitive book, by Bethany McLean and Peter Elkind, on the company's fraud and collapse. Its senior managers devised energy trading strategies and other ruses that were so complex that the company's top executives, most notably Kenneth Lay, golf buddy of President Bill Clinton and megabucks fundraiser for President George W. Bush, didn't understand them. But if you're good friends with presidents of both political persuasions, who needs technical trading expertise?

The one thing that eventually became transparent, though, was that whatever the managers were up to, it wasn't honest. More than a dozen executives, including Lay himself, pled guilty or were convicted of fraud (Lay died before he was sentenced), and the company's auditors, Arthur Andersen, were found guilty of obstruction of justice, and Anderson was essentially dissolved.

As McLean and Elkind explain, the wider story of Enron was a parable of much of the moral compass of American capitalism in the new century.[4]

> The larger message was that the wealth and power enjoyed by those at the top of the heap in corporate America demand no sense of broader responsibility…Ethical behavior requires nothing more than avoiding the explicitly illegal…refusing to see the bad things happening in front of you makes you innocent, and…telling the truth is the same thing as making sure that no one can prove you lied.

Tyco, a name which itself seems to conjure swashbuckling American economic dynamism, followed soon after. In 2002, Dennis Kozlowski, the chief executive, along with his chief financial officer, resigned and were later convicted of more than thirty counts of fraud after it was alleged they had stolen more than $100 million from the company. In the trial, prosecutors explained how Kozlowski had spent the money he took from Tyco to furnish a Fifth Avenue apartment and to purchase more than $13 million worth of paintings, including a Renoir and a Monet. In a twist worthy of the best detective fiction, it was a ruse he used to avoid paying sales tax on the artwork that led to the discovery of the wider fraud.[5]

Kozlowski's extravagant taste in art was perhaps even better illustrated by a fortieth birthday party he threw for his wife in Sardinia, which featured, among other delights, an ice sculpture replica of Michelangelo's *David*, which spouted vodka from its penis.[6]

It may be hard to imagine a more powerful visual metaphor for the way in which plutocratic American capitalists viewed their relationship to their customers.

As Americans were still digesting the indigestible arcana of the lives of some of its more colorful chief executives, another scandal engulfed the head of one of the largest telecom companies.

Worldcom, founded by Bernard Ebbers, and at one point the second largest telecommunications company in the US after AT&T, had, like Tyco and Enron, grown rapidly through a succession of mergers and acquisitions in the heady boom of the 1990s.

By the middle of 2002, the company was collapsing under a series of accounting frauds engineered by Ebbers. As with almost all these titans of American business, Ebbers was being lionized by the media shortly before his downfall. He was named a member of the "Wired 25" in 1998, and a proud member of *Time* Magazine's Digital 50 in 1999. (The same *Time* magazine, without a hint of irony, subsequently named him the tenth most corrupt CEO of all time.)

The financial crisis that engulfed America and the world between 2008 and 2010 may have been the single most important event in undermining Americans' faith—not just in the banks and other financial institutions that helped bring it about, but in the very model of American capitalism itself. Perhaps worse even than the evidence of the scale of greed and recklessness by financiers in the early years of the twenty-first century was the sense after the fact that no one had really been held accountable.

Millions of ordinary Americans lost their jobs, houses, and livelihoods, thanks in large part to an orgy of excess by the most privileged of people on Wall Street. Hundreds of billions of taxpayer dollars were dispensed to keep the financial system afloat. But other than a few hapless employees of some investment banks, no one responsible was punished.

The experience taught many Americans that the system was rigged in favor of the powerful and monied, and against them. It gave rise initially to the revolt known as the Tea Party and then to a much wider populist reaction that reflected a broad loss of confidence in American elites and led directly to the election of Donald Trump in 2016.

The details of the crisis are sufficiently well known to keep a description here to a minimum. In the early 2000s the combination of a housing market boom, fed by low interest rates and the easy availability of subprime mortgages, together with the invention of new classes of securities that facilitated a complex and ultimately unsustainable level of credit exposure created interlocking financial excesses. As the housing market turned sour starting in 2006 and defaults soared, the institutions that had most aggressively marketed and traded the new securities fell into distress.

In March 2008, the federal government engineered a rescue by J. P. Morgan Chase, America's largest bank, of Bear Stearns, an investment bank led by one of Wall Street's most notoriously rapacious of capitalists, bridge-playing, cigar-chomping Jimmy Cayne, its CEO for two decades. In his final year at the firm, Cayne, who was well known for commandeering the corporate helicopter to take him on three-day golf weekends, was paid more than $40 million.

But Bear Stearns was merely the appetizer. As financial conditions deteriorated further, Lehman Brothers, one of America's oldest financial institutions, founded by German Jewish immigrants in 1847, was trapped in a liquidity and capital crisis of its own making, as the billions of dollars of securities that were supposed to back its own borrowing dwindled in value.

The result was mayhem and the near meltdown of the most famous names in American banking. The crisis also tarnished perhaps forever the reputation of the US government. Regulators had failed to prevent the crisis from happening and then, once it had happened, spent billions bailing out banks while failing to hold their leaders accountable.

The psychic shock of the financial crisis on American attitudes cannot be overstated.

It not only led to a deep recession, the worst since the Great Depression. It changed forever the way people viewed banks and business more widely.[7]

Anti–Wall Street sentiment has long been a powerful influence in American politics. The Occupy Wall Street movement that began shortly after the financial crisis has antecedents in the earliest days of the republic. The tension between financial interests and the rest of the economy goes back to the first disputes over a national bank and continued through the nineteenth century to the populist movement of the early twentieth century.

But the impact of the great financial crisis was arguably more significant because it fit a wider narrative of an economic system as a whole that was increasingly unjust. What was most striking was the near total lack of accountability for those who had been responsible for bringing the US economy to its knees.

While the federal government did manage to extract hundreds of billions of dollars in fines from financial institutions, the sense of injustice was underscored by the fact that no one of seniority was ever held legally liable for the disaster they had helped create. Only one banker, a senior trader at Credit Suisse who was convicted of inflating the value of securities in his portfolio, was jailed, and a handful of others successfully prosecuted. Compare that with the aftermath of the savings and loans crisis in the early 1990s, when more than 1,000 banking and other executives were sentenced.

If these bankers were deemed "too big to jail," as some put it, the larger problem the crisis emphasized was the "too big to fail" phenomenon—banks that were so important to the financial system that allowing them to go bust would produce systemic chaos. But the big banks today are even bigger than they were then. Goldman Sachs, for example, which came within days of having to be rescued at the peak of the crisis in 2008, saw its total assets almost double in the decade that followed, to more than $1.5 trillion in early 2022. The big banks may be better capitalized and more secure financially now than they were then, but they remain behemoths whose power holds even regulators in its thrall.

The lingering effect of the crisis on American attitudes toward Wall Street is palpable. Almost a decade later, a third of Americans said they had "hardly any confidence" in the people running banks and financial institutions, according to a poll by NORC, compared with just 10 percent at the beginning of the century.

The damage done by the crisis to the trust Americans have in Wall Street, the iconic cornerstone of the US economy, may never be fully repaired.

If Wall Street has been the historically dominant sector of the US economy, in the twenty-first century it is technology that has become preeminent. The top four US companies by market capitalization are all tech companies; Apple alone is six times the value of J. P. Morgan.

Even after the dot-com crash of 2000, tech leaders loomed large in the American iconography, but it's still no surprise that some of the largest recent examples of corporate malfeasance have been figures once hailed as emerging Silicon Valley geniuses.

The most symbolic corporate scandal of the last decade is Theranos, the company founded by a Stanford dropout promising to revolutionize the blood-testing business by replacing conventional blood draws with a mere finger pinprick. At its peak in 2015, the company enjoyed a $10 billion valuation, and was the darling of the tech sector, the shiniest and most compelling of the Valley's many "unicorn" start-ups, privately owned firms valued at more than one billion dollars at the time.

But the *Wall Street Journal*'s John Carreyrou, under my editorship, revealed that Elizabeth Holmes, the black turtleneck–wearing, raspy-voiced wunderkind lionized by media, investors and tech people alike, was a fraud. With her partner, Ramesh "Sunny" Bulwani, she initially bamboozled credulous investors, clients, and journalists, and then, as the *Journal* began to expose her deception, attempted to bully and intimidate anyone who challenged the company's claims.

I have vivid personal recollections of sitting in a contentious meeting in the *Journal*'s offices with David Boies, Holmes's superstar lawyer, as her legal team threatened to sue the newspaper if it persisted with its investigation.

The *Journal*'s reporting led to the collapse of Theranos amid a bonfire of its fabulist promises, the loss of billions in investors' and customers' money, and lengthy prison terms for both Holmes and Balwani.

But the episode left a lasting legacy too—as the most powerful and contemporary example of how a devious corporate mastermind can manipulate American capitalism for her own ends, and in the process it further dented the faith Americans place in American business.

A few years later, another icon of the digital age was similarly exposed as a fraud. At the start of 2022, Sam Bankman-Fried was universally lauded as a unique genius, the personification of the digital entrepreneurship transforming the global economy. The business he founded, FTX, was an avatar of the explosive growth of cryptocurrency, a trading platform for the rapidly expanding digital currency business that had many Americans in its thrall.

By the end of the year he was awaiting trial on \$200 million bail, charged with multiple counts of fraud. It turns out the business for which he was so widely lauded was a kind of Ponzi scheme, in which hundreds of millions of dollars of customers' and investors' cash was funneled to another of his companies to fund "investments" in things like beachfront real estate. Bankman-Fried had built his firm's success in part through marketing its cryptocurrency services to audiences not exactly steeped in finance with massive advertising campaigns including expensive Super Bowl ads, but also through the careful cultivation of powerful politicians by making hefty donations to their campaigns.

It is hard to overstate the importance of all these scandals to the damage done to faith in corporate America.

In the space of just two decades, celebrated American companies and entrepreneurs across the economic spectrum—energy, telecoms, manufacturing, finance, technology—had been exposed as practitioners of fraud, abuse, deception, and reckless negligence. The succession of scandals fell like repeated blows upon the faith that Americans once had in many of their business leaders—and even the wider capitalist system as a whole.

Of course these instances of malfeasance are rare. The vast majority of American corporate leaders do their jobs with honesty and competence. They don't deserve the loss of trust that the actions of a few have brought on big business as a whole. But it's hardly surprising that these relatively isolated episodes have led people to doubt the probity and reliability of corporate America more widely.

Here it is worth reiterating something important—in every single one of these cases, the malefactors had, until very recently, been lionized by the media, investors, and their fellow corporate leaders. They had been almost universally praised as models of American capitalism. When those models of success and integrity become symbols of failure and malignity, the fallout is far and wide.

* * *

Every January, thousands of American corporate executives ascend the slopes of the Swiss Alps to attend the annual meeting of the World Economic Forum in Davos, Switzerland. At 5,000 feet above sea level, hemmed in by tight security and often knee-deep in snow, they spend a few days communing with fellow corporate and political leaders from around the world, all committed to, in the words of the forum's slogan, "improving the state of the world."

The WEF, as its habitues call it, is probably the place in the world most visibly identified with the globalization that has defined economics and politics in the decades since the end of the Cold War.

Its astonishing growth, from an initial gathering in 1971 of a small number of executives there to take part in an uninvitingly titled "European Management Forum" to the premier meeting place each year of top chief executives, heads of government, prominent academics, celebrities, journalists, and self-described "opinion leaders," is testament in part to the ingenuity and tenacity of its founder, German engineer Klaus Schwab.

But its ascent as the global economic summit is also a reflection of the way in which the diverse national and regional perspectives of elites from around the world have converged in the last thirty years into one remarkably unified worldview that holds that borders and national identities are bad, and the pursuit of global integration is good.

It was Samuel Huntington, the political scientist, who coined the term "Davos Man" to capture this new class of global technocrat and plutocrat elites. The attendees at Davos, he wrote, "have little need for national loyalty, view national boundaries as obstacles that thankfully are vanishing, and see national governments as residues from the past whose only useful function is to facilitate the elite's global operations."

Davos Men and (despite grand protestations about diversity and inclusion, relatively few numbers of) Davos Women represent a roster of the most powerful and familiar names in the world of global business—a large number of them American: Bill Gates, Jeff Bezos, George Soros, Larry Fink, Michael Bloomberg, and Sheryl Sandberg among them. They are joined by thousands of like-minded camp-followers, eager to demonstrate their loyalty to the cause and hopeful of getting at least a few minutes in the vicinity of one of their leaders.

"Davos is where billionaires go to lecture millionaires on how they should live and lead," one critic quipped some years ago, and it's true. The self-esteem of most of those attending perfectly matches the Alpine landscape—soaring ever skyward. Whatever the circumstances at the time of the meeting—financial crisis or global recession; international tension or all-out war—the one constant is the absolute self-assurance of these elites, the total conviction that they are rightly the elect, positioned to lead the world to better times.

It's not quite as glamorous as you might think. The town itself is far from picturesque. Having been developed with WEF money, its skyline is pockmarked with a mixture of industrial-style modern European architecture and huge cranes in the process of constructing more of it. Accommodation is scarce for the thousands of masters of the universe who arrive. Many chief executives have been forced to bunk down in youth hostel–quality hotels or boxlike apartments. The food, heavy on Swiss meat and dairy, is not up to the gourmet standards the denizens are used to and probably does more damage to their arteries in a week than they suffer the rest of the year. The parties may go on long into the night—and a few revelers have been known to end up stranded in snow banks or nursing broken bones from an icy fall—but for the most part it's long, arduous work—an endless succession of bilateral and multilateral meetings with clients, government officials, peers, and others.

Each year Professor Schwab and his team pick some theme with a suitably ambitious sounding title—"The Great Reset," "The Fourth Industrial Revolution"—and in the congress center and the various hotels, participants debate problems and solutions. "Debate" is a stretch here. What's remarkable—and ultimately stultifying—about the gathering is the unity of outlook and ideological disposition. On all the big issues—climate change; cross-border trade and capital flows; the importance of ethnic, gender, and sexual identity; the role of intergovernmental institutions in ensuring cohesion—the great men and women all think alike.

It's a reminder in fact that globalization has created a genuine community, and its town hall can be found here. The business, political, and cultural leaders represented from almost every country in the world have much more in common with each other than they do with their fellow citizens back home.

Indeed they are not really nationals of their own countries at all, but part of an easygoing global elite that moves effortlessly from country to country, pursuing business opportunities, cozying up to local power brokers, and preaching the Word of the WEF. Leading corporate executives from New York or San Francisco—the various C-suite figures with alphabet soup titles of CEO, CFO, CMO, CIO—generally have a greater commonality with their counterparts in London, Frankfurt, or Singapore than they do with their fellow Americans in Buffalo or Oakland.

Their elevation and separation from their fellow citizens is so extreme that they even have their own language. Wander into a Davos session and you will catch stakeholders dialoguing and mainstreaming multifaceted metrics in a cross-platform environment before actioning toward implementation mode. It's English, Jim, but not as we know it.

Corporate leaders spend a small fortune to attend. To be a coveted "strategic partner" of the WEF and have access to dedicated coffee lounges and meeting rooms will cost you hundreds of thousands of dollars. These little shrines of global capitalism are dominated by American companies that span the alphabet from Accenture, Bloomberg, and Chevron to Salesforce, Uber, and Verizon.

It's probably wise here to explode the myth that Davos is the nerve center of some sinister global conspiracy in which the elites come together every year to plot how to subjugate the world's citizens to their globalist authoritarian agenda. It's much less exciting than that. This is a gathering of true believers in the global system—unsurprisingly, since they have been its principal beneficiaries. The opening of the world's economies after the end of the Cold War—achieved by a sharp reduction of trade barriers, the removal of obstacles to international capital flows, and the facilitation of large-scale human migration—was no secret plot. It was the policy pursued by almost all governments around the world.

And to be sure, it has had beneficial consequences—especially for the developing world. Countries like China, Indonesia, Thailand, and latterly India and a number of sub-Saharan African economies experienced phenomenal growth rates thanks to the accelerated globalization practiced by Davos Man, lifting hundreds of millions of their citizens out of subsistence-level poverty, slashing infant mortality, and improving health and overall life expectancy.

But while it created unprecedented prosperity for millions of the poor, it engendered even greater prosperity for the owners and top executives of the world's largest companies—most of them American. The vast middle class of ordinary citizens in the developed world got squeezed.

Secure in their own success, focused on their own idealistic goals of "climate justice" and "equity, diversity, and inclusion," the Davos crowd failed to understand the backlash they were unleashing back home.

One of the most memorable moments in recent years came at the 2016 annual meeting, as the US presidential contest that year was kicking off. At one of the exclusive lunches a few hundred of the world's elite listened as various experts and commentators offered predictions for the coming year. When a prominent American political analyst soberly informed the guests that there was a real possibility that Donald Trump would be elected president the following November, the room was filled with a mixture of audible gasps and laughter. Half the attendees—seriously—thought it was a joke, and the other half thought they were hearing someone tell them the world was going to end in a matter of months. The irony, of course, was in the complete lack of self-awareness. It didn't even occur to them that it might have been the policies, outlooks, and attitudes of the stunned crowd gathered in that Alpine hotel conference room that had engendered the very political conditions that now so horrified them. They were living in their own multicultural, supranational country, one in which Hillary Clinton was president and no vulgar outsider should ever be allowed to challenge their self-comforting worldview.

To be fair, the Davos crowd has belatedly recognized the peril their supranation has helped create. There is greater discussion at the forum these days of inequality in developed countries and how to alleviate it. They reluctantly acknowledge that globalization has produced losers as well as winners, even if they don't actually know any of them.

But they can't really hide the depth of the contempt they continue to have for the deplorable people left behind at home who don't see the world as they do—the kind of people who haven't been to an expensive university, who don't specify their preferred pronouns, and don't understand the importance of carbon neutrality.

It's oddly apt that this annual gathering to promote and celebrate globalization meets in this little town in the Bernese Alps. Fifty years before the first gathering, Thomas Mann chose it as the setting for *The Magic Mountain*, his epic novel that depicts the corruption and decay of European bourgeois society in the years leading up to the First World War, a thinly disguised metaphor for the descent into disorder that led to that epoch-making conflict.

Modern Davos is a perfect metaphor for the world the modern elites have created. The place has the feeling of a secure redoubt, like a medieval castle where the royal court gathers behind the high walls to make the critical decisions for the peasants outside, whose angry cries can be heard in the distance, growing steadily and ominously louder.

* * *

Globalization has created a new world order, a kind of virtual borderless empire, with a supranational hierarchy of CEOs and top government and intergovernmental officials. If this is a twenty-first century global realm, Davos represents the symbolic imperial capital. Like all imperial sovereign classes, the global elite need a belief system, a kind of secular faith, something that suggests a moral purpose to their existence, both to justify their own rule and to ensure their subjects adhere to its authority.

And so they have developed their own form of theology—a temporal canon, with its own moral and doctrinal heft. As observance of traditional religion has declined in the west, this secular theology has come to serve as a kind of postmodern unifying belief system—with a whole catechism of progressive ideas and values.

Its paramount article of faith, its defining dogma, is belief in climate alarmism—the idea that man-made global warming is advancing so rapidly that the Earth is in mortal peril—and a moral and practical commitment to addressing it.

Fifty years ago many of our leading scientists and anthropologists were expressing alarm about the prospect of a new ice age. But in the last few decades a wide scientific consensus has coalesced around the proposition that the planet is steadily warming, mostly from the production of greenhouse gases.

There is solid evidence for this, but there is—or ought to be—legitimate debate over the pace at which the planet is warming, over the benefits as well as the costs of climate change, and, especially, over the measures that should be taken to counter it.

This legitimate debate, however, one that could produce a diverse range of practical options for dealing with the climate challenge, has essentially been shut down by the elites who control most of the public discourse in the west. The authorized truth is that the planet is on course for a rapid escalation in temperatures that will result—in short order—in catastrophic weather events, drought, devastating sea level rises, and other calamities. The only way to avert this disaster is to achieve "net zero" carbon emissions—within a decade.

As extreme, implausible, and impractical as this alarmism is, any dissent from it is discredited and delegitimized as "climate denialism" and anti-science, and adherence to the most extreme version of climate change theology is enforced by the media and leading cultural institutions.

That progressive thinkers and activists would embrace this extremism is hardly surprising—the kind of regulation of all aspects of economic activity required to achieve "net zero" would be beyond even the wildest imaginings of the most passionate advocates of socialism in its heyday.

That corporations, especially American corporations, should have bought into it almost as enthusiastically is an extraordinary development. But that is more or less exactly what has happened in the last decade.

At the instigation of governments and international agencies like the United Nations, beginning in the early 2000s companies began to be encouraged to make "sustainability" a key objective in their operations and planning. Soon afterward, a new framework for investing principles was born—"Environmental, Social, and Corporate Governance"—ESG.

The aim was to factor into investing decisions by the institutions that allocate the bulk of the world's capital specific objectives that go way beyond companies' traditional aims of maximizing shareholder value.

So, for example, fund managers controlling billions of dollars in pension fund savings would begin to demand that the companies they invested in make particular, achievable reductions in their carbon footprint, and ensure a certain level of representation of women and ethnic minorities in their senior management and board positions.

No institution has been a more enthusiastic and effective advocate for ESG investing than BlackRock, the world's largest fund management firm.

The company manages about $10 trillion in assets—the pension savings of tens of millions of Americans notable among them—and the power of the purse it controls can force companies to do its bidding, not necessarily to maximize returns for shareholders, but to advance political and social aims mandated by the progressive elites who dominate our public discourse.

All of this has contributed significantly to the decline in trust in American big business.

Vivek Ramaswamy, an entrepreneur who founded Roivant Sciences, a health care and biotech company, and who in 2023 became a Republican presidential candidate, argues that the elevation of ESG by influential business and political leaders represents nothing less than an attempt to enlist American capitalism and the companies that practice it into engines for progressive causes. "America is becoming less and less like itself and more like a bastardized version of the European model of social progress, where elite executives work hand in hand with the government to do what they think is best for society."

Advocates for ESG argue that factoring in social and environmental considerations is not only right for society but can be beneficial financially. Lawrence Fink, the chief executive of BlackRock, has repeatedly argued that his firm's strategy of prioritizing these objectives results in better returns for investors—you can do well by doing good.

But the evidence is flimsy.

Terence Keeley, a former senior manager at BlackRock who left the firm in 2022, published a book that year that captured his growing disillusionment with ESG. In *Sustainable*, he points out in fact that not only does the focus on ESG distract companies from the primary objective of achieving the best return for their shareholders, it is highly ineffective:

> To date, ESG equity strategies have been broadly disappointing. They have underperformed broad indices while failing to generate any meaningful progress against their primary, non-financial target: climate change. Many ESG strategies haven't been win-win; they've been lose-lose.

Keeley notes that in the five years between 2017 and 2022, ESG funds underperformed the broader market—securing an average 6.3 percent return compared with the market's 8.9 percent return. An investor who put $10,000 into an average global ESG fund in 2017 would have $13,500 five years later, compared with $15,250 if he had put his money into the broader market.

No wonder Americans feel literally shortchanged by their business leaders. Not only are they forced to watch as their corporate overlords use their powerful positions to pursue ideological goals many do not approve of, but they are actually paying for the privilege of it.

Though its adherents claim it promotes good business and investing practices, ESG is often merely a ploy to pursue political and cultural objectives. This is reflected in some of the financial and business lunacies it ends up promoting. All companies are now given ESG ratings by highly influential analysis firms like S&P and MSCI, which are used by major pension funds and other asset allocators, as the benchmarks by which they determine how they distribute their investments.

But the indicators they use—especially for the "social," or "S" goals, in ESG analysis are often nothing more than subjective assessments of how a company is supposedly making critical contributions to society, by, for example, having a certain number of women or ethnic minorities on its board.

This often results in notorious absurdities. In 2022, Tesla, Elon Musk's electric car maker, was dropped from S&P's ESG 500 index—a basket of supposedly top companies for ESG performance—while S&P continued to rank a company such as Exxon Mobil in the top ten. The index's compilers explained that the reason the world's largest maker of battery-powered cars ranked lower in the rating agency's estimation of contributions to the health of the planet than America's largest oil producer was in part to do with stories about racial discrimination and workplace conditions at Tesla.[8]

We've seen this trend toward prioritizing political and social considerations in corporate policies across the American business world.

After the riots that followed the murder of George Floyd in the summer of 2022, large American companies raced to associate themselves with the Black Lives Matter movement—an ideologically extreme organization that has long had overtly Marxist objectives. In 2020 alone BLM raised $90 million from American companies such as Amazon, Apple, Coca Cola, and Nike.

While there was widespread support for campaign to combat racial injustice in the United States at the time, it was also clear that many Americans felt that BLM was a political organization with goals very much at odds with their own. As it became clear that BLM leaders had siphoned off a significant amount for their own use, public support of the organization fell sharply, and by 2022 Americans were evenly split on the merits of the organization. Big business, though, continued to pledge rhetorical and financial support.

The nation's most powerful chief executives have also committed their companies, which depend for their revenue on the custom of ordinary Americans, to support other extreme progressive political causes.

In 2016 the National Basketball Association pulled its annual All-Star Game from North Carolina after the state legislature passed a law that banned transgender people from using bathrooms they choose according to their identity. In 2021, Delta's and Coca Cola's CEOs denounced legislation governing voting procedures in Georgia, capitulating to demands from Democrats, including President Joe Biden, who described the law as "Jim Crow 2.0"; this despite the fact that the law, while tightening some of the permissive measures that had been put in place for voting during the COVID pandemic, made voting significantly easier than it was in, for example, Biden's own state of Delaware.

"I want to be crystal clear," said James Quincey, Coca Cola's CEO, "the Coca Cola Company does not support this legislation, as it makes it harder for people to vote, not easier."

Curiously, this supposedly restrictive law that incurred the displeasure (and threats of reprisals) from corporate leaders resulted in the highest level of voter turnout in 2022 in midterm elections in Georgia's history.

In 2022, the Walt Disney Company enmeshed itself in Florida politics when it came out against a state law that would ban schools from teaching about sexual orientation or gender identity to children in kindergarten through third grade.

In each of these cases, polls indicated heavy support among the state's citizens for the measures taken, and yet major corporate entities in the states, under pressure from Democratic politicians, progressive activists, and many of their own woke employees, opted to deliberately insert themselves on one side of the argument, essentially raising a middle finger to millions of their customers.

In the past, American companies generally avoided political controversy, mindful that it is not in their shareholders' interests to risk alienating a large number of their customers.

In the 1980s, as Nike, the sportswear company, was seeking to establish itself as the premier brand in its market, it struck a deal with Michael Jordan, then an emerging basketball talent for the Chicago Bulls of the National Basketball Association. By the end of the decade Jordan had become such a star that his endorsement was worth not only tens of millions of dollars, it was also believed to be worth votes.

According to Sam Smith's 1995 book, *Second Coming*, about Jordan's return to the NBA after a short spell away, the star was asked to deploy his popularity in a political cause.

> He was approached by US Senate hopeful Harvey Gantt, a black politician who was running against Jesse Helms in North Carolina, Jordan's home state. Gannt had hoped that Jordan's name would help him defeat Helms, widely regarded as a virulent racist. But Jordan declined. He wasn't into politics, he explained, didn't really know the issues. And, as he later told a friend,
> "Republicans buy shoes too."

Jordan had a much better understanding of the proper role of a corporation than either his successors in the NBA or most of today's leadership of corporate America.

In the last decade, the corporate rulebook has been rewritten to make explicit pursuit of a highly partisan set of political objectives company policy.

How has this happened?

It's doubtless partly the increasingly partisan media environment these companies operate in. Support for BLM, transgender causes, or liberal arguments about voting rules helps companies get favorable treatment in the media.

But a large part of it may be simple cynical political calculation by chief executives.

As we have seen, trust in corporate leadership has dropped sharply in the early years of the twenty-first century in response to scandals, malfeasance, the failure to address the consequences of the global financial crisis, and soaring inequality.

As Vivek Ramaswamy argues, support for woke, progressive causes by business leaders is a way of buying the support, or at least the acquiescence, of liberal progressive groups that dominate the public discourse. In the process companies can shield themselves from criticism about their true misbehavior.

Wokenomics is a powerful weapon for CEOs, which they can readily deploy as a smoke screen to distract from greed, fraud, and malfeasance.

If this is correct it is a Faustian pact. By allying themselves with the prevailing causes of the cultural and political elites, CEOs are likely in the process only further undermining their standing with the wider American public who are, after all, their customers, and ultimately shareholders.

One reason perhaps that chief executives have been able to get away with turning their companies into vehicles for left wing causes in the last couple of decades is that the companies themselves have become much more immune to market forces. Across the American economy there has been a dramatic decline in competition between companies, as the number of firms in many of the biggest markets for goods and services has shrunk significantly

In sector after sector of the economy—from airlines and telecommunications to cable television and breweries—waves of mergers and acquisition have increased significantly what economists call industrial concentration, the domination of each market by a small number of companies. The narrowing of choice caused by this merger mania has been exacerbated by a steep decline in the number of new start-up businesses in the US economy. The firms that remain end up with greater market power, and the consumer enjoys fewer choices.

"The market share of the four largest public and private firms has grown significantly for most industries, and the average and median size of public firms, i.e., the largest players in the economy, has tripled in real terms," wrote economists Gustavo Grullon, Yelena Larkin, and Roni Michaely in a study published in 2017 for the Mendoza Business School of the University of Notre Dame.[9]

The authors found that more than three-quarters of US industries had seen an increase in concentration between the late 1990s and 2017.

What this means, of course, is not just fewer options if you want to fly, sign up for a mobile phone contract, or buy a beer. It leads inevitably to higher prices.

In his 2019 book *The Great Reversal, How America Gave up on Free Markets*, NYU professor of economics Thomas Philippon, a Frenchman who had moved to the United States, traced how the prices American consumers paid for basic goods and services had become much higher than those paid by their counterparts in Europe.

Philippon began his research with a simple question:

"Why on earth are US cell phone plans so expensive?"

The answer, he discovered, was diminished competition:

This lack of competition has hurt US consumers and workers: it has led to higher prices, lower investment and lower productivity growth.

The evidence is compelling—broadband prices in the United States are double what European consumers pay; profits per passenger among US airlines are far higher than for their European counterparts.

All this is heavily counterintuitive—the United States is supposed to be the land of free markets and intense competition. But perhaps most intriguing is what Philippon says is the reason for these anti-consumer trends in the United States.

Contrary to common wisdom, the main explanation is political, not technological: I have traced the decrease in competition to increasing barriers to entry and weak antitrust enforcement, sustained by heavy lobbying and campaign contributions.

In other words, much of modern American capitalism is a vicious circle of cronyism: big companies buy political influence through large-scale donations and lobbying at the federal and state level. This political largesse lubricates the system of business rules and regulations in such a way that those companies get favorable treatment from politicians and regulators. That in turn enables them to get bigger—by avoiding antitrust and other regulatory interventions, which means they can then buy even more political influence. The biggest loser in all this is the consumer who gets less choice, poorer quality goods and services, and higher prices. Corporations, meanwhile, enjoy higher profits, and the political classes who make the policies and the rules that govern the way markets operate get buckets of money to ensure their own reelection.

The total amount spent on lobbying firms by corporations grew from $1.4 billion a year in 1999 to more than $3.71 billion in 2021—more than twice the rate of overall inflation in the economy. But even this figure only scratches the surface of big company spending on politics—when you factor in donations to political campaigns the number rises to more than $9 billion.

As Philippon explains, the process is so critical to big companies' success that lobbying and political spending is now a core—and highly efficient—component of their costs.

> Lobbying expenditures are three times more concentrated than revenues, which are themselves already fairly concentrated. This means that large firms play an even more outsized role in the political system than they do in the economy itself.

This is crony capitalism—rigging the political system for their own advantage by moneyed corporations—and it's a critical reason for the decline in trust Americans have in the corporate sector.

* * *

The three decades since the end of the Cold War have seen a historic shift in the balance of economic rewards that go to capital and labor.

The so-called labor share—the proportion of total business revenues that goes to workers—declined from 63.3 percent in 2000 to 56.7 percent in 2016—its lowest level since before the Second World War.

There are multiple reasons for this, and not all of them necessarily reflect ill on American capitalism. It's true that powerful labor unions in the 1960s and 1970s helped drive labor's share to higher levels and in the process fueled inflation and weakened American productivity. The rise in corporate profits isn't all a story of fat-cat capitalists getting the gold while workers get the shaft. Profits are reinvested in businesses to improve their long-run performance, and, with most American workers now owning pension plans or 401ks, some of the gains from increased profitability find their way into workers' pockets eventually. And profitability is the way to attract new investment and new jobs and opportunities—allowing business to make money has always been central to America's long-term economic success.

But whatever the rights and wrongs of the shift and the widening inequality in the United States it has produced, there's no escaping the role that this change has played in the way Americans view their corporate leadership.

The loss of high-wage manufacturing jobs in the United States to the developing world, the growing scale of American companies through crushing competition, the manipulation of the political system to favor them—all may have improved their profitability but they have contributed also to a strong sense that America's corporate leaders no longer care about Americans.

The sense of injustice induced by the failure of political leaders to hold banks and other big firms accountable for the most disastrous financial and economic crisis of the modern era has further diminished the trust Americans had in big business.

Above all, it is the way big American companies have become vehicles for an ideological agenda that significant numbers of Americans oppose that has most damaged the sense of solidarity citizens feel with their business elites. Insisting on green environmental policies while most Americans still want the freedom to drive cars or fly cross country and while millions of their fellow citizens are employed in traditional energy extraction. Pushing woke ideas about gender and sexuality, which polls suggest a large majority of Americans find at odds with their own understanding of morals and science. Promoting a culture of intolerance for dissenting ideas in their own workplaces and in the wider society.

Perhaps worst of all is the hypocrisy these extraordinarily successful and privileged corporate leaders display.

Global chief executives lecturing Americans on the need for environmental sacrifices while flying off to Davos in their private jets. Wall Street firms demanding bailouts while pushing their hardpressed borrowers into bankruptcy and financial ruin. Sports teams and Hollywood studios denouncing discrimination and injustice in the United States while kowtowing to the Chinese Communist Party in pursuit of business opportunity.

No one ever said, "What's good for General Motors is good for America." It is another of those many mischievously misquoted observations.

But in its curious way it was once true. There was a time when the interests of great American companies seemed closely aligned with the interests of the people. That's an idea that rings hollow in twenty-first century America.

CHAPTER 4

Bad News

I N LATE 2016, shortly after Donald Trump's surprise election to the presidency, I was approached by a distraught young editor at the *Wall Street Journal* who asked to come and see me for an urgent private discussion. I was editor-in-chief of the paper at the time and had been aware of a rising level of consternation among some members of the *Journal* staff about our coverage of the election and the president-elect.

Throughout the campaign and immediately afterward, as hysteria about this unusually controversial candidate had escalated in much of the media, I had reminded the *Journal*'s staff to, as it were, Keep Calm and Carry On. We would treat Trump like other political and public figures. We would do tough, probing journalism, investigating his business background and political stances, rigorously pursuing all aspects of his life, career, and speech, and we would publish what we could confirm. That we duly did. In fact we wound up winning a Pulitzer Prize for some of our more consequential reporting on the candidate's dubious behavior. But, I insisted, we would not adopt, as other news organizations had done, an explicitly oppositional or confrontational posture. Our job was to hold all public figures, especially popular and successful ones, accountable through our reporting, not to become crusaders for or against a particular party or candidate. Above all, we would hew to our near-sacred commitment to our readers that we would pursue objectivity—the truth, as far as we could possibly ascertain it—in our reporting.

This, apparently, was a source of dismay for some on the *Journal* staff, who thought we should be like other newspapers and be aggressively opposing and undermining Trump. So, at the appointed time the young editor, passionate and emotional, stopped by my office, sat on my sofa, and harangued me for half an hour.

Respectfully, she said, I didn't understand what was going on. Now that Trump was about to be president I should recognize my error and mobilize all available *Journal* resources for a full-scale editorial assault on the man. She had studied the history of Nazi Germany in college, she told me in all earnestness, and she believed that this was how genocide starts. What we were witnessing was essentially an eerily precise replay of the late stages of the Weimar Republic; America 2016 was Germany 1933. If the press had been more aggressive in opposing them back then, the Nazis would never have succeeded in their evil designs. It was no longer our duty simply to report on what was happening, to try to be objective. We now had to wade into the fray on the side of moral virtue in order to save democracy and the republic from fascism.

I listened politely and told her I disagreed. Aside from the flawed comparison of a 240-year-old republic and the most successful democracy in the world with a 1930s Germany whose Weimar constitution had been around for little more than a decade, forged in the humiliation of defeat in the most devastating war in the nation's history, and which had been battered by unprecedented economic stress and domestic political violence, there was a much more important point about the role of journalism.

We couldn't know at this stage how Trump would govern, but we had had a taste of the strange and intoxicating cocktail of narcissistic bombast, vaudeville shtick, mesmerizing showmanship, and shameless mendacity that had characterized his campaign. We had covered all that critically and would continue to do so. But 63 million Americans had voted for him, and for reasons, it seemed to me, which we should not dismiss or disdain, that had to do with rising disgust at the American political establishment. Whatever she, or I, thought of him, the notion that by becoming another news organization devoted to destroying him we would somehow convince readers that he should be removed from office struck me as naive. More likely, the abandonment of the values and principles that we had always stood for—objective reporting, fact- and evidence-based analysis—would forfeit the trust our readers placed in us. They would assume, rightly, that every story we did would be selected and reported in a way that would portray Trump and his administration in the worst possible light—that we would have ceased to report things as they are but instead become a motivated protagonist in a cultural and political war.

The best way for a newspaper to combat ignorance is with reason, I told her. The most effective way to combat propaganda is with facts. The right way to combat lies is with truth.

Evidently, I didn't convince her. As memory serves, she joined another news organization shortly afterward, part of a large exodus of ideological discontents around that time who left the *Journal* for more comfortable quarters. Helping facilitate that migration still ranks among my proudest achievements as editor of the *Journal*.

I recount all this not to denigrate a former conscientious colleague or demonstrate any great virtue on my part but rather to offer a small but perfect allegory of what has gone so catastrophically wrong with the American news media in the last decade or so.

It's no exaggeration to say that trust in American journalism has collapsed. According to a 2022 survey by the Reuters Institute for the Study of Journalism, only 26 percent of Americans said they trust the news in general.[1]

This is the lowest share recorded and is down 12 percentage points since 2017 alone.

Rasmussen Reports, which regularly surveys American opinion, notes that in 2021, 83 percent of Americans saw "fake news" as a problem. Fifty-six percent—most Republicans and independents—actually agreed with the statement that the media were "the enemy of the people."

While the erosion of trust has accelerated sharply in the last few years—especially during the Trump presidency and its aftermath—the decline in the public's faith has been going on for many years.

The reasons for this startling collapse are many and varied—and will be the subject of this chapter. But the anecdote about the distressed young editor at the *Journal* a few years ago captures the fundamental problem of modern journalism.

Back in its heyday, when people trusted the news, most journalists saw their job as to ferret out the truth, the objective facts and context of a story, an event, a person. Obviously, no one could ever hope to attain a perfect, comprehensively accurate account of every aspect of every story. But the truth was out there somewhere, and it was our job to get as close to it as we could. It could be discovered through diligent reporting, an attempt to investigate and interrogate all sides of a story until we could, within our limited time and resources, tell our readers, listeners, and viewers: this is what, to the best of our ability, we believe objectively happened.

That's seen as quaintly old-fashioned by the people who run most of the news today. The most influential journalists now see themselves not as neutral, independent gatherers of fact, information, and testimony in the pursuit of reporting the truth. They see themselves as protagonists in a moral struggle. The truth is not something to be uncovered by objective reporting. The truth is something that has been revealed to them—in their high school and undergraduate studies, by their inculcation with progressive values, through their ideological beliefs—and is then to be disseminated by them to a mostly ignorant public. Stories are to be chosen and reported in ways that fit the narrative. Their role today in the modern establishment hierarchy is somewhat akin to that of a priesthood in less secular times—spreading light in the unknowing darkness with their unique vocational training in divining and disseminating eternal truths and meaning.

Journalists have long had an elevated sense of their own importance in society. One of my favorite stories that captures the self-belief of the typical American newsman dates from the moments after the first planes hit the World Trade Center on September 11, 2001, according to an account published later in the *New Yorker*. The then managing editor of the *New York Times*, briefly in charge that morning, immediately called in his senior editors to figure out what they would do for an emergency plan if the newspaper's offices in midtown Manhattan were the next target of al Qaeda's terrorists.

Because, of course, after the World Trade Center, the Pentagon, the US Capitol Building, and the White House, it was natural for a *New York Times* editor to assume that next on any self-respecting terrorist's list of iconic American institutions to destroy would be The World's Most Important Newspaper.[2]

But this self-importance is much worse now than it ever was—and not just at that institution—because even as they see their own role as ever more essential to the health of democracy, their audience trusts journalists less than ever. There's been an inverse relationship at work over the last few years between the media's self-belief and the trust their audience reposes in them.

Not that journalists are unaware that they now rank somewhere between ambulance-chasing trial lawyers and automated call-center respondents when Americans are asked to rank professions by the level of trust they place in them. They understand that the level of trust people have has dropped sharply. Indeed they spend acres of print, hours of air time, and trillions of bytes examining the decline of faith in news reporting. Nobody does self-reflection like the American media type. It's less navel-gazing, more self-proctology, and yet, for all their intestinal probing, they still miss the real problem. They generally ascribe the decline in trust to a host of malevolent forces who, it is said, tarnished the reputation of upstanding reporters and editors. This list includes, but is not limited to, Donald Trump, Facebook, Fox News, Russian intelligence agents, and Elon Musk.

They don't seem to understand—or to want to understand—that the loss of confidence in most of what appears in the media these days is a direct function of their own successful attempts to turn much of the news into propaganda.

The Trump years—with their high-intensity running street battles between the president and his opponents in the media—doubtless accelerated the decline in much of the public's faith in news. Like that editorial colleague of mine, so many journalists decided that Trump was such a threat to democracy that, in the words of a prominent magazine editor at the time, we were now in a "state of emergency" that warranted new rules for how journalists should operate.

Some of this may have been a reasonable reaction to the character of the president himself. All presidents find much to make their blood boil about the reporters who cover them. The often confrontational back-and-forth between the White House press corps and the president has long been a feature of political journalism; and most presidents have at times been less than truthful in their communications with the American people. Trump was certainly an extreme manifestation of this tendency; his capacity to pronounce evident falsehoods without compunction or shame is almost unique in the modern presidency.

But none of that justified the hostility of a press corps that essentially lost its mind over the president.

The tone of the media's coverage of the presidency was set even before he entered office with the almost ubiquitous allegation that he had won election thanks to an elaborate campaign of collusion with the Kremlin—supposedly some form of quid pro quo between him and Vladimir Putin, the Russian president, that made Trump—in the eyes of most of the media—essentially a Russian asset, a "Siberian Candidate," as *New York Times* columnist Paul Krugman described him.

But as we now know, the allegation of collusion with Russia— "reported" ad nauseam by the *New York Times*, the *Washington Post*, CNN, and virtually every other media outlet—was false. Trump and his team had surely shown an unwise and improper openness to Russian efforts to discredit Hillary Clinton, his opponent, as when members of his team agreed to give a hearing to some shady figure promising "dirt" on the Democratic candidate.

Yet evidence of any actual collaboration between the campaign and the Kremlin was nonexistent, as Robert Mueller, the special counsel appointed to investigate the claims, concluded in a long report published in 2019. That never stopped many in the media from constantly seeking it and occasionally peddling damning allegations that were flimsy at best, wholly indefensible at worst.

In a devastating piece of reporting for *Columbia Journalism Review* published in January 2023, Jeff Gerth, a former investigative reporter for the *New York Times*, documented in excruciating detail the willful deception and dishonesty of so much of the coverage of Trump by news organizations. He discovered that reporters and editors at some of America's most storied news institutions had abandoned the basic principles of journalism that had always been designed to ensure fairness, objectivity, and accuracy. They had become essentially partisan players in the political contest.

> My main conclusion is that journalism's primary missions, informing the public and holding powerful interests accountable, have been undermined by the erosion of journalistic norms and the media's own lack of transparency about its work. This combination adds to people's distrust about the media and exacerbates frayed political and social differences.

(I should say at this point that the vast majority of my colleagues at the *Wall Street Journal* never succumbed to this lunacy and continue to pursue old-fashioned objectivity in reporting—it's the main reason the *Journal* is the most trusted newspaper in America.)

But if Trump was a tipping point for the descent into outright advocacy journalism, his campaign and presidency were far from the beginning of the decline in trust in American media. Faith in American news had been sliding for years before Trump. To understand what has gone wrong with American journalism we need to understand what it was about Trump that made his candidacy and his presidency such a fiery crucible for the relationship between the media and much of the public—and how it became a raging bonfire of distrust in modern news.

It was in part Trump's character and behavior that inspired so much animosity among the people who covered him—the falsehoods, the boorishness, the casual disdain for the niceties of Washington politics.

But it's hard to escape the conclusion that it was something else that turned them instantly into his foes: he represented a cultural and political affront to their sensibilities, the likes of which they had not confronted in mainstream politics before, a man whose ideas and words should not be allowed to have a place in American public discourse.

From the moment he declared his candidacy for president in June 2015, in the famous escalator ride in Trump Tower, it was obvious that the candidate held views and represented values that were wildly at odds with those deemed permissible by most influential national media figures. He was aggressively hostile to illegal immigration and open borders—a restrictionist on immigration generally, defensive of traditional American values on issues such as sex and gender, and held strongly nationalist views that elevated America and American exceptionalism above other nations and the modern creed of globalism.

Indeed, you could argue that a critical reason for Trump's success was precisely that he articulated ideas and beliefs held by many Americans that the mainstream media had denounced, derided, or ignored. And it's this that points us to the reason that trust in the media has been sliding for so long.

Trump merely crystallized a process that had been trending for more than four decades. Half a century ago, in what we might now see as its golden age, the media was widely trusted. Newspapers such as the *New York Times* and the *Washington Post* enjoyed a degree of trust among the public that meant their reporting was believed—and highly consequential. The Pentagon Papers and Watergate changed the course of history—because the reporting that produced them was believed and trusted.

In 1976, in retrospect, the very highest point in the standing of American journalism, the Gallup survey found that 72 percent of respondents had trust in the media. It's been sharply downhill since then.

This collapse in trust has grave consequences for the health of American democracy.

A widely trusted, free press is essential to the functioning of a democratic society, one in which the people are the ultimate decision-makers. Trust in the information they are supplied enables the people to make informed judgments, confident that those judgments are based on facts and the truth. This is vital to the operation of accountability in democracy—of government, corporations, powerful institutions, and individuals.

As Thomas Jefferson wrote:

> The people are the only censors of the governors...The basis of our governments being the opinion of the people, the very first object should be to keep that right [of access to information]; and, were it left to me to decide whether we should have a government without newspapers or newspapers without a government, I should not hesitate a moment to prefer the latter.

But for that accountability to work, the people must trust the information they are being given. If they are fed information they see as false or dishonest, they won't know whether to believe it. They won't know if the story it purports to tell warrants action on their part or should inform their decision-making.

Imagine if a Watergate were to happen today; the press reporting malfeasance by a president on a large scale. Would readers believe it, given the source of the information? It's highly likely that half the audience—the half that was politically motivated to believe it—would do so, and the other half would not. You don't even have to have a vivid imagination to consider the question. In many ways this has been the story of the last few decades in American politics—as both political parties have sought to impeach presidents on the basis of information that was initially reported by the media. Levels of trust have been so low that the efforts dissolved into routine partisan fights.

Donald Trump once famously said, "I could stand in the middle of Fifth Avenue and shoot someone and not lose any votes." In a lifetime of highly dubious assertions, that may have been the most truthful thing the man ever said. Think about how it would play out. Half his supporters wouldn't believe reports of the shooting, or insist that there must be some context to the incident that the media were not covering. The other half would probably shrug their shoulders and say, so what?

How did this happen? How did we go in less than half a century from an age when reporters were trusted enough that their journalism brought down a presidency to an age when much of the country doesn't trust a word they say or write?

The media people themselves have a ready answer. They want us to believe that the collapse in trust is all the result of the rise of alternative sources of information that have fed a section of the public a steady diet of falsehoods—"misinformation," as it is called. A form of what economists call "Gresham's Law" then takes hold—where bad money in circulation drives out good money, and all cash is tainted.

The argument goes that people trusted the news until—beginning in the 1980s—the arrival on the scene of a toxic combination of new media: conservative talk radio, Fox News, and "fake news" catalyzed by conspiracy theory-laden social media.

Talk radio—pioneered by people like Rush Limbaugh, the bombastic iconoclast who garnered a vast following for his daily trashing of the regular news outlets, "the drive-by media," as he called them, developed a hyperpartisan approach to politics and culture. This was supposedly in contrast to the "objectivity" of the rest of the media at the time. Conservatives gravitated to this form of commentary and, in the eyes of the traditional intendants of mainstream news, bought into a steadily more intoxicating diet of ideological extremism, half-truths, and hyperbole. Limbaugh spawned an entire genre of similar highly partisan commentators.

The second wave of shock troops storming the bastions of "objective news" came in 1996 when Rupert Murdoch and Roger Ailes created Fox News. Again, the content and direction of the programming was clearly right-leaning and partisan, and Fox's audience grew rapidly until it quickly dominated cable news programming. Its "fair and balanced" slogan seemed to the traditional media companies and outlets like an Orwellian representation of its ideologically distinctive content.

Then in the early years of the new century, with the onset of the digital revolution, social media became a dominant source of news and information. In its immediacy and reach it fostered the growth of communities of the like-minded, and became a bounteous source of stories and commentary—some of it wildly inaccurate, or plainly made up. Platforms such as Facebook became the fount of ideologically sympathetic content for conservatives, who increasingly could find news that suited their beliefs and reinforced their prejudices, and this digital delivery of news turbo-charged the partisan nature of news.

In the view of the people who had controlled the media for decades, these developments undid the trust that people had always placed in them. Journalists had previously seen themselves as "gatekeepers" of news, through their professional approach to newsgathering, protecting the ears and eyes of citizens from harmful error, propaganda, and lies. Now the gates had been breached, the walls were down, and any old unscrupulous bandit with ideological leanings and a yen for profit could build a platform in the town square to spread misinformation.

Writing in Vox in 2016, Jason Mittell, a professor of film and media culture at Middlebury College, and Chuck Tryon, an associate professor at Fayetteville State University, sought to explain how the benign traditional media had been usurped by bad right-wing news, as the latter succeeded in "normalizing" falsehood.[3]

> The mainstreaming of conservative fake news is a clear case of the dangers of such normalization. As we increasingly accept inaccurate peddlers of politicized misinformation as "news," we allow our citizenry to be horrifically misinformed as part of this new normal.

It's a convenient and in some ways appealing narrative, purporting to explain how the loss of trust in the media is the result of corruption from outside, and ascribing the blame to a bunch of malignant outsiders.

But it's flawed, of course, in one critical respect.

It fails to account for the reason that listeners, viewers, and readers sought these alternative sources of information in the first place.

These outlets didn't emerge in a vacuum, the product of the mind of some evil genius out to destroy the business model of the media. They arose because tens of millions of Americans thought they were being badly served by the media they had.

Rupert Murdoch is famously said to have quipped that he founded Fox News because he believed there was a niche in the market—and discovered that the niche turned out to be fifty percent.

As they ponder the low esteem in which their activities are held today, many modern mainstream media folk like to think of the news in the 1960s and 1970s as operating in a kind of state of grace—pure and uncorrupted reporting, believed by everyone. But it isn't true.

The media was already exhibiting signs of bias in its supposed glory days.

The process began with political and cultural developments in the 1960s that opened a widening gulf between the nation's elites and many of its regular citizens. Opposition to the Vietnam War, the civil rights movement, a succession of Supreme Court rulings—most notably *Roe v. Wade*, which discovered a Constitutional right to abortion—were all embraced by the culturally progressive establishment, heavily overrepresented in the news media.

At the time it might have seemed that icons such as Walter Cronkite or David Brinkley or the front page of the *New York Times* were some Voice of God, neutral daily interpreters of the warp and weft of history, judiciously assessing the unfolding of events objectively for the nation.

As Ted Koppel, himself a famous exponent of the school of the journalist as the voice of unimpeachable authority, wrote in a column in 2010:[4]

> Much of the American public used to gather before the electronic hearth every evening, separate but together, while Walter Cronkite, Chet Huntley, David Brinkley, Frank Reynolds and Howard K. Smith offered relatively unbiased accounts of information that their respective news organizations believed the public needed to

know...It was an imperfect, untidy little Eden of journalism where reporters were motivated to gather facts about important issues.

But there was already something rotten in this little Eden.

It became increasingly evident in fact that these neutral arbiters of objectivity were part of an elite that had their own biases, shared values, and ideas that were at odds with many of their audience.

To be sure the biases were subtle at first but became more obvious over time.

In his biography of Walter Cronkite, the historian Douglas Brinkley acknowledges how liberal his political views were.

While he mostly refrained from outright advocacy on the air, his views were increasingly obvious—and revealed clearly in a conversion on air after the defeat of Michael Dukakis, the Democratic presidential candidate in the 1988 election:[5]

> Liberalism isn't dead in this country. It isn't even comatose. It simply has an acute case of laryngitis. It simply has temporarily—we hope—lost its voice...But God Almighty, God Almighty, we've got to shout these truths in which we believe from the rooftops.... We've got to throw open our windows and shout these truth to the streets and to the heavens.

He wouldn't have to wait long for the truth-shouting.

At the time, the contemporary avatar of the media's Voice of God was Dan Rather, his successor at CBS news, who soon established himself as a progressive protagonist in the culture wars, and was eventually disgraced by his crude attempt to manipulate a false story to political advantage in an effort to destroy the presidential campaign of George W. Bush in 2000.

So the arrival of Fox News in the 1990s or conservative channels on social media in the 2000s was not some rude intrusion into the prelapsarian world of objective journalism. They were responses to demand from at least half the population who were tired of being ignored or demeaned.

If it's clear that American journalism became steadily more partisan and tendentious throughout the 1970s and 1980s, the question remains: how and why did this happen?

Several factors contributed to the change, but two—one demographic, one economic—were key.

The demographic change involved a transformation in the kind of people who became journalists.

Until the 1950s–60s, journalism was viewed more or less as a craft, performed by skilled craftsmen, trained, like other craftsmen, to execute a task. You didn't need a university degree or professional qualification to do the job, at least in part because the task was the realization of something objective, in this case, the truth.

Walter Lippmann, the pioneering journalist of the first half of the twentieth century, is often credited with establishing the goal of objectivity in reporting. In his book *Public Opinion*, published in 1922, he defined the journalist's function, and was fiercely critical of contemporary "yellow journalism," the pursuit of subjective, agenda-driven reporting.

The most destructive form of untruth is sophistry and propaganda by those whose profession it is to report the news. The news columns are common carriers. When those who control them arrogate to themselves the right to determine by their consciences what shall be reported and for what purpose, democracy is unworkable.

But even before Lippmann, other prominent figures in news had helped guide American journalism toward a focus on objective facts and not subjective opinion.

The first edition of the *Wall Street Journal* in 1889 carried a note from Charles Dow, Edward Jones, and Charles Bergstresser, its publishers and editor, which laid out the paper's mission. At a time when much journalism was speculative, conjectural, and highly partisan, the *Journal* would seek just the facts.

"Its object is to give fully and fairly the daily news...It will aim steadily at being a paper of news and not opinions," they wrote.

These principles guided journalism to much of its success and built steadily rising levels of trust in its work.

But beginning sometime in the 1960s, journalism ceased to be a craft performed by talented people with a clear and relatively simple objective of discovering facts and became more of an opportunity for the dissemination of ideas.

As journalism became more influential, highly and expensively educated young men and women—often from the best universities—were drawn to it.

In the 1950s a relatively small proportion of journalists employed by major news organizations had a degree of any sort. Today that number is around 90 percent.[6]

And in the most influential news organizations, not only do most journalists have a bachelor's degree, vast numbers of them graduated from the nation's top universities.

A study in the brilliantly aptly titled publication *Journal of Expertise* discovered that in 2016, more than 40 percent of the reporters and editors at the *New York Times* (and the *Wall Street Journal*) were graduates of elite universities.[7]

For these elites, simply uncovering facts and reporting objective reality was never going to be enough for a career choice. Finding out merely what happened was insufficient. Taking their cue from Karl Marx, who wrote of philosophers that they had "merely sought to interpret the world; the point is to change it," they need to be able to give people a full lesson in why something happened and why it mattered. They need to tell them how to think—and what to think.

In its heyday journalism demanded skepticism and curiosity. The good reporter doubted just about whatever he was told. He'd weigh competing accounts and explanations and actively seek out alternative versions. Read the bios of great reporters from the past and they'll be scattered with adjectives like "ornery" and "insubordinate."

The modern journalist is different. His primary ambition is to belong, not to risk the isolation of independent thought, to be part of the expert class, to identify as a member of the cultural elite, happily swaddled in all their shared nostrums. He's most content when he's wagging a finger at the selfish fools who continue to doubt climate extremism, express skepticism about vaccines, or deny their innate privilege.

This trend toward the professionalization of journalism, and its changed place in the social hierarchy, was intensified by Watergate. The work of Carl Bernstein and Bob Woodward propelled journalists to the status of rock stars. Instead of ink-stained wretches toiling over typewriters in grubby newsrooms, they could now have Hollywood movies made about them.

This might not have been so much of a problem for the question of public trust if it hadn't been for the fact that the vast majority of these well-educated, highly motivated, and very ambitious journalists all thought alike.

This is also the result of social and demographic phenomena.

Journalists, by dint of their intellectual interests and sensibilities, tended to be on the left. If you were interested in making money, being an entrepreneur or a successful capitalist, you were unlikely to want to be a journalist. Steadily the news business attracted and became full of like-minded people with a liberal education—and a liberal outlook.

This demographic trend has intensified since the turn of the century.

Journalism has become a profession dominated by a new generation of young graduates of American universities where—as we shall see in a separate chapter—an ideological hegemony had taken hold. Not only are these, like their immediate predecessors, predominantly left-leaning, they were increasingly intolerant of alternative views.

This is the generation that matured—if that is the word—on college campuses where opinion that did not fit with the prevailing orthodoxies on issues of race, gender, sexuality, American culture, and history, western civilization and the like were actively suppressed.

As Andrew Sullivan has written, they graduated into the workforce and simply brought their radical intolerance with them.[8]

The ascent of this class and cohort of little Maoists perhaps reached its apotheosis in the summer of 2020 during the Black Lives Matter protests following the murder of George Floyd, a black man, by a white police officer in Minneapolis. It was the summer in which newsrooms—abandoning any last vestige of journalistic objectivity—felt compelled to publicly commit themselves to BLM, a radical organization, whose political ideology is well to the left of mainstream American politics.

In the most chilling example of editorial extirpation of views that dissent from their ideology, a large group of journalists at the *New York Times* revolted against their paper's leadership over the publication of an op-ed that summer by Senator Tom Cotton, calling for the deployment of the National Guard to quell the violence that was accompanying many of the protests.

The progressive revolt led to the firing of the opinion page editor, James Bennet, and the reassignment of other editors, and what amounted to a groveling apology by the paper's leadership for having had the temerity to publish a legitimate expression of opinion by a US senator.

Two years later, Bennet—himself no conservative, but an editor who had sat happily within the paper's ideological confines—denounced the *New York Times*, saying he had been treated by colleagues as an "incompetent fascist" and accusing its proprietor of publishing a paper that "exists(s) to tell progressives how progressives should view reality."[9]

Bennet found a place elsewhere, but these are people who largely control now what is allowed to be published in the largest circulation newspaper in the United States—overeducated extremists, imposing their narrow worldview on institutions that once existed to disseminate objectively verifiable truths.

One more factor that has accentuated the declining trust in journalism is commercial in character—a significant change in the business model of most newspapers.

For most of the twentieth century, the news business was largely paid for by advertising. Newspapers—and then later radio and television, with their mass audiences—were a perfect place for businesses looking to sell their products and services to market their goods and services.

In the booming economy of the late 1990s, the volume of advertising was so great that at the *Wall Street Journal,* for example, there would be days when the business side of the company—the people who sold the advertising space—would have to turn away advertisers because the printing presses literally could not handle the volume of newsprint that would be needed.

But with the onset of the digital age, that source of revenue has all but dried up. Advertising is now dominated by the digital giants Google and Facebook. Advertising revenue at major newspapers in the United States has fallen by more than 70 percent since 2000. For television, the decline in ad revenue share is smaller but still significant.

This collapse in the main source of revenue for companies has forced media groups to pursue strategies that unwittingly sharply exacerbated the decline in trust in traditional news.

To deal with the decline in revenue, two approaches were followed. One was to maximize reach, with increasingly sensationalized news reporting designed to appeal to larger and larger audiences, to hold on to the scraps of ad revenue that were still there. This has led to an explosion in mass market digital news, whose journalistic standards are low, where maximizing number of eyeballs far outweighs the importance of reporting accuracy.

The other approach was to prove just as damaging for the quality of journalism: upmarket, "quality" newspapers pursued a subscriber-based model. Instead of being funded by advertising revenue, news would be funded directly by people paying for the product. The *Wall Street Journal* pioneered this strategy, and it has been a considerable success, but for many publications it has made the newspapers increasingly dependent.

To persuade subscribers to part with a sizeable sum of money to finance expensive journalism, news organizations had to tacitly promise them a degree of solidarity in the ideological tint of their output. To get millions of people to pay several hundred dollars a year for a news publication, the easiest route is to promise them stuff they find fits with their ideal and prejudices.

This is now an embedded feature of modern journalism. Publications such as the *New York Times* and the *Washington Post* have significantly expanded their subscriber base, in effect saving their publication from financial ruin that threatened from the loss of advertising revenue.

But in return they have become increasingly driven by their readers to produce news of a particular ideological style.

So a kind of vicious circle developed: increasingly left-leaning staffs at the major news organizations pushed an increasingly progressive agenda in their reporting—this attracts left-leaning readers who demand more coverage aligned with their views—and so on.

Of course this trend has also resulted in partisanship of the right in some news organizations too, so what we have is a dynamic that creates ever more polarized news—which means trust in news as a whole declines—and all of this has been compounded by social media, in which, as we have seen, the audience can find news and information that only suits its own interests and ideology.

It's worth dwelling for a minute on this partisanship in media. Throughout this chapter I have chronicled the decline in trust in news by mostly focusing on what is loosely called "the mainstream media." These are the major urban news outlets—newspapers like the *New York Times*, the *Washington Post*, the *Los Angeles Times*; television like CNN, MSNBC; the news divisions of the major networks, ABC, CBS, and NBC; magazines, such as *Time*, *Newsweek*; but also, in the digital age, along with smaller influential publications read by other journalists like Slate, Salon.com—and, of course, perhaps the vehicle for the most widespread dissemination of ideas and interpretations of news, Twitter, less mainstream since acquired by Elon Musk.

But it's also true that a conservative ecosystem has built up in response—as we have denoted, Fox News, but also newer outlets such as Breitbart, OAN, Newsmax, and a host of digital properties.

But it's important to note that this does not mean that the media is somehow perfectly balanced between left and right—and that therefore the "mainstream media" is somehow no more significant in shaping the cultural and political narrative than conservative media.

Even with the growth of conservative and far-right outlets, the news that dominates the political agenda is still largely developed and channeled by progressive voices.

This is in part because of the sheer preponderance of left-leaning journalists across all news outlets.

Frequent surveys of reporter and editor show a large majority of them are liberal or progressive. In a survey by two professors at Indiana University in 2014, the researchers found that only 7 percent of journalists at major publications were registered Republican or Republican supporters. Nearly 30 percent were Democrats.

What's more, this advantage for the left has increased dramatically in the last fifty years. In 1971 Democrats outnumbered Republicans by a ratio of about one and a half to one. Now the gap is four times.[10]

Another study by researchers published in 2017 found that liberals outnumbered conservatives among journalists also by four to one.[11]

The major mainstream liberal-leaning outlets also have the lion's share of reporting resources. This is critical in determining overall bias in media coverage.

Among them the *New York Times*, *Washington Post*, CNN, NBC, etc., have thousands of staff—the work of these outlets tends to dominate the news agenda.

While bias in the media is often exemplified by distorted coverage of a particular subject—the Trump-Russia collusion story is an obvious example, but others abound too—think about the coverage of the Supreme Court nominations of Brett Kavanaugh in 2019 and Amy Coney Barrett in 2020—the legacy media produced an unending barrage of negative stories about them.

But it is not what we might call reporting bias—the tendency of journalists to skew their reporting in a particular direction that is most effective in promoting a particular worldview. It is rather, editorial bias—the selection of stories to cover and report on. By choosing to report on certain stories and ignore others, editors can drive the terms of public discourse.

When a publication such as the *New Yorker* publishes a long, highly damaging but dubiously sourced story about a Republican president's nominee for a Supreme Court position, it will get retold and disseminated and become the defining word for millions more words of reporting. Conservative-leaning outlets, for all the reasons outlined in this chapter, simply do not have the resources and reach to match that, so, irrespective of the fact that there may be apparent balance between left and right in reach, there is no such balance in editorial output.

For the most part, what I have described here in tracking the reasons for the decline in trust in the news media among Americans has been an abandonment of objectivity. For all their faults, left-leaning journalists (and right-leaning journalists, for that matter) still believed they were at least trying to convey objective truth to their audiences.

But of late an even more pernicious trend has taken hold—an idea steadily gaining ground that the very idea of objectivity is to be discarded.

Perhaps stung by all the criticism that they have forfeited trust in their journalism through dressing up subjective opinion as objective, large numbers of journalists at the most influential publications in America now reject even the idea that they should strive to be more objective.

In an eye-opening opinion column in the *Washington Post* in early 2023, Leonard Downie Jr., the former top editor at that paper, called for an end to the attempt to find objective reality in reporting.

The piece was titled, "Newsrooms That Move Beyond Objectivity Can Build Trust" (yes—perhaps the first thing the *Post* could usefully do is fire its headline writers).

It enjoined journalists to reject the outdated idea of "objectivity" because it was a standard that was "dictated over decades by male editors in predominantly white newsrooms and reinforced their view of the world." The very idea of objectivity, in other words—that there is objective truth out there about a story that it is a reporter's job to discover—is racist.

This fits with the wider postmodern rejection of objective reality that we have come to see in other aspects of the public discourse. It reflects in part some of the teaching of critical race theory—based on the idea that supposedly objective judgments are in fact rooted in prejudice and the structural hegemony of white male supremacy.

The modern breed of journalists that increasingly subscribe to this idea think reporters should now favor "moral clarity" in their work over the old-fashioned, problematic idea of objectivity.

They think objectivity means unthinkingly reflecting two sides to every story—mistaking the pursuit of absolute balance in reporting for the pursuit of truth—for example, providing equal coverage to people who say the Earth is flat as to those who insist it is round.

But objectivity was never about that—neutral, noncommittal on the one hand, on the other hand spurious balance. It was about acknowledging that there is truth in the world—in politics, in business, in international affairs; in culture, art, entertainment, and science; and that through hard work, extensive reporting, and investigation, it can be discovered.

If the media has now finally abandoned that idea, then whatever remaining trust there is in its work is likely to disappear completely.

CHAPTER 5

Struggle Sessions

I N OCTOBER 2017 William Jacobson, a distinguished professor
of law at Cornell University and, as a conservative, something of
an endangered species among Ivy League academics, was invited to
deliver a lecture at Vassar College in upstate New York. The event had
been organized by a group of conservative students and was intended
to challenge the climate of ideological repression at colleges and universities that had been steadily banishing opinions that dissent from
the mandatory progressive orthodoxies. The title of the talk was, as
it happens, "An Examination of Hate Speech and Free Speech on
College Campuses."

The notification of the event on campus was met with a burst of
unironic and denunciatory rage. Student groups organized to protest
and to try to get the talk canceled. The Vassar authorities, in a typical
display of amoeba-like spinelessness, quickly sided with the protesters,
and the college president condemned the speech.

The lecture nevertheless went ahead, under heavy security. College
administrators arranged for students both to protest and to retreat to
"safe spaces" where they could be insulated from the offending views.
One of these spaces was the library, where distraught students were
led by guides bearing torches and offering comfort. In a cordoned-off

section they were given coloring books and pencils to help channel and resolve the trauma of finding themselves in the vicinity of someone with ideas they found objectionable. Back at Cornell after the event, the professor met further hostility from his own faculty members. "Twenty-one of my colleagues, alumni groups, the dean, all denounced me. Their goal was to marginalize me and silence me," he says.

It used to be easy to laugh at the snowflakes on college campuses. Extreme left-wing political dogma and attempts to ostracize those who oppose it have long been a prominent feature of university life, and perhaps immature minds can be forgiven a little passion and intolerance.

But the slide into ideological totalitarianism has taken a headlong plunge in recent years. And, in a development that has dark implications for the maintenance of democracy, the intolerant creed that commands adherence to its nostrums about race, gender, and sexual identity increasingly dominates not just universities but high schools and is even creeping into American elementary education.

Nothing has done more to undermine the trust the public has in education that the advance of this intolerant extremism into the nation's classrooms.

Jacobson became something of a bête noire. Shunned by his colleagues, demonized by his college administration, he is, however, protected by academic tenure. But he is in no doubt about the threat to those who don't have such security. "People are scared of losing their jobs and the left has weaponized this to drive people out... most people don't have the option of doing something else," he says. "They couldn't get me but they can silence others."

And they have. Joshua Katz, a professor of classics at Princeton University, is one such example.

In the summer of 2020, at the height of the national meltdown over the killing by a Minneapolis police officer of George Floyd, a black man, and the often violent Black Lives Matter protests that followed, Princeton, like many other prestigious American universities, found itself besieged by radical extremists with wild-eyed proposals about race on campus and in society.

On July 4, a date presumably chosen for its symbolism, a group of several hundred faculty and students published an open letter to the university's leadership, demanding changes to combat what they called a long-standing culture of "anti-Blackness" at Princeton and in the United States as a whole. These changes included the conferral of a range of preferential treatments on black and minority faculty, such as additional pay, time off, and other benefits based on the color of a teacher's skin.

But beyond these demands for what amounted to little more than an obvious shakedown of university resources for a large group of already extraordinarily privileged academics (Princeton professors are among the most richly rewarded in America) was a call for much more sinister changes. Most strikingly, the signatories wanted to establish a committee that would "oversee the investigation and discipline of racist behaviors, incidents, research, and publication on the part of faculty…" In other words, any research or publication that didn't fit the increasingly radical (and continually moving) ideological precepts of the anti-racist fanatics in the senior common room could be canceled—along with its author.

Katz, a tenured professor of distinction who had taught students for twenty years, objected to this transparent attempt at academic censorship, an idea about as alien to the concept of a university as is possible.

Writing in Quillette, an online intellectual journal, Katz lambasted the proposals, especially the idea of a disciplinary committee for way-ward thought.[1]

> For colleagues to police one another's research and publications in this way would be outrageous. Let me be clear: racist slurs and clear and documentable bias against someone because of skin color are reprehensible and should lead to disciplinary action...But is there anyone who doesn't believe that this committee would be a star chamber with a low bar for cancellation, punishment, suspension, even dismissal?

Katz also objected to a proposal in the letter that the university publicly apologize to an extremist black activist group, the Black Justice League, what he called a "terrorist" group whose aggressive tactics a few years earlier had "made life miserable for the many (including the many black students) who did not agree with its members' demands."

The article provoked predictable outrage from activist anti-racist groups. Perhaps less predictable was that Katz found himself depicted as literally an official poster child for intolerable racism and white supremacism by his own employer. Shortly afterward, a website hosted by the university as part of its anti-racist commitments and intended as a helpful guide for college first years cited Katz's article as an example of rancid bigotry.[2]

If that sounds like the stuff of totalitarian fantasy, what happened next was like something out of a Franz Kafka novel.

The university's authorities, with the connivance of the president—Christopher Eisgruber, of all things, a leading legal scholar—dredged up an old complaint lodged against Katz more than a decade earlier of an inappropriate relationship with a student. Katz had already been duly disciplined over the episode—a consensual affair—years before, but the university now decided he had to be fired.

Katz's evidently contrived dismissal was greeted by defenders of free speech at Princeton and elsewhere with horror.

Writing in the Tablet, Sergiu Klainerman, a professor of mathematics at the university with decades of standing, excoriated the leadership and the culture of intolerance it had created.[3]

> It is painfully obvious by now that Katz's only real crime was his criticism of the 2020 faculty letter, which made him the first member of the Princeton community who publicly objected to Eisgruber's attempts to replace freedom of thought, speech, inquiry and association with fashionable woke fanaticism. Katz had to be punished as an example to the rest of us not to interfere with the university's plans to remake itself as a factory of partisan ideology.

The irony of all this is that American universities, especially Ivy league and other elite institutions, are among the least institutionally racist places in the United States, if not on the entire planet. The idea that students and faculty at these colleges, which have elevated ideas of systemic racism and structural inequality, and pursued aggressive affirmative action policies in admissions and hiring for decades, are somehow dominated by white supremacists conducting vigilante campaigns of prejudice and discrimination against ethnic minorities is about as farcical as the idea that the state of Utah persecutes Mormons.

The stories of Jacobson and Katz are just two of a proliferating number of examples of how the vast majority of American universities have betrayed the principles of free expression on which the United States and its globally preeminent system of education were built.

They call to mind Mao Zedong's Cultural Revolution in communist China in the 1960s, in which an ideological purification was conducted to rid institutions such as schools and universities of heretical, "old" thinking. Today's versions of "struggle sessions" involve students and compliant faculty being encouraged to denounce teachers. The victims are not forced to wear dunce caps or face more lethal penalties, but the humiliation inflicted on them is intended to have the same effect on anyone contemplating dissent.

Take the example of James Sweet, the president of the American Historical Society. In the summer of 2022, Sweet, a distinguished historian at the University of Wisconsin, published a thoughtful column in the association's magazine on the problem of "presentism" in contemporary historical work. Sweet suggested, with only the merest hint of disapprobation, that too many scholars today allowed their current political views to distort their interpretations of the past.

"Too many Americans have become accustomed to the idea of history as an evidentiary grab bag to articulate their political positions," he wrote. The article also took a gentle sideswipe at the "1619 Project," a recent *New York Times* invention that had gathered much favorable attention. Its central argument was that the true founding of the United States occurred with the arrival of the first slave ship to the continent in 1619, not with the American Revolution in 1776, an exercise, the authors argued, that was designed in large part to preserve the institution of slavery.

The uproar that greeted this gently and appropriately critical commentary of much so-called history was deafening. The massed ranks of professors and teachers of African American studies and other disciplines denounced Sweet for daring to (implicitly) criticize them.

In a move reminiscent of the forced confessions uttered by victims of the cultural revolution, Sweet issued an abject apology.

He acknowledged the "anger and dismay" his "ham-fisted attempt at provocation" had caused. He "sincerely regret[ted]" the alienation he had brought about. He was "deeply sorry" for his "clumsy efforts," and "apologize[d] again," promising to attempt to "redeem" himself in future.

American higher education has been in many ways central to the nation's success in the last century. Universities and colleges have not only educated some of the nation's most influential men and women and incubated the research that has powered so much world-beating American innovation. They have flourished as idea factories, institutions where people of different backgrounds, outlooks, and traditions have come together to generate the intellectual currents that drive the way we come to better understand the world.

But, central as it is to the continued expansion of the country's collective mind, higher education rests on a fragile base of public trust. Universities depend on the continued willing support of taxpayers, alumni, parents, and businesses to thrive. To exert influence on the nation's economy, culture, and politics, they must be widely respected, their educators and staff believed. Their work has to command the confidence of the American public.

But, just as we have seen with many of the key institutions in American life, trust in higher education, in many of the institutions that have been central to the nation's intellectual development, is crumbling.

According to a Pew Research Center survey, as recently as 2010, 61 percent of Americans thought colleges and universities had a positive effect on American life, with just 26 percent saying their effect was negative. Less than a decade later, in 2019, the proportion saying the effect was positive had dropped to 50 percent. Thirty-eight percent said it was negative.[4]

This decline is mostly based on a steep loss of confidence by the conservative half of the nation. The same survey found that in that nine-year period the proportion of Republicans and Republican-leaning voters who believed colleges and university had a positive effect on American life dropped from 58 percent to 33 percent. Democrats' views were largely unchanged.

Other surveys have suggested the pace of decline in trust is accelerating.

A Gallup survey found that the proportion of respondents saying they had confidence in institutions of higher education dropped from 57 to 48 percent between 2015 and 2018.[5]

Another survey found that the percentage of people saying college had a positive impact on the country dropped by fourteen percentage points in the two years from 2020 to 2022.[6]

Since it has been in the last few years that we have seen the most egregious examples of intolerance and ideological monomania on university campuses, it makes sense that the decline in trust of a large proportion of the population has been accelerating recently.

Faith in the nation's public schools as a whole—from kindergarten right through to college—has also been declining, and again the deterioration has accelerated in recent years. The proportion of people saying they had a "great deal" or "quite a lot" of confidence in public schools was in the high 40 percent range in the Gallup surveys of the 1980s. In 2022 the number was 28 percent.

Large numbers of Americans now see the institutions that are responsible for educating their children as essentially indoctrination centers, inculcating extreme ideas in the nation's youth.

In the case of public high schools, this fear has resulted in a backlash by parents. Over the last decade or so the teaching of certain topics—race and gender studies, courses in civics and history and others—has given a distinct ideological taint to what many high schoolers learn.

But in K–12 education, parents and elected officials seem to enjoy a higher degree of accountability over what is taught.

In 2023 the College Board was forced to withdraw a curriculum for a new Advanced Placement course in African-American studies that would have given prominence to writers associated with so-called critical race theory (more on this later), as well as to the "queer experience and black feminism." After protests and threats of reprisals from Ron DeSantis, the Republican governor of Florida, the curriculum was withdrawn and replaced with one rooted in a much less ideologically slanted version of history and literature.

DeSantis and his fellow Republicans were also successful in barring the teaching of sexuality, and sexual and gender identity to very young children, passing a Florida law that barred discussion of such topics in teaching context before the age of seven.

A parental pushback against the advance of radical ideology in elementary and high school teaching was also evident in various elections in the last few years. In Virginia, Republican Glenn Youngkin won election for governor in 2021, in part because of his effective articulation of parents' concerns about what was being taught in the state's public schools. In the 2022 midterm elections, Republican candidates pushing for the removal of radical teaching curricula and ideologies were successful in a number of school board elections across the country.

But at the college level—in both the public and private sector—if anything, the ideological homogeneity and increasing intolerance of heterodox opinion appears to be increasing.

Students themselves are often eager enforcers of speech codes, or at least feel compelled to restrict expression of differing opinions from the majority.

In a 2021 survey of more than 37,000 students at 159 colleges, for Real Clear Education, College Pulse, and the Foundation for Individual Rights in Education, more than 80 percent of students said they self-censor at least some of the time on campus. Two-thirds of respondents thought it acceptable to shout down a speaker or prevent him or her from speaking on campus, and a quarter said it was acceptable to use violence to stop a speech. More than half said they found racial inequality to be a difficult topic to discuss on campus.[7]

The reason colleges seem so much more intolerant these days is presumably largely because they have become so much more ideologically monolithic.

Several studies have confirmed this trend over the last three decades.

Regular surveys for the Higher Education Research Institute (HERI) have found a lurch to the left in the last thirty years.

In 1989–90, when the institute first surveyed hundreds of academic staff at major colleges and universities, it found that 42 percent of faculty identified as being on the left, 40 percent were moderate, and 18 percent on the right.

By 2016–17 HERI found that 60 percent of faculty were left or far left, compared with 12 percent who identified as right or far right. In less than three decades the ratio of left wing to right wing faculty had gone from 2.1 to one to five to one.[8]

Even this may understate the degree of political uniformity. A more recent study for the Harvard *Crimson* found that more than 80 percent of Harvard's faculty identified as "liberal" or "very liberal." A grand total of 1 percent described themselves as "conservative." Not a single respondent said they were "very conservative."

These are North Korean levels of political conformity.

Lawrence Summers, the leading economist who was US treasury secretary in Bill Clinton's administration in the 1990s, later served as president of Harvard. After a tumultuous few years, and following repeated clashes with the ideologically homogeneous faculty, Summers told me in an interview that this lack of diversity is a serious problem.

> Intellectual diversity is as important to the mission of higher education as demographic diversity and that it's appropriate to make more efforts in our major universities to promote intellectual diversity. And that's certainly something I tried to do during my time as president of Harvard.

What started as college playground antics—politically correct neologisms, consciousness-raising, and anti-bias theology—has become mainstream and deadly serious, a process that is undermining faith in American education itself. The extirpation of dissenting opinion goes beyond simply limiting or "canceling" people who speak out in opposition to prevailing orthodoxies. It is actively and successfully promoting policies that replace America's historical discrimination against minorities with a modern form that sorts Americans into racial identities and then prioritizes some over others.

How did American higher education become host to this monolithic ideological hegemony?

The answer, as Ernest Hemingway wrote of going bankrupt, is in two ways: gradually, then suddenly.

The election of Donald Trump in 2016, with his often crude and belligerent rhetoric, the left's angry backlash to it, and the national turmoil that followed the murder of George Floyd by a police officer in 2020 seem to have provided some of the sparks that lit this ideological conflagration. But there was plenty of kindling that had been laid over the previous few decades.

A significant part of this modern extremism has its roots in the development of a radical intellectual movement that emerged in university faculty common rooms more than three decades ago. Critical race theory, along with other what might be termed structuralist interpretations of history, society, literature, and other intellectual currents and first given a name by Kimberlé Williams Crenshaw, a law professor at University of California Los Angeles, was a successor ideology to traditional Marxist thought. The essence of the theory was that America, and to a large extent all western capitalist societies, is inherently and systemically racist (and patriarchal). Its institutions and rules reflect the hegemony of the white male and the promotion of his distinctive interests to the detriment of others.

The key thesis was that the system itself is structurally flawed and notions of "equality" that well-meaning progressives espoused were invalid. The ideas of what constitutes virtue and value in such a society must be inherently racist and so our concepts of objectivity, fairness, even logic, reason, and scientific method, are all shot through with white oppressive characteristics.

Just as Marxists saw the oppression of workers by capitalism in all aspects of life, so these postmodernists saw racial and gender oppression as the central guiding force in all aspects of economic, political, and social organization.

This emphasis on identity—seeing humans principally as belonging to groups in society—has been augmented by so-called intersectionality, which the dictionary defines as "the interconnected nature of social categorizations such as race, class and gender as they apply to a given individual or group, regarded as creating overlapping and interdependent systems of discrimination or disadvantage."

In short, the dominant idea is that society has been built on systems of oppression—led by white male heterosexuals—and those systems of privilege and advantage still define the character of contemporary society.

Taken to its logical conclusion it has the capacity for—and indeed is succeeding in—essentially delegitimizing all forms of traditional academic study.

This reductio ad absurdum seems to know no bounds. Dan-el Perilla Peralta, a professor of classics at Princeton, wants to abolish classics as a discipline because it inherently propagates whiteness.[9]

He has described the teaching of traditional classics—Latin and Greek history, literature, and civilization—"equal parts vampire and cannibal" and said that throughout history its teaching has served to murder, enslave, and subjugate.

It has been determined that mathematics is inherently racist. According to Rochelle Gutierrez, a professor of math education at the University of Illinois, "Mathematics itself operates as whiteness," according to an article in *Campus Reform*. Algebra and geometry perpetuate "unearned privilege" among whites.[10]

Who gets credit for doing and developing mathematics, who is capable in mathematics, and who is seen as part of the mathematical community is generally viewed as white.

(It should be noted here in fairness that math and the hard sciences have proven to be unsurprisingly more immune to the advance of radical ideology in universities. But that is not for want of trying by some of the more progressive educators.)

A key feature in all this modern ideology is the emphasis on praxis—that this approach to understanding the disposition of power is not simply a critique, a theory, but an organizing principle for society at a micro and macro level. It is essential to this worldview to affirmatively reject the existing order. This explains why it is so exclusionary and intolerant: in a neat circularity it argues that challenges to it are themselves acts of oppression.

Of course no one seriously challenges the proposition that racism persists in America or that minorities have historically and currently continue to suffer from injustice—in business, housing, law and criminal justice, and education. But anti-racism goes well beyond this premise. Anti-discrimination policies, the new thinking says, are incapable of redressing fundamental inequality; that can only be achieved through an immersive rejection of the system itself. Modern proponents of the idea, such as the writer Ibram X. Kendi, insist this means white people must acknowledge their sinfulness. He and fellow peddlers of the theory are paid handsomely by company human resources departments to re-educate their workforces.

It is probably no accident that, as a successor to Marxist thinking, this ideology emerged right at the end of the Cold War. Critiques of fundamental flaws in western capitalism were popular on campuses in the 1960s and 1970s, but the intellectual traction they gained more widely was tempered by the existential threat posed by capitalism's unappealing alternative. The paradox was that, having won the Cold War in large part because of the evident superiority of its liberal values, America and the wider west found itself easier prey to alternative far-left critiques.

Jason Hill, who was born in Jamaica and teaches philosophy at DePaul University in Chicago, faced his cancellation battle defending the Israeli prime minister Benjamin Netanyahu's policies in the West

Bank. Threatened with a student boycott, backed by leaders of the academic community, he sued the university for defamation. "The US has lost its energy," he says. "The West as a whole lost its sense of purpose and meaning and significance and there arose all kinds of alternative ideologies to fill that vacuum."

As academics signed up to critical race and similar theories, they tended to hire like-minded people, and dissonant voices dwindled. The rapid growth in the number of administrators at colleges has played a significant part too. Most colleges have hired vast armies of diversity, equity, and inclusion officers, intendants of racial equality and social justice to ensure compliance with goals for gender, sexual, and ethnic diversity.

As the author Richard Vedder wrote a few years ago, "When I started teaching in the 1960s there were typically around two faculty for every non-faculty support person. Today there are more administrators than faculty at most schools."[11]

According to a study by Ashlynn Warta for the James G. Martin Center for Academic Renewal, at one major public university, the University of North Carolina, "funding for institutional support (i.e., administration) saw a nearly 50 percent, inflation-adjusted increase in eleven short years"—from $2,217 per student in 2006 to $4,069 per student in 2017.[12]

It's become obligatory at most universities for applicants to academic posts now to include a statement of how they plan to address racial and gender diversity challenges in their research and teaching.

As colleges have become populated with radical teachers, the students they admitted were more open to the kind of exclusionary and intolerant pedagogy that delegitimizes opposing views. In their 2018 book *The Coddling of the American Mind*, the social scientists Greg Lukianoff and Jonathan Haidt trace much of the modern intolerance on campus to a climate of "safetyism." In the past twenty years, they say, educators and even parents have become obsessed with emotional fragility. Like those poor suffering students at Vassar who had to be coddled with coloring books and crayons to alleviate their suffering from the words of an unsympathetic professor, students now routinely complain that certain types of speech "hurts" them.

Lukianoff and Haidt cite three "great untruths" that have come to define modern American teaching: "what doesn't kill you makes you weaker," "always trust your feelings," and "life is a battle between good people and evil people."

In 2015 Nicholas Christakis and Erika Christakis, a husband and wife team of professors at Yale, were denounced by students after she criticized cultural hypersensitivity about Halloween costumes. In a confrontation with some of their critics that went viral on YouTube and recalled scenes from China's Cultural Revolution, Mr. Christakis was told that he and his wife had inflicted "pain" and needed to apologize. Needless to say, they did.

The domination of student bodies by fragile young minds has spilled over into the workforce in the past decade. In technology, media, and other companies, they have brought their pathologies and ideologies into the workplace, and our companies, government departments, law firms, and cultural institutions are now increasingly peopled by graduates schooled in the idea that America is systemically racist, sexist, and bigoted and its history one of unrelenting exploitation and harm. The damage to the nation's cohesion and purpose is truly an academic gift that keeps on giving.

Economic factors have also played a role in the widening gap between the exclusionary progressivism on university campuses and the views and outlook of the wider American public.

In the last thirty years the differential between compensation for jobs in the commercial private sector—especially finance, technology, management, and health care—and professors' salaries has mushroomed. A recent study found that, after inflation, salaries for full-time faculty members in higher education increased by just 9 percent between 1971 and 2019. That puts academics a little behind average workers in terms of real income increases in the last fifty years.[13]

But the real gap emerges when seeing how university salaries have diverged over that time compared with salaries for other professionals with comparable qualifications.

The median salary for a university teacher in the early 1970s was around $80,000 in today's money. Back then that represented a competitive salary when measured against other jobs such as lawyers and finance professionals.

But today the median salary for a full-time faculty member is around $90,000. Bear in mind this would be typically for professors with a decade or more of postgraduate experience.

Today, starting salaries for investment bankers straight out of four-year college are over $100,000. New associates at big law firms—typically age twenty-five or so—make more than that.

In short, the compensation for university professors has gone from that of a highly respectable and well remunerated professional to among the lowest that graduates can expect to command. An executive assistant in a top law firm makes more than most tenured professors with twenty years' standing at a major state university.

What has all this got to do with trust?

Sociological studies tell us that highly educated humans who value personal financial reward in vocations tend to be more conservative. It's no accident that entrepreneurs, bankers, business leaders, and others are more conservative in ideological perspective than teachers, journalists, and public sector workers—whose cultural and intellectual interests lean left.

The relative decline in academic salaries compared with finance, technology, and other careers has almost certainly further narrowed the field of ambitious conservative-minded young graduates.

Self-selection plays a role too. Would-be academics of a conservative disposition are turned off by the atmosphere and intolerance they see from the progressives who dominate universities. Why put in the hard work for a PhD at a university where your ideas are likely to be constantly denounced and delegitimized by teachers and fellow students, and the prospect of a tenured position at the end of it is significantly diminished?.

Add to that the suffocating demands of university administrators with their enforcement of vast numbers of diversity, equity, and inclusion rules, and is it any wonder fewer conservatives submit themselves to the process?

The sharp decline in trust in higher education in the last decade probably owes to other factors besides the rising intolerance of heterodox views.

Access to the most elite level universities has become steadily more restricted and subject to increasingly complex admission rules.

Affirmative action programs favor certain ethnic minorities but not others, resulting in a widening disparity between the qualifications of some candidates admitted and many who are rejected.

As this book goes to press, it is expected that the US Supreme Court will strike down affirmative action programs as they have operated at many universities for decades; the ruling is expected in a case brought by an organization representing large numbers of students who say they were unfairly denied admission to colleges such as Harvard.

The ruling should bring to an end increasingly egregious discrimination practices at many elite colleges. Students particularly adversely affected have been from Asian-American families, who, despite high levels of academic achievement and other attainments at high school, have found themselves denied places at top universities.

If the Court decides as many have expected it to, it will be a ruling that may, after four decades, begin restoring some faith in the fairness of university admissions for many millions of Americans.

Other forms of discrimination persist, however, and further cement the idea in the public's mind that, for many people, the chance of admission to an elite college is unfairly loaded against them. Many universities continue with so-called "legacy" admissions policies, favoring the offspring of alumni, especially those who have been fortunate enough to be able to be very generous in their "advancement."

Yale University is just one case of many. One of the oldest and grandest of the Ivy Leagues, Yale likes to emphasize how diverse its student body has become after many years of affirmative action for certain minorities. In its description of its incoming class of 2025, it boasts that more than half identified as students of color. It made less of the fact that 14 percent—one in seven new Yalies—were the offspring of graduates of the university. Yale and other colleges insist that these "legacies" met the same academic and other standards for admission as other applicants, but countless exposés of the process have demonstrated that relatives of Yale alumni—already some of the most privileged people on the planet—get special attention in the application process.

This highlights another way in which top American colleges have become increasingly unmeritocratic and detached from the bulk of the nation they are supposed to serve.

In recent years, economic considerations—the widening gap between the cost and the perceived value of a university degree—have undermined public faith in the role of universities and colleges.

The cost of college has become prohibitively expensive for many American families. Data from the National Center for Education Statistics show that between 1981 and 2021, the cost of four-year college tuition, room and board almost tripled in real, inflation-adjusted terms, from a little over $10,000 a year in today's money to nearly $30,000.[14] While, as we have noted, faculty salaries have stagnated in real terms, much of this additional cost to the student stems from the astronomically rapid growth of the bureaucracy—especially the university administrators who enforce the strict diversity, equity, and inclusion mandates. Not exactly value for money in the eyes of many hard-pressed families.

Levels of student debt incurred to help pay these soaring costs have also surged. The average student loan debt nearly tripled in real terms too over the same period.[15]

While a college degree still represents a significant boost to lifetime earnings potential, the advantage relative to the cost is shrinking. For many students, especially graduates of second-tier private universities, where the cost can match Ivy League levels, the benefit is diminishingly small.

The richer institutions, with endowments the size of medium-size countries in the world (Harvard's was valued at $53 billion in 2022, Yale's $41 billion) make a great deal of the fact that they use their extraordinary wealth to subsidize students from poorer families so they can attend college without incurring a mountain of debt. The wealthiest colleges now generally provide free tuition for anyone from a family with an income below $100,000—a sum substantially in excess of average US family income.

But in practice, this munificence has not resulted in a genuinely economically diverse student body.

In his book *The Tyranny of Merit: What's Become of the Common Good?*, Michael Sandel, a professor of philosophy at Harvard, exposes the degree to which top universities have increasingly become schools for the children of the already very rich.[16]

He points out that more than 70 percent of those who attend the hundred or so most competitive colleges in the United States come from the top quarter of the income scale; only 3 percent come from the bottom quarter.

> The wealth gap in college enrollment is most acute at the top. At Ivy League colleges, Stanford, Duke and other prestigious places, there are more students from the wealthiest one percent of families than from the entire bottom half of the country. At Yale and Princeton only about one student in fifty comes from a family whose income is in the bottom 20 percent of the population. Applicants to the Ivy League from families whose income falls in the top one percent of the country have a probability of admission 77 times greater than those from families in the bottom 20 percent. A majority of children from families in the bottom half of the income scale attend two year colleges or do not go to college at all.
>
> Though far more inclusive in terms of gender, race, and ethnicity, this meritocratic elite has not produced a fluid, mobile society. Instead, today's credentialed, professional classes have figured out how to pass their privileges on to their children, not by bequeathing them large estates but by equipping them with the advantages that determine success in a meritocratic society.

A fascinating phenomenon in the last decade has been the growing discontent of alumni of prestigious universities alarmed at the intolerant progressivism that dominates the culture at their alma mater. Growing numbers of (often very wealthy) graduates have joined what has been termed an "alumni rebellion," withholding donations unless their colleges agree to enforce free speech.[17]

But the campaign has had limited success. This is probably due mainly to the fact that, despite what they view as the intolerant conditions on campus, these alumni know the value that a degree from a top university in an increasingly competitive global marketplace for jobs confers on their beloved children.

Given the rapid advance of authoritarian progressivism on campus, an all-consuming obsession with postmodern ideology about race, gender, and other aspects of social identity, a rigid and still tightening political conformity among faculty and students, exorbitant increases in costs along with diminishing rewards, and diminishing accessibility for the vast majority of people unfortunate enough not to be wealthy or already in possession of an elite college degree, it's hardly surprising that trust has declined sharply in American higher education.

But a cynic may ask, does it matter?

A sanguine answer might be: not that much.

American universities still seem to dominate the top of the global rankings of surveys of higher education.

The worst excesses of woke thought-policing are found in liberal arts, humanities, and social sciences, but in the hard sciences, mathematics, and technology, US universities are still genuine places of learning and discovery.

The quality of research and much of the teaching at America's institutions of higher education is peerless, and cutting-edge work continues to drive innovation. The special relationship developed between universities and business in places like Silicon Valley; Austin, Texas; and along Route 128 outside Boston is still generating an interchange of ideas that places American technology ahead of most of the rest of the world's. Ambitious minds from all over the world still flock to American universities—for bachelor's, master's, doctoral degrees, and for postdoctoral work, the drive of these immigrants contributing incalculably to overall American prosperity. Every fall the list of Nobel Prize winners announced in Stockholm is dominated by professors from American universities.

But the intolerant progressive march through these institutions continues apace. Increasing numbers of academics in the sciences and math—where ideological views remain still relatively diverse—say they find the overall climate at their universities repressive. In October 2021, the Massachusetts Institute of Technology—one of the nation's top science, mathematics, and economics universities—canceled a guest lecture on planetary climate science by Dorian Abbot, an associate professor in geophysical sciences at the University of Chicago. His crime? He had previously publicly criticized affirmative action, arguing that race-based preferences in personnel decisions risked harming true diversity—intellectual diversity—in universities. It's worth remembering that this critique of affirmative action is widely shared—and indeed affirmative action itself may already have been struck down by the time this book goes to press.

In an article he had co-written that was published in *Newsweek*,[18] Abbot argued:

Ninety years ago Germany had the best universities in the world. Then an ideological regime obsessed with race came to power and

drove many of the best scholars out, gutting the faculties and leading to sustained decay that German universities never fully recovered from. We should view this as a warning of the consequences
of viewing group membership as more important than merit, and
correct our course before it is too late.

The Nazi analogy in contemporary debate is often an overwrought
one, and perhaps the sentiment could have been better expressed, but
the central thrust of the argument is a good one: the insistence on
conformity in universities and colleges is inconsistent with the idea of
freedom of thought and academic rigor.

* * *

"A university training is the great ordinary means to a great but ordinary end; it aims at raising the intellectual tone of society," wrote
the nineteenth-century English prelate and scholar John Henry Newman, in his book *The Idea of a University*. "It is the education which
gives a man a clear conscious view of his own opinions and judgments, a truth in developing them, an eloquence in expressing them,
and a force in urging them."

Even more important than the many practical benefits that a rich,
diverse system of higher education bestows upon a country is the role
that universities and colleges play in developing the mind of a nation.
They are supposed to represent the pinnacle of the education process—the route by which the country's finest brains are brought to
realize their potential. In many ways, the strength of a nation's intellectual self-confidence and the health of its ambition can be measured
directly by the quality of scholarship and learning at its universities.

For several hundred years the great institutions of American learning fostered a climate of inquiry, debate, and discovery that embodied the very ideals of freedom of thought and expression central to the American ideal.

But in the first few decades of this century, the character of much of American higher education has changed in ways that reflect and amplify the wider deterioration in the trust that Americans have in the institutions that hold so much influence over their lives. Universities have a unique role in American life. They must not only restore public trust in themselves; they have a crucial part to play in rebuilding trust in America.

CHAPTER 6

Subscribe, Follow, Like, Distrust

I N THE SUMMER of 2020, Republican congressman Greg Steube started to notice something odd about his campaign emails.

As a candidate running for reelection in his Florida congressional district, as with all candidates in an age dominated by electronic communication, daily direct emails to voters and potential supporters were an important part of his campaign. But after a while, his parents, who were eagerly following his election prospects, noticed that they weren't receiving his emails in their Gmail inboxes. When they dug a little deeper, they realized they were missing their son's communications because the emails were going directly to the Gmail spam folder.

The congressman began to hear from other Republican candidates that they too were being alerted that their emails to Gmail accounts were going straight to spam.

As it happened, not long after the discovery, Sundar Pichai, the chief executive of Alphabet, the company that owns Google, was testifying before the congressional committee of which Steube was a member, alongside the chiefs of other leading technology companies. Most of the questioning that day focused on bipartisan concerns about the scale of big tech and whether the Silicon Valley giants were abusing their market power.

But when Steube got the chance for a question, he pitched it out of left field for the Alphabet boss—what was happening to his emails?

The guy from Google was evidently nonplussed and explained that the company's algorithms simply did what users wanted—sorting emails from friends and family sometimes differently from those from official accounts.

But, the congressman persisted, pointing out, this couldn't apply here, since the emails from son to father were just going straight to spam. Could this not be a case of algorithmic discrimination—with Google disproportionately diverting emails from conservatives and Republicans away from users' attention?

Pichai demurred; the allegation certainly seemed farfetched, even a little paranoid, and didn't get much attention. Just another batty right-winger discovering conspiracies where there weren't any. Most of us hate getting unsolicited political emails anyway and are quite happy to see them go to spam. Perhaps Google was just being helpfully zealous.

But the story did get the attention of some data researchers at North Carolina State University. Hassan Iqbal, Usman Mahmood Khan, Hassan Ali Khan, and Muhammad Shahzad, decided to test the proposition that Gmail was biased. Over the course of five months that summer and fall they examined whether tech companies' "spam filtering algorithms" were indeed politically slanted.[1]

They created 102 email accounts and subscribed to two presidential, seventy-eight senate, and 156 house candidates' campaign newsletters. To control for the possibility that non-political factors such as demographics, geography, and age of users might account for any differences in spam filtering, they posed as a range of subscribers.

They discovered that Gmail did in fact display a remarkable differential in how it treated the emails of candidates of different political parties. Google's email system retained in the user's inbox a very high proportion of emails from left-of-center candidates, marking only 10 percent as spam. But more than 77 percent of conservative candidates' emails got channeled to the spam folder.

The study "further observed that the percentage of emails marked by Gmail as spam from the right-wing candidates grew steadily as the election date approached, while the percentage of emails marked as spam from the left-wing candidates remained about the same."

Intriguingly, the study also found that while Google leaned heavily left, two other email providers, Microsoft and Yahoo, leaned to the right, though not by anything as much as Google in the opposite direction.

Google insisted that there was no political choice at work in its algorithms.

The researchers also said they had "no reason to believe that there were deliberate attempts from these email services to create these biases to influence the voters." But they added, "as many of the voters today rely on the information they see (or don't see) online such biases may have an unignorable impact on the outcomes of an election."

Representative Steube won reelection handily, without any help or hindrance from his parents' strangely behaving Gmail account, and perhaps the company is right that no conscious bias had been installed in the spam algorithm.

But the odd episode captured in microcosm the wave of mistrust with which many Americans now regard the technology companies that increasingly facilitate our communications, expand our knowledge, and even shape our lives.

Reasonable suspicions of political bias are just one reason why people have become wary of big technology companies. The evidence is indisputable. Beneath the uncertainty about Google's email is a vast mountain of certainties about how the tech firms manipulate our politics: the suppressing and outright blocking by Facebook and Twitter of embarrassing and potentially explosive stories about Hunter Biden in the days before his father was elected president in 2020; the cancellation by payment processor Stripe of campaign contributions to candidates of which it disapproved; the suspension of fundraising by GoFundMe, the leading crowdfunding site, by supporters of the Canadian truckers' protests in 2022 against vaccine mandates; the cancellation of contracts with the US defense department by Google and others because of protests by their employees.

At the same time as conservatives allege political bias against them, many other Americans insist that the technology companies promote "misinformation" that advances right-wing causes and feeds conspiracy theories—involving everything from alleged Russian interference in US elections to false claims about vaccines and wild claims about pedophile rings run by powerful Democratic politicians.

The combination of companies whose leadership and workforces are dominated by people with highly motivated political objectives and ideologies, and the ease of sharing and transmitting false information with a wide audience has led to a collapse in trust in technology companies in just a few years.

But deepening political divisions generated by suspicions of partisan ideologues and unscrupulous manipulators of information are just one way in which the ubiquity of the internet has undermined faith in the very basis of our information technology–driven culture and society.

Fears about privacy, the security of financial transactions and communications, concern about the automation of jobs through information technology and artificial intelligence, and growing alarm about the damage that the universal fixation with smartphones and the apps that run on them is doing to our mental health—these have all contributed to a profound loss in confidence in modern technology and, more importantly, in the wider bonds that tie the very nation together.

The modern technology that is now intrinsic to almost all our daily activities has been with us a relatively short time, so measures of public trust don't go back as far as they do for other institutions, but even in a decade, the decline is startling.

According to an annual trust survey conducted by Edelman, a public relations firm, trust in the technology sector reached an all-time low in 2022, with a 57 percent rating among respondents. That's down from 78 percent in 2012 when the survey began.[2]

That puts the tech sector roughly in the middle of the full range of American business, behind health care, retail, and manufacturing but ahead of the energy and automotive sectors. Just a year earlier, tech had been the top-ranked sector in the survey—in 2021 it had fallen to ninth. Social media companies recorded a score of 46, placing them below all other business sectors in the survey.

The decline in trust in modern technology is different in critical respects from the loss of faith in other institutions in America. First, its sheer scale and reach—and the fact that it cuts across all sectors and aspects of our culture—means that it dominates our economy and society in ways no other business, political, or cultural institution does.

But second, the decline in trust represents a precipitous fall from grace for the promises of the internet revolution. In not much more than a single generation, we have gone from widely shared expectations that modern technology would transform our lives incomparably for the better to the contemporary reality that for many Americans it has made politics, culture, and life itself worse. It's these two things that make the loss of trust in the applications of technology so pervasive and harmful.

First, consider the scale.

The speed at which the US economy and society has been transformed by the information technology revolution of the last half century can be measured in all kinds of ways: most obviously by the domination of the economy and financial markets by big tech companies.

In 2000, the four biggest US corporations by value were household names whose brands had been staples of American life for generations: General Electric, which had been making light bulbs and much more since 1892; Exxon Mobil, pumping oil for America's factories and vehicles since 1911; Pfizer, producing pharmaceuticals since 1849; and Citigroup, a financial services behemoth whose ancestor company started lending money in 1812. Rounding out the top five was Microsoft, an upstart founded in 1975 but whose scale then presaged the transformation to come.

Today, the five largest companies are, along with Microsoft, Apple, Alphabet (the parent company of Google), Amazon, and Nvidia, a graphics designer and creator. Also in the top ten is Meta Platforms, parent of Facebook.

Of these, after Microsoft, Apple is the granddaddy, founded in 1976. The rest were all started after the end of the Cold War: Nvidia in 1993, Amazon in 1994, and Google in 1998. Facebook emerged from Mark Zuckerberg's college dorm room as recently as 2004.

More than two centuries after its founding, America was dominated by businesses that had been around for most of the nation's history. Today, it is dominated by half a dozen companies that mostly didn't exist when half of today's Americans were born.

It's not only the speed of this transformation but its pervasiveness in American life that is so striking. Two-thirds of Americans own an Apple product. Almost a third perform Google searches. Two-fifths buy something on Amazon at least once a month. Almost three-quarters use Facebook, half of them frequently.

Second, the unfulfilled promise.

Throughout history, every wave of technological innovation has been greeted with both outlandish claims for its promise but also deep skepticism about its long-term usefulness.

The story that Henry Ford's banker told his lawyer not to invest in the eponymous motor company because "the horse is here to stay but the automobile is only a novelty—a fad" is probably apocryphal. Darryl Zanuck, the great twentieth-century film producer, may have had his tongue in his cheek when he said of television that it "won't be able to hold onto any market it captures after the first six months" because "people will soon get tired of staring at a plywood box every night."

But it is certainly true that new products, devices, and services generate high expectations that may not be met.

When the internet emerged in the 1990s, building on the arrival of the personal computer and the rapid expansion of fiber-optic cable distribution in the 1980s, the possibilities seemed not only limitless but enormously beneficent.

Some of the forecasts were positively dreamlike.

"If cyberspace is utopian it is because it opens the possibility of using the deterministic platform for unpredictable ends...we might even grow a system large and complex enough to leap across that last possible bifurcation—autopoetically—into that strangest of all possible attractors—the godmind," wrote David Porush, a prominent author at the time.

More prosaically—or at least comprehensibly—forecasters had high hopes that in short order the internet would transform the way we read and write; learn and study; love and work; play and shop; live and even die.

"A...metaphor that I think comes closer to describing a lot of the activities that will take place is that of the ultimate market," wrote Bill Gates in 1995. "Markets from trading floors to malls are fundamental to human society, and I believe this new one will eventually be the world's central department store. It will be where we social animals sell, trade, invest, haggle, pick stuff up, argue, meet new people and hang out."

More powerfully still, the possibility of instant access to every book, article, movie, television show, work of art, and piece of research ever published, along with an infinitely expanding universe of globally communicated thoughts and ideas, seemed to presage a world of knowledge beyond the wildest imaginings of any of our ancestors since time began.

Some of the most important hopes revolved around the world of politics—domestic and international.

The widespread and instant availability of information would make citizens of democracies better informed. That would enable them to make better decisions, not just about their consumption and investment habits, but about their political choices. There would be dramatically improved communication so that, as in some giant Socratic adventure, citizens would hear arguments and evidence, assess their validity and relevance, reach logical conclusions, and make choices that reflected the best possible knowledge set. Social media would greatly enhance the ability of citizens to come together in voluntary groups, and disseminate information and data that would make them more collaborative.

"We will derive robust and sustainable economic progress, strong democracies, better solutions to global and local environmental challenges, improved health care, and—ultimately—a greater sense of shared stewardship of our small planet," declaimed Vice President Al Gore in 1995, adding that the internet would not only spread participatory democracy, but also forge "a new Athenian Age of democracy."

But wait. Things would be even better than that. We would not just have Periclean democracy on a global scale; unlike those pesky warring ancients, we would have world peace too. As the internet shrank global geography, our planetary interdependence would become greater, and all around the world, undemocratic regimes would be exposed to good democratic ideas. Swords would be beaten into electronic plowshares.

"On balance, the death of distance will be a force for peace," wrote Frances Cairncross in her 1997 book, *The Death of Distance: How the Communications Revolution is Changing Our Lives.* "Because it favors democracy, and democracies are more reluctant to fight than dictatorships, it will reduce the potential for conflict."

So how's all that working out for you?

With elevated expectations like that for a future of freedom, democracy, and peace, it's little wonder that disappointment was in our future. With so much trust placed in rapidly evolving technology to deliver a twenty-first century of unimagined contentment, it's no wonder at all that the realities of the succeeding thirty years have undone so much of that trust.

You would need the pinkest of rose-tinted spectacles to see democracy in the 2020s as being in better shape than it was in the 1990s.

Confident forecasts that democracy would spread rapidly in the information age as people who lived under tyranny would be empowered by instant access to the truth their governments denied them have been confounded.

In fact totalitarian governments have proved adept at exploiting the possibilities of information technology to tighten their grip on their people.

In China today, the ubiquitous use of smartphones has enabled a system of social control unlike anything Mao Zedong could have imagined. Constant surveillance and examination of every aspect of a Chinese citizen's activities presents the Communist Party with a system of incentives and punishments to ensure near universal compliance with the party line. A system of "social credit" rewards good behavior—on everything from obeying traffic signals to staying out of too much debt—and penalizes breaches.

The reach is extraordinary. Beijing maintains regional and national blacklists for various violations of social order. It can take from two to five years to be removed from the list. Offenses that will get you on the list include late tax payments or disobeying environmental rules.

Punishment for offenses by individuals can include travel bans and even reduced employment opportunities as well as constant audits by intrusive authorities. Good behavior is rewarded by discounts on energy bills, the freedom to rent bikes or hotel rooms without the need for a deposit, shorter waiting times at hospitals, and better savings and borrowing rates at banks.[3]

Central monitoring of samizdat websites enables easy suppression of dissenting political or cultural views. China's repression is much more extensive and tighter thanks to the internet and other modern technologies—such as artificial intelligence—than it has ever been.

The best example of the antidemocratic paradox of the internet and social media came probably in the so-called Arab Spring from 2011 to 2012, when repressive governments in the Middle East and North Africa came under intense revolutionary pressure from their peoples.

Initially, the use of social media in spreading information about regime abuses, alternative manifestos, and practical information about the timing and venues of protests facilitated the revolutionary movements. In places like Tunisia and Egypt, people even talked of the insurrections as "Facebook Revolutions."

But gradually, as the despots asserted control over the technologies, they were actually able to use modern digital techniques to intensify suppression. Under pressure from governments, social media and other tech companies suspended or closed accounts of some prominent protestors. It was subsequently discovered that Microsoft had earlier agreed to train law enforcement officers in Tunisia in the ways of information technology in exchange for cooperation from the government there on the company's commercial objectives.

Other big US tech companies earned valuable contracts helping repressive governments develop their means of surveillance, monitoring, and censorship.

In Myanmar in 2013, Facebook hosted accounts of the country's military and authoritarian leaders that incited hatred against the country's minority Rohingya population, helping facilitate what the United States and other countries later declared to be a genocide.

All this did profound damage to the reputation of America's big tech companies. In the space of a few years these giants of Silicon Valley, which had been widely lionized as facilitators of a new era of entertainment, information, and social communication, were suddenly seen by many as all-seeing, all-powerful instruments of oppression, hatred, and division.

But it was at home in the United States that the worst damage was done to the faith people placed in technology.

"Fake news" and "misinformation" have circulated in American political discourse since the early days of the republic—indeed well before that. Before Mark Zuckerberg was born, wild conspiracy theories were part of the currency of politics—from ancient antisemitic calumnies about blood libels to the various claims about who killed President John F. Kennedy.

But the great virtue of the internet—and social media especially—is also its great vice: its unprecedented reach and the unprecedented speed with which false or malicious stories could travel.

In a country increasingly prone to hyperpartisanship, and one so closely and bitterly divided along ideological lines (as we have documented in an earlier chapter), the potential of misinformation in shaping opinion and thereby the outcome of close elections was suddenly enormous.

By now, the stories of how social media circulated fake or misleading stories—or failed to circulate accurate stories—at critical phases of recent US election campaigns are well documented.

Democrats continue to insist that Hillary Clinton lost the 2016 presidential election to Donald Trump mainly because of the distribution of false stories about her, on Facebook especially, many of them planted by a Russian intelligence operation.

In 2020, the suppression by Facebook of a *New York Post* story about Hunter Biden, Joe Biden's son, and his alleged nefarious activities is blamed by Republicans for costing Trump the election.

In fact, detailed studies have shown that the Russian campaign against Clinton likely had very little effect on the outcome of the 2016 election. Likewise, it's highly uncertain whether the Biden revelations would have made much difference in 2020 if they had not been digitally blocked.

But neither judgment matters much. What the Russia allegations did was unleash a storm of accusations about Facebook that changed forever the way social media and tech companies more generally were perceived by many Americans. Their efforts to avoid accusations in the future that they had been manipulated by a foreign power, combined with intense pressure from their employees and the traditional media, made them take actions that only deepened suspicions that they were politically committed and inherently untrustworthy.

Bipartisan distrust of media has been further enhanced as conservatives have further pushed back against the appearance of bias against them. When the billionaire entrepreneur Elon Musk acquired Twitter in 2022, he explicitly promised to end what he and most conservatives viewed as politically skewed information on the platform. This in turn led progressives to doubt whether Twitter could be trusted—and so the cycle of bipartisan mistrust turned again.

Further alarms about the trustworthiness of technology have been aroused by the rapid advances made in artificial intelligence in recent years. While this technology seems to have the potential to achieve extraordinary advances for the frontiers of human knowledge, again it has been tainted by suspicions that the algorithms underpinning it are themselves ideologically determined.

When OpenAI launched its ChatGPT product in late 2022, a chatbot capable of providing extraordinarily sophisticated responses to questions and challenges from users, it was met with a mixture of awe and alarm, as users saw for the first time the vast potential of generative artificial intelligence that could make our lives infinitely easier, but could also turf us all out of our jobs. But the excitement was tempered and the fear magnified when it was discovered that much of the content it generated betrayed—like, presumably, its programmers, and the bosses of the company that produced it—a distinctly progressive bias.

What we have increasingly now in so much of the technology that Americans interact with on a daily basis—social media and search engines especially—is widespread bipartisan mistrust, with something similar to what has happened in traditional media. Instead of an ideal in which these tech giants are believed to provide products that generate objective truths, we seem to operate in a context in which one side has its own set of trustworthy platforms, and the other side has its own.

If you think about it this is no form of trust at all. The very concept underpinning trust is that we believe things we can't verify ourselves; we put our faith in sources of information whose judgments we don't judge. If we only believe sources that we are predisposed to believe, it is essentially the same as only believing things we can verify ourselves. That represents the absence of trust.

But news—fake, misinforming, partisan—is not the sole reason that Americans have lost trust in the technology that dominates their lives—and the people and companies who supply it.

The ubiquity of tech, and our very dependence on it, has created its own trust gap. It may not be true that you always hurt the one you love, but it's almost certainly true that you come to hate the thing you depend on. Our dependency on our devices creates its own resentment. It's the sheer power and utility of modern tech—smartphones, tablets, digital televisions, social media, apps—that leaves us deeply unsettled about what it is doing to us.

The most obvious manifestation of this is rising alarm about privacy. This is a phenomenon that captures precisely the ambivalence Americans feel about technology. The data collected in every encounter and experience we have online helps make our lives much more efficient, enjoyable, and even healthier—enabling companies to divine our tastes and needs and better supply them with more targeted goods and services. But that same accumulation of data that makes life so much more efficient is also a terrifying example of how we have surrendered our most precious possession—our privacy—to technology companies.

A Pew survey in 2019 found that well over half of Americans believe it is not possible to go through their daily lives without having their private data collected.[4]

And of course they would be right.

Stories of misuse of private data, of the dissemination of users' data without permission are legion.

In 2020, in the early stages of the COVID pandemic, the *New York Times* revealed that a data mining feature on the Zoom video-conferencing platform allowed some participants on calls to access profile data about other participants on the business networking site LinkedIn.

The company disabled the feature when the story was published, but it was a reminder of the almost unbridled access to our information tech companies have.

In 2019, Twitter acknowledged allowing advertisers to access users' personal data to improve the effectiveness of their marketing. Without obtaining users' permission, ad buyers on Twitter could mine their email addresses and phone numbers, and cross-reference their marketing databases with Twitter's to identify shared customers and serve them targeted ads. The company claimed the incident was the result of an internal error.

In 2016 Reuters reported that Yahoo had been scanning the email of hundreds of millions of users at the behest of the National Security Agency and the Federal Bureau of Investigation.[5] The company insisted that it was merely complying with the law and a directive from the intelligence agencies, but the demand itself was highly unusual in the breadth of its targeting, and the company's decision was highly controversial internally and led to the resignation of its chief information security officer.

For years apps have been able to track users on their cell phones even when they are not using the app, and have used the data then obtained for commercial purposes. Facebook, for example, claims that it doesn't sell its users' data to third parties. But it does acknowledge that it may share information about users with other apps, advertisers, and other vendors, as well as with other platforms it owns, such as Instagram.

There have been repeated interventions by regulators and legislators to improve protection for users' data, but these have barely impacted the ability of platforms to exploit information without the permission or knowledge of the user. The pervasive sense we all have that our devices are constantly monitoring our online activity, collecting the most detailed information about it, and using that information for commercial or even worse nefarious reasons is inescapable.

Even when tech users can have limited confidence that companies won't misuse their data, they can have little security that their data won't be stolen by a hacker.

Worries about the security of data have risen sharply in the last few years. The same Pew survey cited earlier found that 70 percent of adults say their personal data is less secure than it was five years ago.

Again, it's hard not to conclude that the worries are justified. In the last few years the number of prominent companies and institutions whose security has been breached has been multiplying.

In 2020, Marriott International, the world's largest hotel operator, revealed that its network had been infiltrated by attackers who obtained the login credentials of two Marriott employees. The breach resulted in the potential exposure of data of more than 300 million customers of the hotel group, including some personal information.

Government agencies—even in what are deemed to be the most secure places on earth—have proven no less vulnerable.

Between 2012 and 2015, the Office of Personnel Management, a department of the federal government in Washington, was hacked, and cybercriminals stole 22 million personal records, including Social Security numbers, addresses, and even some fingerprint data.

Enterprising criminals are one thing—cyberhacking by enemy governments is another entirely.

Perhaps the most unsettling conversation I ever had as an editor was when I asked the head of a major bank with hundreds of millions of personal accounts how strong their security protocols were.

Noting that we were seated in the *Wall Street Journal*'s office building in midtown Manhattan, a well-protected edifice guarded by the New York Police Department and our own robust corporate security team, the chief executive offered the following analogy.

"You can be reasonably confident you have enough security in place to withstand an attempt to break into this building by even the most well-armed and determined criminals," he said. "But how do you think you'd manage to defend against an attack by a foreign military—carried out not by men wielding M-16s but by pilots flying F-16s? That's what cybersecurity is like. We handle thousands of attacks a day from enterprising hackers. But if a foreign government decided to come after us, we'd be in deep trouble."

Of course that's exactly what happens. A few years later we at the *Journal* learned that the Chinese government had succeeded in hacking into the emails of some of our journalists, risking exposing key sources and stories they were working on.

To these long-standing but still largely unresolved fears about the privacy and security of personal data have been added in recent years growing alarm about the damage ubiquitous personal technology is doing to mental health and well-being.

Few novel technologies have changed basic daily human behavior as the introduction of the iPhone in 2007. The transformation it wrought is so immersive in human lives that it is genuinely difficult to recollect how life worked before it. The smartphone's utility (the iPhone was followed shortly afterward by various similar products, most successfully devices running on Google's Android operating system) is so expansive that it has literally altered almost every routine activity—from reading to viewing to listening to playing, navigation, working, entertainment, dating, and so on.

In addition to the extraordinary benefits and efficiency it has brought, it is inevitable that such a fundamental change in human behavior—for the first time in the history of *Homo sapiens*, the typical person spends many hours a day engaged with a small screen that connects them to just about every human and nonhuman activity on the planet—would have deep psychological, mental, and cognitive effects on its users.

Medical researchers have found many connections between this extended exposure to smartphones and multiple behavioral problems—sleeping, cognitive awareness, social interactivity.

By far the largest problems associated with almost continuous access to the web have been attributed to engagement with social media apps.

And most affected, both because of the time spent immersed in the internet, and because of the developmental stage of psychic growth, have been teenagers, especially girls.

As Jonathan Haidt, a social psychologist, has written about extensively, beginning in 2012–2013, a marked increase in rates of depression, anxiety, and self-harm has been recorded among adolescent girls.

According to data from the US National Survey on Drug Use and Health, the proportion of teenage girls who reported experiencing major episodes of depression almost doubled between 2011 and 2018—from 12 to 22 percent.

As Haidt says, "Only one suspect was in the right place at the right time to account for this sudden change: social media. Its use by teenagers increased most quickly between 2009 and 2011, by which point two thirds of 15–17-year-olds were using it on a daily basis."[6]

There are many ways in which activity on social media leads to mental health problems for girls. There is evidence from behavioral science that connecting with peers online is less fulfilling than connecting in person. Hours spent gazing at a screen have been shown to dramatically increase feelings of isolation and disconnection from society. Girls' self-esteem is also adversely impacted by seeing endless images of supposedly perfect teenagers, endlessly having fun, seeming happy, fulfilled, and beautiful. Social media also distracts from physical activity such as traditional play or exercise, a known protective against mental health problems.

Tragically, the most extreme consequences of these damaging mental health effects are increasing sharply. Suicides by American teenage girls increased by 134 percent between 2010 and 2020. For boys, the increase was 109 percent. Of course other factors may have played a role, especially the isolation brought about by the COVID-19 pandemic in 2020, but the data are clear—these trends were already in place, and the incidence of suicide truly took off at the dawn of the social media era.[7]

Big tech companies, especially the social media platforms, initially pushed back against suggestions that their products were harming and even killing young people.

But in 2021, the *Wall Street Journal* revealed that Facebook had known for years that Instagram, the photo-sharing app it owns, had been contributing to negative feelings experienced by teenage girls.

The *Journal* reported the contents of internal company documents from Meta, which was then called Facebook, that showed the results of its own research.[8]

"We make body image issues worse for one in three teenage girls," said one slide from 2019, based on data Facebook had found.

"Teens blame Instagram for increases in the rate of anxiety and depression," said another. "This reaction was unprompted and consistent across all groups."

It's no accident that social media use becomes addictive. Indeed addictiveness is a feature and not a bug of the software the platforms use to attract and keep users. While the big companies have been coy about sharing their algorithms publicly, evidence that they are specifically created to maintain and increase engagement is now copious.

Researchers have compared the "like" button on a Facebook or Instagram page to a slot machine or casino video game paying out rewards for players. The apps are built deliberately to target the dopamine center in the human brain in ways that develop addictions. These are especially effective when aimed at children. The appeal and ubiquity of social media then are literally creating an entire generation afflicted with a profound psychological disorder. It is as though we have built an entire sector of the economy dedicated to turning our children into junkies. Who would trust such a sector?

New waves of tech apps and platforms create new challenges. In the last few years the explosive growth of TikTok, the social media video sharing app has generated additional concerns to those associated with traditional social media. The app—with its particular appeal to children and young adults—has perfected particularly addictive content around short videos. By early 2023 the app had more than a billion monthly active users. But this is not just another case of clever Silicon Valley software engineers creating a new form of digital obsession. TikTok is owned by Bytedance, a Chinese company based in Beijing. While it enjoys the financial backing of major US private equity firms, it is controlled by the Chinese government, through a golden share investment, and as with all big Chinese companies, a member of the Communist Party is appointed to its board of directors.

Bytedance, through TikTok, harvests the data of tens of millions of American users, which can then be accessed by its owners, and ultimately the Chinese government.

With US policymakers growing increasingly alarmed by the scale and reach of TikTok, in March 2023, Shou Chew, the company's chief executive, appeared at a congressional hearing. In an extremely rare display of bipartisanship, representatives from both the Democratic and Republican side peppered him with questions about how the company used Americans' data. They were particularly concerned that the company had acknowledged accessing the data of two journalists to pursue an investigation against some of its own employees suspected of leaking confidential information.

When one congressman asked Chew to explain the spying the company had done, he replied, to general disbelief, "I don't think spying is the right way to describe it."

The hearing, and the growing alarm about TikTok, captured the range of concerns that Americans have about social media companies—from mental health, to privacy, and even now to national security—and explained why so many don't trust them.

But the trust problem is not just confined to social media. Psychological problems associated with extended smartphone usage have been widely documented—the extensive screen time on which many young people spend their days has inflicted all kinds of mental damage.

As the writer Abigail Shrier puts it in her book *Irreversible Damage: The Transgender Craze Seducing Our Daughters*: "Nearly every novel problem teenagers face traces itself back to 2007 and the introduction of Steve Jobs's iPhone. In fact, the explosion in self-harm can be so precisely pinpointed to the introduction of this one device that researchers have little doubt that it is the cause... The statistical explosion of bullying, cutting, anorexia, depression, and the rise of sudden transgender identification is owed to the... relentless harassment supplied by a single smartphone."

More recently, new and troubling evidence has emerged that suggest the problems are not just confined to young people. Internet use—of all sorts—has in fact reached the level of something like addiction for tens of millions of US adults.

Social media again is a major culprit. Researchers Hunt Allcott, Luca Braghieri, Sarah Eichmeyer, and Matthew Gentzkow followed a group of 2,700 Facebook users in the month after the 2018 US midterm elections, some of whom deactivated Facebook for that period and some of whom did not.[9]

They found that "deactivation caused small but significant improvements in well-being, and in particular in self-reported happiness, life satisfaction, depression, and anxiety."

In aggregate, many more people of all ages in the last decade have reported mental health problems. Data from the Centers for Disease Control and Prevention have shown increases in reported anxiety and depression in almost all age groups over the last few years. At least some of this may be a form of digital contagion. In their book *Connected: The Surprising Power of Our Social Networks*, James H. Fowler and Nicholas Christakis traced the way in which behaviors spread from individual to individual depending on their proximity. "Students with studious roommates become more studious. Diners sitting next to heavy eaters eat more food." As historian and commentator Niall Ferguson has noted, perhaps digital spread is responsible for a part of our rising epidemic of misery.[10]

Of course digital networks, social media, and smartphones are not wholly or perhaps even mainly responsible for the deterioration in Americans' mental health over the last decade. It seems probable that the COVID-19 pandemic played a critical role too—and there the availability of digital networking may even be said to have reduced the isolation and loneliness that were the inevitable consequence of lockdowns and social distancing.

But the evidence is also overwhelming that our immersive use of digital technology has had far-reaching effects. It is at least clear that the great expectations that attended the arrival of this technological revolution have been offset in substantial part by growing familiarity with the bleaker consequences. And it's this realization that has been such an important factor in diminishing the trust that people have in the tools and devices that have become so important to them. Given the centrality of digital devices to their lives, the decline in trust in much modern technology and its practitioners is likely to have had an outsized effect on the overall level of trust Americans feel in their society and one another.

* * *

Of course, ubiquitous digital technology has transformed our lives, our health, our prosperity, and our relationships in many ways for the better. Consider the number of happily married couples who met on an online dating app, or the simple joy that a grandparent experiences seeing a grandchild for the first time on FaceTime.

And though economists continue to struggle to find hard data to support the contention that the information technology revolution of the last thirty years has improved business productivity, few would doubt that digitization, the collation and manipulation of exponentially expanding quantities of data, the arrival of the personal computer and the internet, satellite technology, the smartphone, artificial intelligence, and all the other innovations of the last few decades have dramatically increased the efficiency with which most personal and business tasks are performed.

In any case, there's no going back now. Digital technology is so embedded in our lives that we just have to accept its deleterious qualities along with the many advantages it brings.

But it's also clear that the way modern technology has developed and been exploited has played a profoundly important role in undermining trust among Americans—and in other societies. There is no reason that, whether through policy, regulation, or voluntary action by tech companies, measures cannot be taken to help restore some of that lost confidence. Social networks and search engines could be managed in ways that remove some of the suspicions that they are vehicles of a particular political ideology. Social networks could do a better job of managing information they publish—and perhaps be held responsible for it. Consumers' concerns about data privacy could be allayed in part by digital firms compensating them for using it. Young girls could be protected from some of the harmful effects of social media by better filtering and perhaps even through the imposition of age limits or electronic ways of limiting exposure to certain apps. Big tech companies may simply have too much power and may need breaking up.

Without action on all these fronts, the risk that technology plays an ever larger and more destructive role in undoing the bonds of trust that bind a society together grows ever larger.

CHAPTER 7

Trust Me, I'm a Doctor

TEXAS TECH UNIVERSITY in Lubbock in the northwestern corner of the Lone Star State has long had a reputation for world-class scientific and medical research. Its engineers have led the world in electronics and computer science. Its biologists have helped develop some of the most important breakthroughs in the treatment of respiratory illness.

Only the very best applicants can expect to get coveted faculty or research posts. But a few years ago administrators introduced a new requirement for candidates—they would need to submit a "diversity statement" outlining their commitment to anti-discrimination and the promotion of "diversity, equity, and inclusion" in their work. In the biology department, staff would "strongly weight" such a statement in considering applications.

As John Sailer, senior fellow and director of university policy at the National Association of Scholars, revealed in an article in the *Wall Street Journal*, in 2022, the requirement became a political litmus test used to filter out scientists whose views did not fully comport with the prevailing progressive orthodoxies.[1]

One cell biology candidate was flagged for "microaggressions towards women faculty." Two examples were given: "assuming one junior faculty was a graduate student" and "minimizing the difficulties of women in the US comparing to worse citations elsewhere."

As Sailer wrote, "DEI connotes a set of highly contestable social and political views. Requiring faculty to catalog their commitment to those views necessarily blackballs anybody who dissents from an orthodoxy that has nothing to do with scientific competence."

The day after Sailer's article was published, Texas Tech announced it would end its use of such statements in hiring decisions. But the practice continues throughout many of the nation's most prestigious scientific institutions, for whom, it seems, having the right kind of political and cultural views is at least as important for a candidate as being a competent scientist.

Until recently, practitioners of science and medicine seemed immune to the broad decline in trust Americans have displayed toward their elites.

This seems blindingly obvious. Who wouldn't "trust" science and the scientists who produce it? Governments might be led increasingly by partisan ideologues and dishonest politicians; the news may be dominated these days by activists with a crusading agenda; universities might have become factories for radical progressive dogma; big business may look like it's run largely by cadres of self-indulgent plutocrats who put the pursuit of global profit ahead of their duties to workers and fellow citizens, but surely science is science, pursued by people with objectives rooted in hard data, evidence and physically verifiable phenomena?

There have of course always been legitimate, nagging concerns in the public's mind about the methods and goals of the scientific process. Difficult ethical decisions arise in everything from stem-cell research to the development of artificial intelligence, and lurid stories from science fact and fiction have always haunted the imagination:

with out-of-control scientists creating doomsday machines, Franken-stein's monsters, or Brave New Worlds. And there have always been certain types of people attracted to crank science or quack medicine; followers of mad or unscrupulous pseudoscientists with outlandish claims about sex with space aliens or unproven allegations about the risks of certain vaccines have from time to time raised unwarranted questions about the wider profession.

But few people seriously doubted that scientists and medical pro-fessionals were first and foremost technicians, benevolent nerds in white coats, interested only in following the trail of data and experi-mentation wherever it took them, irrespective of any ideological con-victions they may have or political or social pressures placed on them. There is no such thing as progressive physics or conservative chem-istry. In science and medicine, the decisions you make are driven by observation of real-world facts, objective data, and perceptible cause-and-effect relationships. Whatever your priors, as they call them, the conclusions you reach are the result of a methodical process of testing hypotheses against real observation, not preordained by some larger policy goal.

Widespread public confidence in the work of scientists is more essential to the health and prosperity of a society than trust in just about any other institution or people. Decisions made by scientists are not reversible decisions about the right level of taxes and spending, what story you might read first on a smartphone app, or how the latest brand of toothpaste is sold to you. These are literally life-and-death decisions made on a daily basis by people who hold extraordinary influence over our health, safety, and welfare. If large numbers of peo-ple don't trust our scientists, doctors, and lab researchers to follow the facts and tell us the truth about medicine, human biology, or the climate, we literally lose our ability to make scientifically informed decisions about our health, our lives, and the planet itself.

"Science is the great antidote to the poison of enthusiasm and superstition," wrote Adam Smith almost 250 years ago, and that judgment has underpinned public perceptions of science throughout American history.

But in the last decade or so, large numbers of Americans have lost faith in scientists and much of the science they produce. Unlike the other institutions of American society that have lost the trust of Americans in the recent past, however, this decline in confidence has been almost entirely along partisan lines.

Overall levels of trust in the scientific community among the American population haven't changed much, according to public opinion surveys. And it's noticeable that trust in science remains much higher than in most other institutions, such as the government, the media, and big business.

The General Social Survey conducted each year by NORC–University of Chicago found that among all adults, the proportion saying they have a "great deal" of confidence in the scientific community has been roughly steady—up a smidge from 45 percent in 2000 to 48 percent in early 2021.

But this stability masks a startling divergence in levels of trust depending on partisan affiliation. The percentage of Republican-identifying voters expressing trust in scientists dropped from 47 to 34 percent in that time. The number of Democrats rose from 46 percent to 64 percent.[2]

There's some evidence that the decline in trust has accelerated more recently, especially among Republicans. A survey by the Pew Foundation found that the overall proportion of respondents saying they had a "great deal of confidence in science" dropped by ten percentage points from early 2021 to the end of the year. The proportion saying they had similar confidence in medical science dropped even more—by 14 percentage points.[3]

As we shall see, the COVID pandemic from 2020 to 2022 and the public health community's response to it severely damaged trust in medical science and in science more generally. But it is not the only factor: a growing number of Americans are now suspicious of much of what they hear from the leadership of the scientific community, seeing it as consistently skewed toward a particular ideological viewpoint with the aim of achieving wider social objectives in line with the tenets of modern progressivism.

This rising mistrust on the part of almost half the American population is dismissed by the leading lights of the scientific and public health policy fields as the product of hag-ridden, superstitious, and ignorant people misinformed by a nefarious coalition of Republican politicians, right-wing news organizations, and social media who spread false information about COVID, climate change, and other topics on which they claim the science is "settled."

They point to evidence of a growing educational divide between Democratic voters and Republican voters—liberals and progressives are more likely to be college educated; conservatives more likely to have finished education with high school diplomas—and claim that rising science-skepticism among the latter is the natural result of lower intelligence or, at least, learning.

Skepticism of much of what they are told about science by experts is the result of "a clear convergence of fear, lack of critical thinking, confirmation bias and political tribalism," Marshall Shepherd, a meteorology professor at the University of Georgia, told the Associated Press in 2022.

But that dismissal of the widespread and escalating mistrust felt by much of the public demonstrates a misplaced arrogance among many scientific and medical professionals—and unwittingly only underscores the larger problems. In fact, while irrational fear and loathing may have played some part in the declining confidence people have in science, there are also ample reasons why rational citizens might have cause to doubt what they are being told by the professionals.

As we shall see in this chapter, the behavior, public pronouncements, and actions of leaders of the scientific and medical communities in four key areas have directly undermined public confidence—and have reinforced the view among many members of the public that science is often subordinated to political or ideological objectives in ways that fatally alienate almost half the population: the COVID-19 pandemic and policymakers' response to it; the prioritization of an ideology that promotes racial "equity" in medical outcomes; the racial justice; the twisting by policymakers and some health professional of basic science on the reality of biological sex; and the mobilization of much of the scientific community around the most extreme and alarmist interpretations of the threat from climate change.

*   *   *

The notion that public health officials and the media and other outlets who dutifully channeled their messaging were motivated purely by science and data in their response to the COVID-19 pandemic doesn't stand up to much scrutiny.

When the respiratory virus began to circulate in the United States in early 2020, the immediate reaction was less measured, science-based reasoning and calculation, and more blind panic.

To be fair, in the early days of the pandemic, confidence about the scale of COVID's severity and the mortal threat it posed to most humans and our way of life was low. Public health officials across the country—of all political persuasions—reacted on the precautionary principle, that when you don't know how bad something is going to be, you plan and prepare for the worst.

Not only did Donald Trump, whose later apparent insouciance about the threat from the virus caused him significant political damage, take draconian measures at the federal level, such as the closing of US ports of entry to most foreigners, but states like Florida, whose Republican governor Ron DeSantis later became a folk hero for many conservatives for his public criticism of the more extreme measures, as well as California and New York, home to two of the most prominent Democratic governors in the country, responded in much the same way—with a comprehensive lockdown of businesses, hotels, restaurants, and bars, and instructions to their citizens to stay at home as much as possible.

The early coverage by major news organizations, which like to present themselves as cool, sober purveyors of authoritative science to their audiences, could be summed up as "We're all going to die!" as they filled their pages and air time with story after lurid story of otherwise healthy young men and women in their thirties, who had never been sick in their life, succumbing in the most gruesome way to the deadly virus.

Beyond stoking widespread terror, the most important implications of this alarmism spread by public health officials at the state, national, and international level, vividly illuminated by media organizations, and initially believed by the public, were clear: the only proper response to the emergency was a maximalist series of measures to restrict the spread of the disease—so called non-pharmaceutical interventions: social distancing, face masks, and above all, lockdowns and stay-at-home orders.

The wider social and economic costs of these measures—especially lockdowns—were downplayed or ignored entirely. The objective of "stopping the spread" was established as paramount. That in itself represented a failure of scientific method, the proper execution of which would have offered a more balanced and comprehensive assessment of the risks of different types of policy response.

While concerns about the danger of overloading the hospital and health care system with COVID cases were understandable, any proper assessment of the right response to the pandemic should have weighed the great longer-term costs to public health—the medical conditions that went ignored or untreated because patients were scared or ordered not to go out; the effects on public health of in effect shutting down an economy for months; the damage to children's education done by enforced stay-at-home rules; and the cost to millions of people's mental health from the isolation from normal social life caused by lockdowns.

What's more, it was already becoming clear in those early days that, while serious, especially for older and more vulnerable members of the population, the lethality of the COVID virus was quite low, especially compared with earlier, though less widely transmitted, viruses over the previous fifty years or so.

Critics of the extreme measures began to emerge to challenge the authorities. Some states began reopening businesses after a few months. A number of well-credentialed scientists stepped up to raise concerns—backed by scientific data.

John Ioannidis, a professor of epidemiology at Stanford University, began calculating the infection fatality rate (IFR)—the number of deaths expressed as a percentage of everyone infected with COVID. Even in the early stages of the pandemic—before the availability of vaccines and when the initial strain of the virus was at its most dangerous—the number was a little over 1 percent, only a little higher than for a seasonal flu. Given that the virus could be transmitted much more easily than the flu this meant a significantly higher number of people might die from COVID than from a typical seasonal flu outbreak. But it was also clear that the disease disproportionately affected certain categories of the population, especially the elderly, and given all these data, growing numbers of skeptics questioned whether, given this scientific knowledge, a complete shutdown of the economy and society was really justified. It was especially questionable whether, given the infinitesimally small risk to children from the virus, that the wholesale shutdown of schools should continue.

But public health officials—from the federal government down to individual states and counties—not only persisted with their worst-case interpretation of the risks and the most extreme lockdowns to deal with it, they sought actively to discredit and actively suppress alternative scientific views and approaches.

In October 2020, hundreds of leading epidemiologists, physicians, and public health scientists, including at least one Nobel Prize winner, published the Great Barrington Declaration, a call for a rethink of these extreme COVID measures.[4]

"Current lockdown policies are producing devastating effects on short- and long-term public health," they wrote. "The results (to name a few) include lower childhood vaccinations, worsening cardiovascular disease outcomes, fewer cancer screenings and deteriorating mental health—leading to greater excess mortality in years to come, with the working class and younger members of society carrying the heaviest burden. Keeping students out of school is a grave injustice."

Legitimate debate and disagreement is part of the scientific method, of course. But the response from the leading scientists in government was not to engage but to undermine and submerge the critics.

> This proposal…seems to be getting a lot of attention—and even
> a co-signature from Nobel Prize winner Mike Leavitt at Stanford.
> There needs to be a quick and devastating published take down of
> its premises. Is it underway?

So wrote Francis Collins, director of the National Institutes of Health in an email to Anthony Fauci, director of the National Institute of Allergy and Infectious Diseases.[5]

Later, as the lockdowns took their toll, we learned just how damaging they were, with higher excess mortality, reduced levels of educational attainment, increased mental illness, and other deleterious effects on society and the economy. Instead of listening to criticism from distinguished scientists citing unimpeachable data and evidence that challenged them, the men and women in government who claimed scientific authority sought to shut down debate.

The full arrogance of the approach taken by these public scientists was captured a little later when Dr. Fauci told a television interviewer that Republicans who criticized him were "really criticizing science, because I represent science. That's dangerous."[6]

"L'état, c'est moi," Louis XIV of France is supposed to have said. There is no surer way to undermine faith in public health than for a fallible human being to declare, without irony: "I am science."

The rejection of any criticism of public officials' claims of omniscience was dutifully taken up by a complaisant media, whose so-called science and health writers rushed to denounce any demurral from the voices of authority.

When Georgia's governor, weighing the risks, decided to reopen the state after a couple of months of the pandemic, a headline in the magazine *The Atlantic* described the decision as "Georgia's Experiment in Human Sacrifice."[7]

The same insistence that "following the science" meant that Americans had no choice but to accept the judgments of their public health experts and bureaucrats was reflected in further episodes that undermined the faith a large number of Americans placed in their scientific leadership.

The science supposedly assured us that face masks were essential to stop the spread, and for more than a year many tens of millions were required by administrative order to wear masks in public places. A subsequent comprehensive study found that the masked had enjoyed in fact no better protection than the unmasked.[8]

When the first COVID vaccines were launched in late 2020, public health officials claimed that they were effective not only in reducing serious illness and death but that they would succeed in stopping the transmission of the virus.

In fact, while it is true that they significantly reduced the risk of serious infection—and claims that they were ineffective or even harmful are bogus—they proved much less successful at stopping transmission.

This mattered because, under the guidance of public health scientists, many jurisdictions introduced mandatory vaccinations for people who were to return to work, on the grounds that an unvaccinated employee was more likely to spread the virus than a vaccinated one. Indeed, many employees who refused to be vaccinated were fired because of such rules. But this turned out to be based on faulty science too.

Rochelle Walensky, head of the Centers for Disease Control and

Prevention under President Joe Biden, declared in April 2021 that "vaccinated people do not carry the virus." In fact, the vaccine manufacturers, while rightly claiming that their products reduced the severity of COVID infection, had been careful to note that they could not say that vaccines had any effect on transmission.[9]

Then there was the question of the scientific evidence for the origins of the coronavirus.

Right from the start of the pandemic, officials publicly accepted the word of China's communist government that the virus had "zoonotic" origins, meaning it had, like other viruses before it, originated in an animal, jumping in some way to humans, probably by someone eating an infected creature such as a bat or pangolin. The most commonly cited culprit was a "wet" market in Wuhan, central China, where various species of animals are sold for human consumption.

Independent scientific investigators quickly began to question this official version of events. A number of researchers pointed to evidence in the genetic makeup of the virus, among other things, to cast doubt on this account. In their book *Viral*, Matt Ridley and Alina Chan examine the evidence and argue that the most likely origin of the virus was in fact that it escaped from a laboratory. Wuhan just happens to host two of the largest centers of virology research in the world, and researchers there worked with large numbers of live viruses in conditions that are often described as less than secure.

It wasn't just the Chinese authorities who vehemently denounced this possible explanation. Strikingly, American public health officials did so too. Dr. Fauci was critical early on of claims that COVID might have anything other than a zoonotic origin. And in a paper published in the magazine *Nature* on March 2020, a group of scientists poured cold water on the lab leak hypothesis.

It was only sometime later that it emerged that a number of leading researchers were much more open to the idea that the virus might have started in a Chinese lab. In emails between Dr. Fauci and some of these researchers that subsequently became public, it's clear that in the very early days the lab leak was considered a serious possibility. But in the course of the next few weeks a campaign by some of these researchers and government officials sought to downplay it.

It also emerged that the National Institutes of Health—whose work Dr. Fauci helped oversee—had for some time been funding research into virology at the Wuhan lab.[10]

To this day there is no certainty about how the virus started. Several US government agencies, including the Energy Department and the Federal Bureau of Investigation, have concluded that it was probably the result of a lab leak, while others think it was more likely zoonotic. Nor is it clear, if the virus did come from a Chinese lab, whether the US government bears some responsibility for funding research at the Chinese lab.

But it is clear that initial efforts to explore the possibility of a leak were quashed—and not for reasons of lack of scientific evidence. Supposed authorities on science such as the editor of *Scientific American* denounced those, including some government officials, who raised the possibility of the hypothesis.

"Former CDC director Robert Redfield shared the conspiracy theory that the virus came from the Wuhan lab," Laura Helmuth wrote on Twitter. "Epidemiologists and virologists are doing heroic and urgent work on social media debunking everything he said. Thanks so much to them."

The "heroic" work, it turns out, was the highly uncertain conclusions of a group of motivated scientists promoting their own views and attempting to suppress and discredit any alternative hypotheses.

Matt Ridley, an authoritative science writer and journalist, was initially persuaded by the scientists' published words and in the early stages of the pandemic used his standing to endorse the claims that the virus must have come from an animal. But as he delved further into the story, he discovered that expressions of skepticism about the theory by some of the epidemiologists who had been consulted had been removed before these pieces were published.

As Ridley wrote later of his initial response to the denials that a lab could have been responsible:[11]

At the time, I trusted senior virologists who told me the lab leak could be dismissed. Frankly, I was duped.

At almost every stage of the COVID pandemic and with almost every public policy decision, an "official" scientific view was reached and promulgated, and any attempt to challenge it was fiercely opposed.

Perhaps most troubling of all the eagerness with which the media participated in the suppression of alternative arguments and evidence. Both legacy media firms and the modern social media giants like Twitter and Facebook eagerly joined in articles questioning lockdown or vaccine efficacy were flagged by the tech companies as potential "misinformation." Claims that the virus might have emerged from a Chinese lab were dismissed and derided by the mainstream media.

A paper published by a group of Israeli researchers in the journal *Minerva* found countless examples of successful efforts by official authorities and media to suppress the widespread circulation of alternative views on the science and policy measures of COVID offered by highly qualified scientists and doctors.

"In place of open and fair discussion, censorship and suppression of scientific dissent has deleterious and far-reaching implications for medicine, science, and public health," the paper by Yaffa Shir-Raz, Ety Elisha, Brian Martin, Natti Ronel, and Jiosh Guetzkow said.

The real reason so much trust in science and medicine was lost during the pandemic was this: leading figures in public health across the country essentially inverted the scientific method. Normally in the scientific process, a hypothesis is advanced, tested, and then either proved or disproved in conclusion. But in the case of COVID, officials—while citing scientific authority all the time—determined the conclusion first, then made sure that the data produced the answer they wanted—and ignored or actively suppressed data that contradicted it.

It takes Sigmund Freud to explain the mind of those who seek to exploit the patina of scientific authority to make the case for their prescriptions:

> It would be a mistake to suppose that a science consists entirely of strictly proved theses, and it would be unjust to require this. Only a disposition with a passion for authority will raise such a demand, someone with a craving to replace his religious catechism by another, though it is a scientific one.

It is of course true that COVID was a serious health threat that demanded extraordinary and urgent measures from authorities in circumstances at times in which sufficient scientific data was not available. But it is also true that public health officials—and their political masters—seized repeatedly on often flimsy scientific evidence to impose restrictive measures that had never before been imposed on free societies. As Freud says, it is hard to resist the conclusion that for many in the public health bureaucracy and the wider government COVID was a rare opportunity to realize their long-cherished objectives of administrative rule. Ordering people to stay in their homes, not to gather in social groups, to wear masks, to get vaccinated, requiring business to obey stringent rules all fit well with a mindset that believes government and regulators know best.

In the process, in advancing their political cause, they damaged trust in the science they claimed was driving their decisions.

As Martin Kulldorf, an epidemiologist and professor of medicine at Harvard University, succinctly put it in a December 2022 tweet:

> Trust in medicine is broken. The culprits? A vocal minority of MDs who got the pandemic wrong, promoting school closure and other lockdowns, not protecting high-risk elderly, pushing mask and vaccine mandates and slandering opponents.

* * *

As most of the United States was locked down by strict COVID regulations in the early summer of 2020, another event illustrated vividly the way in which some scientific authorities deployed distortions of science to advance a political cause.

Following the killing of George Floyd, a black man, by four police officers in Minneapolis, protests erupted across the country against what many Americans saw as widespread police brutality against black people. Many of these protests were peaceful demonstrations by large crowds, united in a desire to right what was termed "systemic" racial injustice in America. Some turned violent, and a number of cities that summer were host to scenes of burning of businesses and government buildings, looting, and instances of assault and murder.

For months since the start of the pandemic, public health officials had been warning people not to gather in large groups for fear of spreading the virus, which was killing thousands of Americans a week. Churches had been ordered to close since March. Sporting events had been canceled. Conferences, weddings, family celebrations had all been banned—on the orders of officials citing unimpeachable science.

But as millions of Americans spilled onto the streets in the early summer of 2020, medical professionals—including many who had been vocal in support of lockdowns—rushed to defend the gatherings.

In an open letter at the time more than 1,200 medical professionals defended the racial justice protests.[12] They claimed that these large gatherings were justified—not *despite* their implications for public health, but *because* of their implications for it.

> As public health advocates, we do not condemn these gatherings as risky for COVID-19 transmission. We support them as vital to the national public health and to the threatened health specifically of Black people in the United States.

Public health professionals, who had condemned earlier antilockdown protests by many people who had lost their jobs or their businesses because of the mandated closures as threat to the nation's health, now said the demonstrations orchestrated by Black Lives Matter were praiseworthy.

In a series of posts typical of the outpourings of many medical professionals at the time, Abraar Khan, a doctor at Stanford University, who had warned repeatedly of the dangers of large gatherings, now actively urged his fellow doctors to get out on the streets.

> For those who see Covid-19 and the (BLM) protests as separate— they are not, they are deeply interlinked. Until the deepest inequities

are addressed—racism being at the center of these, Covid will go away... It's beyond time for us in public health to step up.

None of this made any scientific or epidemiological sense, of course. If large gatherings significantly increased the risk of COVID transmission, and black people were being hit especially hard by COVID (and there was some evidence for that), how would taking to the streets in a dense crowd advance the cause of equity? It may well be true that there are deep racial inequalities in health outcomes in America, but how would they be addressed by large gatherings that these same people had described as health risks?

Somehow it was suggested that if you were protesting against lock-down, or gathering with friends on a beach, you were accelerating the spread of a virus that was killing Americans, but if you were doing it in service of racial equity, you were contributing to public safety. It was almost as if the people taking part in these protests were protected by some magical or spiritual force field against the spread of infection.

As Peter Sandman, a writer on environmental issues, put it:[13]

Racial inequality is an important public health issue. Economic privation is also an important public health issue. Everyone is entitled to believe as a citizen that one of these issues is more important than the other. No one is entitled to claim as a public health professional that demonstrating on behalf of one of these issues is more important—or somehow safer—than demonstrating on behalf of the other. To the extent that we have done that, we were wrong.

This prioritization of wider social goals over the traditional pledges contained in the Hippocratic Oath has been manifest in other places in the medical establishment.

In an article in *Commentary* magazine in November 2021 the writer Tevi Troy cited numerous examples—an experimental program at Boston's Brigham and Women's Hospital that would offer "preferential treatment" to patients of color; instances of public hostility to doctors who had challenged affirmative action programs in medical school admissions; the promotion of dubious research claiming that some doctors treat certain patients of color less favorably than white patients.[14]

Whatever the merits of placing larger social and political goals ahead of immediate medical obligations, we can't be surprised that it weakens the confidence many people have in the health care system and the professionals who run it. As Troy writes,

> If doctors become known for making decisions on politics, if the training regimen weakens considerably, if scientific judgments disappear in the face of woke political pronouncements, we will lose more than a generation of dedicated professionals, we will also lose a broader sense of trust in our medical system.

The capture of significant parts of the scientific establishment by partisan activists prompting an ideological agenda can be seen in the sudden transformation in recent years of once eminent—and nerdy—scientific publications into propaganda mouthpieces for progressive causes.

Nothing better illustrates this than the trajectory of *Scientific American*. The magazine, founded in 1845 by an inventor and publisher, used to be known for its lengthy reports on astronomers discovering some new star or biologists explaining how cells work.

In the last few years it has read more like a monthly mouthpiece for the most achingly woke of progressive causes, with article after pseudoscientific article about systemic injustice.

In January 2023, it published a piece about how the collapse of an African American National Football League player during a game in Cincinnati somehow encapsulated racism. The incident it said "highlights the violence black men experience in football"—as though somehow football is an activity whose intrinsic violence somehow only affects black players.

The article was so self-evidently demented that a number of prominent black former players denounced it.

"As a black man and former NFL player I can say this article is absolutely ridiculous," Tony Dungy, a former player and Super Bowl–winning head coach, responded on Twitter.

The capture of much of the medical and scientific profession by this extremist ideology now threatens to impact the delivery of health care to Americans in a much more pernicious way.

To be clear: the continuing struggle to tackle racism in all aspects of life is legitimate and necessary. But in recent years the progress through key institutions of an extreme ideology on race has subverted science, weaponizing it as a tool for advancing a political agenda.

The clear corollary has been a sharp decline in trust in scientists and their work among many Americans.

* * *

The subordination of objective scientific discovery to contemporary progressive ideology can also be seen in the modern movement to eliminate the idea of natural sex.

During her nomination hearing for a position on the US Supreme

Court in 2022, Judge Ketanji Brown Jackson was asked by a Republican senator if she could define the word "woman."

The judge demurred: "I'm not a biologist."

Even just a few years ago the idea that one needed formal scientific qualifications at an advanced level to define what a woman was would have seemed ludicrous to most people. But it has become the currency of modern discourse on gender.

Judge Jackson of course was simply demonstrating an advanced lawyerly skill at dodging a potential political minefield.

But the fact that a successful nominee for the nation's top court considers it prudent not to give an answer on what most people view as among the most basic questions of human biology demonstrates the degree to which progressive ideology has succeeded in undoing the fundamental tenets of commonly agreed science.

The movement to recognize the rights of transgendered people and to liberate them from stigma and discrimination has moved rapidly in recent years from proselytizing the case that gender dysphoria is a genuine phenomenon that needs to be acknowledged and dealt with sympathetically to embracing a set of radical and extreme claims that gender is an entirely social and environmental construct, not rooted in basic biology.

The extent to which this fringe position has much of the establishment in its grip is reflected in the success it has had in changing the national discourse—and even language—on gender. Joe Biden's administration officially referred to mothers in government documents as "birthing people." Leading Democratic members of congress have talked about "a menstruating person's body." In another congressional hearing in 2022 a witness described as an expert on reproductive rights denounced another senator as "transphobic" when he questioned her on her use of the term "people with a capacity for pregnancy," rather than "women."[15]

The litany of inelegant verbal constructions by which these modern ideologues seek to banish familiar gender terminology from the dictionary is by now well known, and it might be argued that the semantics are largely empty gestures, perhaps even solicitous efforts at avoiding the marginalization of transgendered people.

But of course this perversion of traditional science doesn't stop there. It is in fact practiced in increasingly more reckless and damaging ways. The practical science of gender reassignment and regendering is focused heavily on the relatively young—when most experiences of gender dysphoria occur—and in recent years there have been startling revelations of the extent to which children are being helped and indeed encouraged to undergo irreversible medical treatments and procedures to change gender.

In 2023, a whistleblower at one of the biggest centers for transgender and nonbinary people, at Washington University at St. Louis, revealed, among other things, that instead of providing mental health care to children, the facility gave them puberty blockers or cross-sex hormones and that it routinely referred minors for gender-transition surgery.

"Hypotheses are supposed to be tested ethically," she wrote. "The doctors I worked with at the Transgender Center said frequently about the treatment of our patients: 'We are building the plane while we are flying it.'"

No one should be a passenger on that plane. This is a near-textbook definition of the misuse of science by professionals.

In her book *The End of Gender*, Debra Soh, a psychologist, explains the risks for many young people, especially girls.

It's not unusual for a young woman to feel this way—discomfort at having female body and feeling as though she is not like other girls. I certainly felt that way growing up. But instead of reassuring young women that this is completely okay and there is no "correct" way to be a woman, society is now convincing girls who are different that they are really men or another gender.

Like many other women who have raised concerns about the promotion of radical transgender ideology, Dr. Soh has faced recrimination. For many, like the Harry Potter author, J. K. Rowling, questioning the right of any man to declare himself a woman at any time has resulted in efforts at cancellation—attempts to have their work suppressed or sequestered.

Abigail Shrier, a writer on gender issues, has written extensively on the dangers of these trends. She is a supporter of medical gender transitions for adults and opposes discrimination against transgendered people. But in her book *Irreversible Damage*, she cites the evidence of a prominent British psychotherapist to explain how:

> "I think the whole area has become politicized," said...Marcus Evans who resigned from England's national gender clinic, the Tavistock Foundation, over the lack of careful protocols in its treatment of transgender-identified children. "The drugs, you know, the hormone blockers, first of all, they say it's a natural act. What are they talking about? You're going to powerfully interfere with a person's biological development."

The push for transgender equality has also resulted in some troubling developments for women's sports. In recent years a number of male student athletes have changed genders and have been permitted to compete in women's events. In some cases these former males have wound up dominating their sport, to the disadvantage of cisgendered females.

When professionals and elite institutions insist on these radical, revolutionary changes in what most people understand about simple biology, the effect on public confidence is profound. The widespread suspicion is that science is being hijacked by ideologues in furtherance of an agenda, that they are reinventing the most fundamental scientific principles for reasons that have nothing to do with biology. This can only further undermine trust in science and its practitioners.

* * *

One other field in which science has been heavily infected by ideology—with predictable effects on public trust—is climate change.

There's a wide scientific consensus that the earth has been warming for several decades and that a significant part of that warming is man-made—through the emission of greenhouse gases. But the extent of the warming—and the scale of the damage it poses to life on Earth, through extreme heat, changes in weather patterns, and rises in sea levels—remains highly uncertain.

And yet throughout this time scientists themselves—and the public policymakers they advise—have consistently characterized the threat in the most extreme terms—with misplaced certainty.

The Intergovernmental Panel on Climate Change of the United Nations has been the official body collating the work of climate science for decades. In 2022 it issued its latest warning that the world had only a few years to bring about a peak in carbon emissions or else catastrophe awaited.

But the panel has been doing this consistently and with remarkable regularity for decades.

In 1990, the head of the UN environment program said the world must fix climate change by 1995.

In 2007, the head of the IPCC said there were five years to save the planet.[16] "If there's no action before 2012, it's too late."

Every time these dire warnings are issued and the world doesn't end a few years later, the credibility of scientists takes another hit.

To deal with the inconvenient truth that the world hasn't ended on time, as they repeatedly said it would, climate scientists have taken to attributing every natural disaster in the world to man-made global warming.

"Is this the end of summer as we've known it?" a *New York Times* headline asked in the, yes, summer of 2021.[17] (It's an old truth in journalism circles: when a newspaper headline asks a question the answer is almost always "No": "Has this man found a cure for baldness? Are we all going to be vegans?")

In this case the self-evidently refutable proposition in the question was prompted by the summer of meteorologically fraught events the United States had been experiencing: record temperatures and wildfires, droughts and ocean surges, wild storms and flash flooding.

But a cursory knowledge of human history suggests extreme weather events have been with us for some time and did not arrive in the few short years since the saintly Greta Thunberg of Sweden became incarnate. The Bible is full of them. Herodotus tells us that the massive Persian fleet sent to conquer Greece lost half its ships thanks to a freak storm before the Battle of Salamis in 480 BCE. In 1935 CE flooding of the Yangtze River in China may have killed as many as half a million people.

Now everything we have in our skies, rivers, seas, and forests are affirmatory episodes of climate change. It's extremely hot: climate change. It's extremely cold: climate change. It's raining a little: climate change. It's dry with a slight chance of rain but absolutely no prospect of a severe weather event anywhere in the foreseeable future: climate change.

With the definitive affirmation comes the lurid panic followed by the stern lecture: the Earth is going to combust (or drown, or freeze, or starve).

Bjorn Lomborg, an environmental scientist who concurs with the consensus that climate change is both happening and is a threat, nevertheless makes the point that the alarmism is dramatically overdone. According to reliable official data, he noted in a 2021 article in the *Wall Street Journal*, climate-related events such as hurricanes and floods killed almost half a million people on average each year.[18]

> The current climate narrative would suggest that natural disasters are ever deadlier but that isn't true. Over the past century, climate-related deaths have dropped to fewer than 20,000 on average each year, even though the global population has quadrupled since 1920.

All this hysteria merely damages public confidence in scientists.

In 2021 a physicist at New York University, Steven Koonin, published a book titled *Unsettled: What Climate Science Tells Us, What It Doesn't and Why It Matters*. Koonin is no climate change denier, apologist for oil companies, or right-wing ideologue. He served in Barack Obama's administration as a senior energy policy official and adviser on climate policy. The book took issue—backed by data—with many of the most extreme interpretations and forecasts about climate change. But it also skewered scientists who willfully distort evidence in furtherance of what they see to be a higher objective.

> There should be no question about "what the right balance is between being effective and being honest." It is the height of hubris

189

for a scientist even to consider deliberately misinforming policy discussions in service of what they believe to be ethical. This would seem obvious in other contexts: imagine the outcry if it were discovered that scientists were misrepresenting data on birth control because of their religious beliefs.

*   *   *

Scientists—and the work they do—remain more trusted than almost all of the major groups of elites who shape the society we live in. "Trust me, I'm a doctor" hasn't completely lost its validity as a call to authority. Scientific inquiry still enjoys the confidence that ensures its advances are adopted; the technological progress it produces still reverberate with benefit for the rest of us.

But scientists—doctors, professional researchers, public health experts, and others—have fallen prey to one of the principal temptations of the modern culture, the tendency to see everything through the prism of a set of political or ideological prejudices. As they have done so, the trust that is essential not just to their work but to the health and safety of all of us is endangered.

COVID lockdowns, masks, vaccines; racial justice and public health; the biology of gender and sex; climate change. In a short period of time, over the last decade or so, in all these fields—and others—scientists with the highest credentials from the most distinguished institutions in America and the world have manipulated evidence, massaged data, obscured facts, and sometimes simply told lies to the public in pursuit of some political or administrative agenda.

When people stop trusting the work of scientists, they start to believe their own science; wild conspiracy theories about medicines and vaccines; pseudo-scientific explanations for unusual phenomena;

strange hypotheses about the motivations of pharmaceutical companies, medical professionals, and government officials. Bad science gets as much of a hearing as good science, the invaluable work of real science gets discredited, and steadily the most important tools of human knowledge are blunted. Restoring the inviolable integrity of scientific enquiry over the ambitions of ideologues and charlatans is a vital and urgent task.

CHAPTER 8

Mutual Mistrust

WHEN RONALD REAGAN was shot by an attention-seeking madman just weeks into his presidency in 1981, he was taken to the nearby George Washington University Hospital. Minutes later, in the operating theater, as surgeons were about to go to work to remove the bullet and save his life, the president pulled down his oxygen mask and quipped, "I hope you're all Republicans."

The lead surgeon, Joseph Giordano, who as it happened was a registered Democrat, immediately responded: "Today, Mr. President, we are *all* Republicans."

It's a famous anecdote that neatly captures the irrepressibly sunny disposition of the fortieth president, always ready with a disarming joke even in the most dire of circumstances.

But it's also a vignette that now seems frozen in time, a quaint story from another age when the nation could overcome its deep differences and unite around some common sense of duty and patriotism in a crisis. We can only hope that a similar scene would unfold today in the awful event of something like that happening again. But would it? If some young emergency room doctor of typically modern progressive views were called on to save the life of Donald Trump, for example, her Hippocratic obligation to perform the best possible professional care would presumably overcome any temptation to finish him off. But it's highly unlikely she—or half the nation—would articulate the kind of proud and gentle solidarity voiced by Dr. Giordano.

The story—and its antiquity—prompts a deeper thought about the condition of trust in contemporary America. On that day, Dr. Giordano was right. The nation was momentarily united with its Republican leader—but it was, more importantly, American. Identification with the nation back then trumped partisan politics, and for that matter, just about everything else that divides us—religion, race, gender, sexual identity. People fundamentally trusted one another because they were American. And they were American because they trusted one another.

In some ways this seems antithetical to the perceived ideals of what it means to be American. The United States has traditionally been seen as a relatively low-trust society; the cliched ideals of American virtues in fact seem almost to rely on a certain lack of trust in others. Americans, to themselves, and especially to the rest of the world, have cultivated an idea of "rugged individualism," the sense that in this country, more than elsewhere, society is more atomized, citizens less dependent on the group or government, therefore less dependent on trust and mutual confidence. "In God We Trust, Everyone else pays cash" is a sign that has graced the wall of many a bar in the American heartland.

But throughout American history, in fact, its citizens have demonstrated a strong capacity for mutual association—and an investment in the trust that goes with it. In his *Democracy in America* Alexis de Tocqueville identified this tendency of early Americans to club together for mutual benefit in voluntary associations, whether formally, in the various civic groups that have always been a central feature of American society, or informally, by simply being good neighbors and upstanding members of local communities.

But in the last thirty years, just as institutional trust has collapsed, the mutual trust Americans have in one another has been declining sharply. A perusal of some of the most important and widely read sociological works in the last few decades captures this change—*Coming Apart* by Charles Murray, *Bowling Alone* by Robert Putnam, *Disintegration* by Andre Martyanov.

Mutual trust—the confidence people have in their fellow citizens to do the right thing, to behave honorably, to honor the interests, beliefs, and concerns of one another—is the most essential form of trust there is. It binds people to one another, provides them with a sense of common purpose. Social trust—the expectation that citizens operate by agreed standards—forms the basis for a stable society, the rule of law, relations within and between businesses.

Economists call this trust a form of "social capital," the network of relationships between individuals and communities that enables a society to function effectively and prosperously. Research has shown that high levels of social capital—built on social trust—are a firm predictor of a nation's economic performance. In America this most basic level of trust has been waning for almost half a century.

In the 1970s the General Social Survey found that roughly half of Americans said they thought that most people could be trusted. Today, a variety of polls find that number is around one-third. What's more, the levels of trust today decline sharply by age group. Older people are far more trusting than the young. In a 2018 Pew poll, only 29 percent of Americans over the age of sixty-five said most people could *not* be trusted. But that percentage grows going down the age cohorts, until, of American adults under the age of twenty-nine, fully 60 percent said most people were untrustworthy.[1] If today's younger generation maintains those attitudes as they age, in a generation a large majority of people in the country will be suspicious of one another.

What's especially troubling for America is that this steadily escalating mutual mistrust is not a global phenomenon. As Kevin Vallier, a professor of philosophy at Bowling Green State University, has
pointed out in his book *Trust in a Polarized Age*, it is almost unique
to the United States. In Sweden and Germany levels of social trust
recorded in surveys actually rose in the first fifteen years of the twenty-
first century. The United States used to enjoy the levels of trust associated with cohesive societies like these. Now it looks closer to the kind
of societies that exist in Italy or France.

Vallier examines the social science research on what makes societies
high- or low-trust. There are broadly three sets of explanations for the
difference. Higher levels of trust are typically associated with relatively
low levels of corruption, economic inequality, and racial diversity and
segregation. Sweden and Norway, for example, are notable for the trust
their citizens have in one another. They have long been societies that
are generally clean of corrupt practices, have a much more equal distribution of income than the global average, and have not been heavily
segregated or—until recently—even ethnically diverse. Countries like
Brazil and India, where mutual trust is low, have much higher levels of
corruption and inequality and are widely segregated by race.

So could any or all of these three factors have played a part in
pushing the United States down the global trust standings?

Corruption is hard to measure accurately. Various international
institutions publish indexes of perceived corruption. Perhaps the most
widely followed is Transparency International's Corruption Perceptions Index, which draws on data from the World Bank and other
official and private sector sources, and has been published annually
since 1995. Other, less reliable data go back as far as the 1980s.

On these measures the United States does seem to have slipped
a little in the global rankings for clean government and business.

According to the Internet Center for Corruption Research, a body that analyzes data from various sources, the United States dropped from a joint second equal ranking in terms of the cleanest countries in the early 1980s to fifteenth in 1996.[2] In Transparency International's estimation, more recently there has been a further decline in the United States' position—especially in the decade after 2012.[3]

As we have seen in an earlier chapter, this perception fits well with concerns among the American public about the cleanliness of the US political and business climate in America itself. The increased incidence of major financial scandals in the news in the last twenty years has led to rising mistrust of big business and may have contributed to wider social mistrust.

Yet this is unlikely to account for much of the trust deficit of recent years. The United States is still by most global standards comfortably among the least corrupt countries in the world (24th out of 180 in 2022 according to Transparency International) and the still relatively low level of corruption would hardly be consistent with the kind of social mistrust that now pervades the country.

* * *

Rising economic inequality, as noted in an earlier chapter, has probably played a much larger role in the decline of social trust in the United States.

The distribution of income and wealth affects trust in multiple ways. Inequality also reduces social solidarity, a key factor in social capital. People feel much closer socially and emotionally to people of similar income levels. When a section of society becomes immeasurably richer than others, the less well-off question whether the wealth has been gained fairly. Inequality of outcome also significantly affects equality of opportunity. The better-off can afford to send their children to better schools, giving them better educational and employment opportunities that reinforce the advantages those families already have. This further strengthens the sense of injustice those at the bottom feel, the lack of faith they have in the system as a whole, and the reduced trust in the more privileged. At the same time, as Michael Sandel, professor of philosophy at Harvard, has written in his book *The Tyranny of Merit*, the better-off put their success down to a combination of merit and hard work and ascribe others' less successful outcome to a lack of those qualities.[4]

> Even a fair meritocracy, one without cheating or bribery or special privileges for the wealthy, induces the mistaken impression that we have made it on our own.

Rising inequality has been a defining feature of the US economy in the last few decades. The share of after-tax income of the top 1 percent of earners rose from 9 percent in 1972 to 16 percent in 2011. The share of the bottom 50 percent declined over that time from 25 percent to 19 percent. Pre-tax income levels diverged even more, but tax changes reduced the gap.[5]

Wealth inequality has risen even more. Between 1983 and 2016, the share of aggregate wealth owned by upper income families (roughly the top 10 percent) grew from under 60 percent to almost 80 percent.

The share of middle-income households went from 32 percent to 17 percent. Lower-income families saw their wealth decline from 7 to 4 percent.[6]

Matching income data with surveys of social trust, in 2016, economists at the International Monetary Fund found a clear link between the two.

Their results, they said, "provide robust evidence that overall inequality substantially lowers an individual's sense of trust in others in the United States as well as in other advanced economies. The results for the United States indicate that the increase in inequality between 1980 and 2000 explains 44 percent of the observed decline in trust."[7]

Non-economists might flinch at such a precise estimate, but few would dispute that the broad direction seems right. Given what we know about the way income affects social relationships, it doesn't seem like a wildly unsupported inference to assert that, as inequality has risen in the United States, trust has declined.

But the relationship isn't completely clear. While income inequality rose sharply in the United States between the 1970s and 2011, it actually stalled thereafter. Between 2011 and 2021, in fact, on an income basis, the United States actually became a slightly more equal society, and yet, levels of social trust have continued to decline over that time. Indeed the last decade has seen a particularly sharp increase in almost all types of mistrust—in political institutions, business, media, and information technology. So while the rise in inequality surely offers a clue to why people have less faith in one another, it can't supply the whole answer.

* * *

Race has been the most consistent and painful source of friction in American society from its founding. The long, baleful history of prejudice toward and oppression of blacks is a scar on the nation's claim to be a republic founded on principles of freedom and equal opportunity. While the United States has moved beyond slavery and Jim Crow, discrimination has persisted, and the racial tension that is just below the surface and frequently erupts would certainly be considered a factor in the high and rising mutual mistrust in American society.

In the last few years high-profile events such as the murder of George Floyd by police officers in Minneapolis have dramatically reignited the charge that America remains a systemically racist society. The prominence of the Black Lives Matter movement and the protests that followed the Floyd killing led to widespread acceptance of the idea that much more radical reform was needed to address racism. Floyd's murder—along with other violent incidents—certainly increased mistrust of police and law enforcement, as we shall examine in a few pages. But could this be a source of the wider decline in social trust?

To believe that, you'd have to demonstrate that racial tension has gotten worse over the last fifty years, the time frame over which social trust has deteriorated. Is this the case?

While most people would surely concede that racism persists and that minorities continue to suffer disadvantages, it's a stretch to argue that these conditions have actually worsened.

For one thing, the general condition of black Americans has improved in the last fifty years. While on average black Americans still lag far behind whites, in economic terms there have been significant gains.

Take one key measure: unemployment. At the peak of the economic cycle in the 1970s, the unemployment rate for black men over the age of twenty dropped to 8.6 percent. At the same stage in the cycle of the 2010s—in 2019—it was 5.1 percent. For all Americans the numbers were 5.6 and 3.5 percent respectively, suggesting that while there was still a clear gap in the jobless rate, it had narrowed significantly.

What's more there has been a sea change in the last fifty years in the social context in which black and white Americans live. The implementation of affirmative action dramatically altered both the proportion of students at elite colleges that were black and the degree of integration of black and white students. The same has been true in

the workplace, and in the last thirty years the prominence of successful black figures in business, the judiciary, higher education, the military, and politics—including of course the election, with the support
of 43 percent of white voters, of the first black president.

All these changes are reflected in survey data that show a significant shift in attitudes among all Americans toward race over the last
half century or so. Perhaps the most dramatic example is the way the
views of Americans of all races have changed on the subject of the
most intimate of human relations. Polling by Gallup found that, in
2021, 94 percent of Americans said they approved of interracial marriage. In 1973 that number was 29 percent.[8]

As Gallup noted, the big change in the last thirty years has been
among white Americans.

"Non-White Americans have been consistently more approving of
interracial marriages than White Americans—but that gap has narrowed over time and, in the latest reading, has nearly closed," the
polling firm said.

These shifting views are reflected in a changed reality. Fifty years
after the Supreme Court legalized interracial marriage in the *Loving
v. Virginia* case, relationships between blacks and whites have become
commonplace. In the late 1960s only 3 percent of US newlyweds were
mixed-race couples, but by 2015 17 percent were.

There is an important caveat, though, to this suggestion that race
relations have not been a factor in the growing mistrust Americans
feel toward other people. Despite this progress, Americans of all races
seem to have become markedly more pessimistic about racial harmony in the very recent past.

According to Gallup, between 2001 and 2015, consistently large majorities of both blacks and whites said racial relations in the United States
were good. In 2001, 70 percent of black adults and 62 percent of whites

said that relations were very good or somewhat good. By 2013, 72 percent of whites now said relations were good, although there had been a slight decline in the number of blacks saying the same thing, to 66 percent.

But in the next few years there was a sharp decline in the proportions of both races expressing optimism about race relations.[9] By 2021, 43 percent of whites and only 33 percent of blacks described interracial relations this way—and most of this occurred well before the George Floyd murder and Black Lives Matter protests of 2020. It's not clear why there should have been such a sharp deterioration after many years of progress. It may have been the result of some high-profile instances of white supremacist violence, such as the murder of nine African Americans at worship in a church in Charleston, South Carolina, as well as other, earlier episodes of violent encounters between police and black suspects such as the death of Michael Brown in Ferguson, Missouri, in 2015, though police were later exonerated of any racially motivated oppression in that case.

It's too early to say, but it is possible that a resurgence of racial tension has played some role in the increase in wider social mistrust in recent years—though it would not explain the decline in trust over a much longer period.

But what about broader ethnic diversity? Whatever may have happened to relations between blacks and whites in the last fifty years, America has become a much more diverse nation, thanks mainly to large flows of immigration from Hispanic countries. The Latino population has grown by far the fastest of any ethnic group.

In 1970 Hispanics accounted for less than 5 percent of the US population. By 2021 the proportion was 19 percent. Asian Americans, while a smaller proportion overall, have also been growing as a share. As is now well documented, based on current trends whites are on track to be a minority in the United States by mid-century.

Could this increased diversification of US society have contributed to rising levels of mistrust?

The rising role of Hispanics in American politics has been one of the most discussed topics in the last twenty years. Polling evidence that they have tended heavily to vote for Democratic candidates has been cited as a reason to expect long-term Democratic dominance. In their book of the same name published in 2002, political scientists Ruy Teixeira and John Judis posited the rising Hispanic population as a key part of the "Emerging Democratic Majority," and in elections between 2004 and 2016 their prediction seemed to be coming true. Making the same point but in more loaded language, far-right politicians and commentators have warned that successive waves of Latino immigration are cementing Democratic advantages and permanently imperiling the political and cultural objectives of whites who mostly vote Republican.

The political implications of this Democratic demography and this kind of rhetoric could certainly be thought to have damaged social cohesion and weakened social trust. But the evidence is unpersuasive.

For one thing, the assumption that Hispanics would always favor Democrats has been undermined in the last few years. In elections in 2020 and 2022, growing numbers of Latinos voted Republican— according to exit polls, 39 percent in 2022, up from 32 percent in 2020 and 29 percent in 2016.[10]

That suggests that over time Hispanic political preferences are converging toward the nation's as a whole—and if anything would indicate assimilation of another minority into the US population rather than the separation of racial divergence.

In any case, polling suggests that racial attitudes toward Hispanics have also shifted as the population has grown rapidly.

A Pew survey in 2013 found high and rising racial tolerance. Four years earlier, the poll had indicated that the proportion of Americans saying whites and Hispanics get along was 67 percent. In 2013 it was 74 percent. The proportion saying blacks and Hispanics got along well also increased, from 48 to 54 percent.

Furthermore, as Vallier explains, the main contributor to high levels of social mistrust is not national diversity but de facto segregation.[11]

> When ethnic groups are concentrated in small geographical areas and have little contact with one another, distrust is high; with greater contact, the effect shrinks. And while ethnic diversity has increased in the US considerably since 1980—around a 50 percent increase as measured by the National Equity Atlas Diversity (https://nationalequityatlas.org/indicators/Diversity_index#/) ethnic segregation has decreased somewhat.

No one familiar with American history could dismiss the possibility that racial tensions may have contributed to rising overall levels of mistrust in the last half century. Continuing prejudice, the growth of ideologies that place racial identity at the center of all economic, social, and cultural relations, and the growing diversity of the population itself may all have played a part in raising interracial mistrust.

But fortunately the evidence is thin. The clear signs of widening racial divisions in the last few years are troubling but don't fully explain the decline in mutual trust that has been going on for half a century. Polling and election results suggest a growing rather than a declining divide between ethnic groups over the long term.

In any case, the biggest reason to believe that any growth in interethnic mistrust or declining solidarity has played only a small part in the decline in levels of trust between Americans as a whole is the overwhelming evidence that the most important and consequential divides that have opened up in the last fifty years are within, not between, ethnic groups. For this, of course, we have our old friend, increasing partisanship, to blame.

Politics and ideology of course are at the heart of it. According to the Pew survey in late 2020, roughly six in ten adults said they had little or no confidence in the wisdom of the American people when it comes to making political decisions, with 39 percent expressing at least some confidence.[12] This was a sharp reversal in a little over a decade. In 2007, those 57 percent said they were confident in Americans' judgment, against 42 percent who were not confident.

The level of mutual bad faith is so great that Americans actually see those who don't share their views not simply as ill-informed or misguided, but as morally inferior. In a similar survey in 2019, Pew found that 47 percent of registered Democrats say Republicans are more immoral than other Americans, up sharply, from 35 percent in just three years. Fifty-five percent of Republicans say Democrats are more immoral than the rest of the country—up by eight percentage points in three years.[13]

The practical damage this mutual mistrust is having can be seen most vividly in changing views on marriage.

While we noted earlier that attitudes toward interracial marriage have changed dramatically in the last fifty years, Americans have become increasingly hostile to inter-political marriage and dating.

Lynn Vavrick, a professor of political science at UCLA, cites survey evidence that shows how political identity is now reflected in what parents want for their children.[14]

People who identify with a party had even more intense feelings. In 1958, 33 percent of Democrats wanted their daughters to marry a Democrat and 25 percent of Republicans wanted their daughters to marry a Republican. But by 2016, 60 percent of Democrats and 63 percent of Republicans felt that way.

Psychologists have identified a spreading phenomenon called "motive attribution asymmetry"—the assumption that your ideology is based in love, while your opponent's is based in hate—as a key driver of rising mistrust. In a 2014 article in the *Proceedings of the National Academy of Sciences*, Adam Waytz, Liane Young, and Jeremy Ginges analyzed various studies of the views of Democrats and Republicans, along with Israelis and Palestinians, and found a disturbing level of similarity between the attitude of these fiercely opposed pairings toward each other.

As Arthur Brooks noted in his 2019 book, *Love Your Enemies: How Decent People Can Save America from the Culture of Contempt*, the mutual hostility our warring political partisans feel is now so great that, measured by surveys of mutual public trust, the gap between the right and left in America is similar to the gap between Jews and Palestinian Arabs in Israel.

In an article for the *New York Times*, he summarized the problem:

Each side thinks it is driven by benevolence, while the other is evil and motivated by hatred—and is therefore an enemy with whom one cannot negotiate or compromise.

*   *   *

It's likely that these partisan levels of mistrust have been further reinforced by other social changes over the last fifty years.

As we noted in the chapter on technology, Americans report

having become much more isolated since the advent of the internet and the smartphone. Society has become atomized, with less active community engagement, more time spent at home, online glued to screens. The COVID pandemic significantly increased this isolation and reported feelings of loneliness and alienation.

But this is not just a product of the likes of Facebook and Apple or even of the pandemic. The phenomenon of social dissociation has been around for decades.

Since the earliest days of the republic, America has been famous for the individualism of its citizens, but also for the constructive spontaneity in which its people coalesce.

Among the many insights about the fledgling United States for which the French writer Alexis de Tocqueville was famous was his observation about Americans' natural tendency to associate with one another.

> As soon as several of the inhabitants of the United States have conceived a sentiment or an idea that they want to produce in the world, they seek each other out; and when they have found each other, they unite. From then on, they are no longer isolated men, but a power one sees from afar, whose actions serve as an example; a power that speaks, and to which one listens.

These associations rest on a strong foundation of trust. In a society in which so much individual merit and hard work is the way to prosperity, the pooling of individual autonomy requires a high level of faith in the goodwill and honor of others. But these groups built trust too.

And these associations—from small voluntary groups organized at local level such as Lions or 4-H, to great national organizations such as the National Association for the Advancement of Colored People or the National Organization of Women—became essential components of a trust-based system.

But a feature of the last thirty years has been the disaggregation of Americans, the dissolution of so many parts of American civic life.

In his 1995 book *Bowling Alone*, Robert Putnam identified this trend and its damaging implications for cohesion and social capital.

From national survey data and membership numbers for civic organizations such as the Knights of Columbus and B'nai Brith, but also labor unions, veterans' groups, and fraternal organizations, he noted that Americans were increasingly detaching themselves from social engagement.

The title of the book captured the phenomenon. Although, Putnam said, the number of people who went bowling each week had increased in the previous twenty years, the number who took part in bowling leagues had declined.

Putnam cited a number of possible factors responsible for this: the growth in the number of women in the workplace and the focus on the workplace that double-career families tended to emphasize; suburbanization, as people moved out of urban centers and small towns, their sense of locality and the community activities that came with it diminished.

The main explanation, though, he argued, was perhaps the most obvious one—the easy availability of electronic entertainment: the television at first, and, then in its relative infancy, the internet.

As citizens increasingly lived their lives online, exploring the world and society through Google searches and Facebook friends, they lost a critical element of engagement: the serendipity that comes from discovering something they weren't looking for.

Serendipitous connections become less likely as increased communication narrows our tastes and interests. Knowing and caring more and more about less and less. This tendency may increase productivity in a narrow sense while decreasing social cohesion.

As the use of technology has become even more widespread in the last thirty years and the groups with which people interact smaller and more like-minded, this trend has surely accelerated.

Perhaps even more remarkably, the tendency of Americans to find engagement with a narrower group of fellow citizens has been matched by a desire for physical proximity. In his 2022 book *The Big Sort: Why the Clustering of Like-Minded Americans is Tearing Us Apart*, Bill Bishop, a journalist and social commentator, explains how, in the twentieth and early twenty-first century, Americans tended to cluster not virtually but physically.

Majorities have their beliefs reinforced by seeing and hearing their inclinations locally repeated and enhanced. Self-reinforcing majorities grow larger, while isolated and dispirited minorities shrink. Majorities gain confidence in their opinion, which grow more extreme over time.

This could just about directly describe many of our cultural institutions—colleges and universities and media and entertainment business. But it is becoming a daily reality of life for the rest of America too.

A look at the political map of America shows the impact of this trend. It no longer in fact makes much sense to speak purely of "red states" and "blue states." Within states, districts and communities have become much more politically homogeneous. So even though

California is a deep blue state, within the state, counties and congressional districts are becoming more and more politically concentrated with the supporters of one or the other party.

As a *New York Times* nationwide analysis showed, in 1992, just 38 percent of voters lived in a landslide county—defined as one won by the presidential candidate that year by 20 percentage points or more. By 2016 that number had risen to 60 percent.[15]

There is evidence too that the rise of mutual mistrust—or declining social capital—might be a function of the rising distrust in government.

In a 2009 paper in *Social Indicators Research*, Peggy Schyns and Christel Koop discovered a connection between levels of trust people have in institutions and the trust they place in one another. The more people distrust politicians and people in government, the less they trust other people in general, even when controlled for all other variables.[16] "The reverse relationship led us to the same conclusion: the more people tend to trust people in general, the less they distrust politics, a result we found in all countries. This finding refutes the claim that there is no or only a very weak relationship between political and social trust, as some have strongly argued before."

Growing isolation, the narrowing of social and political horizons, the tendency toward increased association online among only like-minded individuals in Facebook groups and other forums, physical clustering with people who think and speak and behave like us—all this represents a disaggregation of American society that has contributed to the decline in social trust among Americans—with profoundly damaging results for the cohesion of the United States as a nation.

One final observation should be made about the deeper roots of social deformation and the erosion of trust we have seen in the last half century. That is the steep decline in the importance to Americans' lives of what were seen for the first two hundred years of the republic as the essential building blocks of civic community—the family and religious faith.

By any measure, traditional family life has been transformed in the United States in the last half century or so. A random selection of data captures the scale of the change. In 1962, according to the Joint Economic Committee of Congress, 71 percent of women were married. By 2019 that number had dropped to 42 percent. Over the same period the proportion of women in their thirties who had never been married rose from 5 percent to 35 percent. In the 1960s the proportion of couples living together who were not married was less than 1 percent. By 2019 it was 12 percent. The percentage of births to unmarried women rose from 5 percent in 1960 to 40 percent in 2018. In 1970 85 percent of children lived with two parents. By 2019 this had fallen to 70 percent.

The so-called "traditional family" in fact is no longer the principal unit of social life in America. Data from the 2020 census showed that the proportion of American households comprised of married parents with children under the age of eighteen was just below 18 percent. In 1970 the number was 40 percent.

There's a lively debate among sociologists about the cost and benefits to society of declining traditional patterns of family life. Some argue that the end of the traditional patriarchal model has generated significant advances for women, with females no longer feeling constrained to fulfill traditional roles and instead leading rewarding lives—single, married with or without children. What's more, the collapse of the traditional family does not necessarily translate into a less cohesive society. The classic nuclear family was not without its own pathologies—for its members and society at large.

But there is social science research that shows there are significant costs in the collapse of the nuclear family. Children who grow up in two-parent families do better at school, are less likely to engage in antisocial activities or crime, find better jobs, have healthier and happier relationships themselves. Families and the relationships they create help to build the emotional and intellectual equipment needed to build relationships of trust.

Studies conducted in multiple countries have identified the same characteristics of trust that flow from the nuclear family. One recent study of German families found the impact on levels of social trust within the traditional family to be much greater than that of civic organizations.[17]

> While it can be difficult to say how important voluntary organizations are in the lives of their members, there can be little doubt about the importance of one's children and marital partner. While having children, and perhaps also a loving marital partner, is a lifelong commitment, people may enter and leave voluntary organizations at short notice. The nuclear family affects the daily lives, identities and futures of its members much more than do voluntary organizations.

What's more, there's a striking and growing gap between more highly educated Americans and those with fewer qualifications.

Researchers at the National Center for Health Statistics estimate that 78 percent of college-educated women who married for the first time between 2006 and 2010 could expect their marriages to last at least twenty years. For women with a high school education or less, the number was 40 percent.

Religion too used to be an important foundation of trust among Americans. But in the last fifty years religious observance has declined sharply.

In 2020 Gallup found, for the first time since the organization had been measuring it, that the proportion of Americans who were members of houses of worship fell below 50 percent.[18] Forty-seven percent said they were members of a church, synagogue, or mosque. The decline has been dramatic in the last two decades—in 1999 the proportion was 70 percent.

This reflects a wider drop in the number of Americans expressing religious beliefs. Over the past twenty years, according to Gallup, the percentage of Americans with no religious belief has grown from 8 percent to 21 percent.

The causes of this change have been widely debated. Some of it may be the result of repeated scandals among the major churches—most notably the Catholic church—the second largest denomination in the United States. Indeed measures of trust in religious institutions show a steep decline in the last twenty years, no doubt in part because of the perceived failures of these institutions.

But there are probably wider social and cultural reasons. Religious belief tends to be associated with lower educational attainment—and overall a higher proportion of Americans with college degrees tend to be non-believers. Many Americans have also found alternative outlets for their spiritual and ideological beliefs—the growing interest in climate change, especially among the young, has been compared by many observers to an alternative, humanist-like religion. The decline may also reflect some of the issues we have discussed elsewhere in this book. The last twenty years have been among the most turbulent and challenging in American history, enough to shake the faith of many people.

Again, there may be many social and cultural benefits from slumping religious observance, but it's hard to escape the conclusion that the disappearance of such an important locus of belief and faith in the lives of millions of Americans may have had a larger impact on their trust in society as a whole.

These large-scale social and cultural changes have surely played some role in rising levels of mistrust. They represent a collapse in the traditional institutions of authority that commanded trust. The stability of the two-parent family, the primacy of faith, and the cohesion of a wider community conferred not only an order on people's lives but established a larger sovereignty of truth on them. Loving but firm parental leadership, the eternal verities of religion, the obligations to a wider social unit of shared values imposed guardrails. It is not that this structure inevitably fostered trust—clearly the many stories of abuse both within families and faith communities did much to undermine trust.

But it is at least plausible that the rapid decline in two of the most important pillars of American society over the last two centuries and the rapid decline in the trust that Americans place in one another are not related.

"When men choose not to believe in God," G. K. Chesterton is supposed to have said, "they do not thereafter believe in nothing, they then become capable of believing in anything."

CHAPTER 9

Conclusions: Rebuilding Trust

F OR MANY PEOPLE, trust is like virginity. Once it's lost, you're never getting it back.

Most of us, sadly, have known friends who have done something to betray us and forfeited our trust. Many of us, shamefully, have betrayed someone at some point in our lives and lost their trust. It can take a lifetime to earn a person's faith and credit and a moment of selfishness or neglect to lose it.

If it can ever be earned back, it is a long and arduous process. It demands a radical change in the ways of those who have forfeited it as well as a generous capacity for forgiveness on the part of those whose trust has been abused. The onus is on those who were once but are no longer trusted to make the changes necessary to rebuild confidence—and even then we can never be sure that they will fully be trusted ever again.

Having lost trust in so many of the people and organizations that purport to lead them, can Americans ever trust them again?

This book has painted a mostly bleak picture of the state of the contemporary United States. It has described a modern pathology of American society: how, in just a few decades—a distressingly short period of time by historical standards—almost all the most important leaders, institutions, and authorities in the country have lost the trust of a large number of Americans. The implications are profound and suggest a grim future. Societies in which the bonds of trust between citizens and their institutions, between citizens and one another have dissolved are failing societies, characterized by discord, dysfunction, and ultimate disintegration.

But if the diagnosis is grim, the prognosis doesn't have to be bleak.

America has overcome epic challenges in its past that repeatedly threatened to destroy it. In fact, given the nation's history, its ability to rise to successive domestic and international threats, it would be unwise to bet that it can't do it again.

There have been trust recessions in the past. While the data on trust we have for the last fifty years is more exhaustive than for any previous period, we know that the United States has experienced previous periods when trust in institutions and in one another dangerously eroded. In the early days of the republic, bitter partisan confrontations fractured national unity. In the mid-nineteenth century, fundamental differences led to a collapse in mutual trust that produced the Civil War. In the late nineteenth and early twentieth centuries, excesses by big business, massive immigration, and periodic economic crises led to a surge in populist sentiment built on distrust of powerful elites. The strife over civil rights, the Vietnam War, and political controversy in the late 1960s and 1970s almost tore the country apart.

Every time, the nation survived, healed its divisions, and made radical changes necessary to restore the community of trust—through political reform, new leadership, common cause in the face of even larger threats.

On one occasion, of course, the nation survived and a level of trust was restored, but only after the bloodiest war in America's history. Is the level of distrust among Americans now so great that a similar conflict is now a serious possibility? That's a view increasingly widely shared, even among some distinguished historians and serious commentators. Two recent book titles, *How Civil Wars Start* and *The Next Civil War,* capture the current febrile mood rather well.[1]

It's impossible to predict with any confidence whether civil war is in America's immediate future. But it ought to be possible—indeed, it ought to be the duty of everyone who wants to see America succeed— to seek urgently for ways to begin rebuilding trust in the nation's institutions and its citizens.

In this final chapter I will offer some possible solutions to the trust deficit, some changes—radical and simple—that can at least begin the process by which many Americans who have lost faith can restore it.

This book has chronicled both the ways in which the major political and civic institutions of American life have forfeited trust and the larger, underlying causes that are sapping the nation's confidence in itself and its leadership.

The restoration of trust demands changes on both fronts. The institutions themselves need to be repaired so that Americans can have confidence in them again. But more importantly, the pervasive sources of distrust among the public will also have to be addressed and removed.

What follows is a brief list of changes that each of the institutions needs, followed by some proposals aimed at addressing the much deeper causes of distrust in America.

GOVERNMENT

Asking politicians to stop lying to us may be too much to ask, since mendacity has long been more or less a requirement for the job in a democracy since the first Athenian stood up in the city's assembly and asked for votes. But it's also true that the quality of political discourse has deteriorated in ways that make the rewards for untruthfulness greater than ever. There is a shamelessness about political untruthfulness today that is new.

Politicians used to lie in ways they hoped could be concealed. When Richard Nixon misled the nation about his role in the Watergate scandal, he did so in the expectation that he could successfully cover up the truth. Even Bill Clinton, who also bears considerable responsibility for the collapse in trust, at least tried to use words that conveyed a different meaning from the underlying truth without actually stating a bare-faced lie. The semantic and moral torment the nation was put through as Clinton sought to justify his claim that he had "not had sex" with the White House intern Monica Lewinsky revolved around endless circumlocutions deployed by the president to convince us that what he had said was technically, if not functionally, true.

But politicians don't even try anymore. They state things that are palpably and provably false, as when Donald Trump insisted that the crowds at his inauguration in 2017 were larger than those for Barack Obama four years earlier. Anyone with access to a photograph could immediately see that this was absurdly false.

So why say it? The answer is the reason why distrust is now so pervasive in American government and politics: the climate of hyperpartisanship.

The common claim that we live in a post-truth society is not quite right, or at least it is incomplete. What we have instead is a two-truth society—which, of course, means a no-truth society. Each side has its own truths, and they are mostly diametrically opposed. The mutual political and cultural hostility is so great that it literally upends the very idea of objective reality, and so, in the Orwellian world we have created, whichever side you are on, war is peace and peace is war;

democracy is tyranny and tyranny is democracy; strength is weakness and weakness is strength; true is false and false is true. In this world objective truth has been replaced by authority-truth. Partisans on both sides will believe what they are told if it comes from their side and disbelieve whatever comes from the other.

The good news is that most Americans are not subscribers to this partisan dystopia.

In its polling that found a sharp decline in trust in government, Pew also discovered that large numbers of Americans believed the problems could be fixed. More than 80 percent of respondents thought reforms could improve the level of Americans' trust and proposed various solutions.

But the nation's public discourse has been increasingly driven by those who are subscribers to the most partisan ideologies.

This is the first and most important task for restoring faith in government: work to dismantle the institutional structures that incentivize polarization. Institutional changes would include reforms that would limit the power of the extreme partisan voices within political parties: changes to districting rules in the states; ending partisan primary elections in favor of so-called jungle primaries—open non-partisan contests.

Greater government transparency would also weaken partisan ideology. Secrecy and lack of accountability breed suspicion and mistrust and fuel the most extreme critiques of government. Way too much official information is designated classified or secret.

But as we shall see later in this chapter, the most effective way to restore some of the lost trust in government and politics will be to raise the quality of political discourse and leadership. Politics needs to focus more on competence and honesty than on partisan identity.

MEDIA

Restoring any semblance of trust to a polarized politics is made much more difficult by media organizations that have increasingly abandoned ideals of objectivity in the last few years. As we saw in Chapter 4, many factors have contributed to the decline in trust in news organizations, but the most important is their embrace of an ideological perspective in the way they report and interpret the world.

The roots of this transformation of the media lie in both commercial and cultural factors. Giving subscribers, who supply more and more of the revenues to big news organizations, exactly what they want has created a dangerous cycle in which newspapers and other media chase more revenue by appealing more and more to the most partisan audiences.

This commercial imperative is hard to break as long as financial incentives drive news organizations in this direction, but there are still changes they can make that will make their content more trustworthy—for all audiences.

A clearer separation between news and opinion will foster an understanding among audiences that there is a difference between objective truth and subjective interpretation of it. Less obsessive coverage of politics, and the tendency to view all news—entertainment, business, sports, and virtually every other topic—through a political lens will further help reduce the ubiquity of partisan ideology that feeds distrust among audiences.

More accountability for news coverage and transparency in how it is created would also improve trust. Too often news organizations publish stories that are mostly or wholly false without any subsequent investigation or public acknowledgment. It is a mark of intellectual strength, not weakness, to acknowledge when errors have been made.

Forgive me if I blow a familiar trumpet, but the example of the *Wall Street Journal*, the newspaper I edited and still work for, is instructive in this. It has achieved commercial success by focusing its news coverage on largely non-partisan coverage—of business, certainly, but also of government, culture, and entertainment too, separate from a conservative editorial page that remains the most influential in the nation.

But the most important change the media needs to make is in the people who produce it. The cultural and demographic transformation of newsrooms in the last thirty years has deepened and accelerated the progressive bias in so much of American news. The hiring of like-minded ideologues from colleges that have become breeding grounds for the regnant progressive cultural theology has turned most news organizations into organs of monolithic left-wing radicalism.

While they prate about the importance of diversity—by which they mean of race, gender, and sexual orientation—these organizations have become monocultural employers whose staff is dedicated to promoting the modern orthodoxies. Hiring staff from outside the predictable college campuses and geographies would widen the range of perspectives they publish and help replenish the trust among large numbers of Americans they have depleted.

BIG BUSINESS

As we have seen throughout this book, scale and remoteness have been a crucial factor in diminishing the confidence Americans have in their key institutions. Globalization—and the pursuit of the opportunities it offers—has not only increased the scale of American corporations but has taken them further away from the Americans who have been employed by them, buy their products and services, and see their pension savings invested in them.

There are many ways in which business—but more importantly policymakers—can begin to restore trust in these behemoths.

The long tide of globalization itself, which began in earnest more than thirty years ago, seems to be receding, and as supply chain concerns grow in the wake of the COVID pandemic and as geopolitical pressures, most obviously with China and Russia, escalate, more companies are "reshoring" in ways that will help reduce some of the alienation that many Americans feel from them. At the policy level, more tax and other measures to encourage investment in the United States should be implemented to further accelerate the process.

But efforts to limit the power of big business domestically are crucial. As we have seen, industrial concentration—the domination of most sectors of the economy by a small handful of firms—has been a critical feature of the United States in the last thirty years. There should be a much more aggressive antitrust approach aimed at encouraging more competition. The power of big corporations to lobby for favorable treatment in Washington and in state and local governments also needs to be addressed. Crony capitalism now characterizes too much of the American economy for its own good—and for the sake of trust in the system itself. Campaign finance reforms aimed at reducing the power of these companies as well as other measures that would make lobbying a more level playing field would also help. It's true that repeated efforts at such reform have either failed or been bypassed, and the Supreme Court has ruled that key reforms represent unacceptable restrictions on free speech. But without weakening the tight relationship between big business and political candidates, crony capitalism will continue to flourish. Corporate governance changes are also essential to ensure better accountability of big companies to their shareholders and would help reduce the seemingly routine instance of corruption, greed, and fraud.

TECHNOLOGY

The loss of trust in big tech companies needs to be remedied if we are to benefit from the full fruits of the technology that plays such a central role in our lives rather than have it master us.

Part of the solution lies as it does with the media—in the need for tech companies to hire more diverse employees and for the managements of those companies to show more backbone in standing up to the little Maoists in their workforces who are insisting their technology is used to promote their ideological goals. This acquiescence to the intolerant progressivism of their workers is damaging not only trust but their own businesses. In 2018 Google announced it was dropping out of a contract to supply artificial intelligence to the Pentagon because its employees objected to it. You couldn't get a clearer example of why so many Americans have come to distrust these companies— one of the world's most powerful and innovative companies refusing to work with the American military because its staff didn't like products that might help the United States defend itself.

It's bad for their business model, because over time competitors not infected by the radical ideology of the left will eat their lunch. We have seen this in spectacular fashion with Twitter, acquired by Elon Musk and removed from the clutches of the progressive Jacobins who used to control it, and in more subtle ways with the growth of AI companies such as Scale AI, whose leadership is primary interested in producing the best products and is not skittish about supporting projects that assist United States national security.

So more competition in tech is essential—and to advance that, some reining in of the giant tech companies' power through regulatory action is needed.

To address the loss of trust caused by growing concerns about privacy, some innovative reforms could be implemented. One idea that is gaining traction among policymakers is requiring tech companies to compensate users for the exploitation of their data. Data is the critical currency of our online lives that is usually not given a value by the people who use it—they get it for free. Establishing a market in data in which users' information earned them some income would help assuage some of the fears digital users have about their privacy and at the same time establish some accountability for tech companies.

EDUCATION

The higher education sector also needs a genuine diversity of ideas and viewpoints if it is to regain trust. Universities and colleges have been dominated in the last few decades by academic and administrative staff who develop them as breeding grounds for ideologies that are directly antithetical to the values on which America was built. Leavening the monocultural orthodoxy with some real diversity of thought would significantly improve not only the confidence they enjoy among US citizens but also their output. Public universities that have allowed this narrow intellectual totalitarianism in the humanities especially should be held accountable by the state governments that fund and nominally administer them. For too long, they have operated as independent fiefdoms immune to the needs and demands of the taxpayers. There are encouraging signs in states such as Florida that lawmakers are beginning to respond to the problem and introduce some proper accountability.

Private universities are mostly beyond the reach of elected officials to impinge on their ideological exclusivity, but here too there are encouraging signs of change. Alumni—on whose beneficence many colleges are dependent for much of their funding—are demanding an end to campus totalitarianism. The many episodes of free speech being suppressed on campus are arousing the concerns not only of those who were educated there, but of employers, to whom campus radicals look for their post-graduation livings. Here's a radical idea: universities should police free speech by identifying those students who attempt to suppress it, and then employers should stop hiring them when they graduate. Colleges like to boast about how many of their alums get big jobs with big companies—let the rewards of a top job be conditioned in part on whether the candidate has shown a commitment to tolerance of views other than his or her own.

SCIENCE AND MEDICINE

As we saw in Chapter 7, rising distrust in science and medicine has also been driven in significant part by partisan loyalties. The advance of progressive ideology through many of the academic, professional, and publishing arms of the scientific world has turned what ought to have been a field of human inquiry that was blind to political opinion or prejudice into merely one more opportunity for the regnant left to advance their ideological prescriptions in the guise of scientific discovery.

Loss of trust in the institutions of medicine and public health has potentially the most devastating consequences. If significant number of people come to distrust doctors and public health officials—either because they believe the science is being distorted for an ideological reason or, even worse, because they believe that the trained professionals who treat them have been selected on grounds other than merit and taught identity-based orthodoxies in their professional education—it will not just be trust that collapses; so too will the health of much of the nation. Skepticism about COVID-19 vaccines may have been largely unwarranted, but the authorities once trusted to inform us of the merits of public health programs had forfeited much of the trust they had previously earned through their political posturing.

Here too the reassertion of objective knowledge and truth in the medical profession and the elimination of ideological objectives and analyses will be essential to the restoration of trust. Something else will be important too—an acknowledgment by officials and other influential figures that science itself is not settled—it is a process, constantly augmented by new data, experimentation, and information. Arrogant assertions that officials must be believed because they alone are "following the science" only serve to weaken trust when it emerges later that the science had evolved toward a different conclusion.

*   *   *

These changes will help to begin to restore trust in each of these damaged institutions. But as we have seen, the trust deficit in America goes much deeper and wider than the actions of any institution or the behavior of their leaders. Underpinning the broad-based decline in public confidence is the deep rift that has opened up within the country over the last thirty years: between increasingly distant and remote elites and regular Americans. To close the trust gap between these two it will be necessary to start reducing that deeper rift.

Four wide gulfs need to be closed: four objectives need to be achieved.

REDUCING ECONOMIC INEQUALITY

As I have argued already, the rise in inequality over the last thirty years has been a critical factor in eroding trust across American institutions and between Americans. Studies have shown that the greater the gap between rich and poor in a society, the higher the levels of distrust.

Inequality is a necessary and indeed desirable feature of successful capitalism. The prospect of creating wealth for oneself and one's family and descendants is one of the most powerful incentives for entrepreneurship, investment, and hard work—all essential contributors to a thriving economy. Immigrants have come to the United States for generations, not because they seek generous welfare payments or the comity that a largely equal community brings, but because they want to enjoy the fruits of their talent and success.

The returns of risk-taking in the United States have always been significantly higher than in most other countries, and the nation as a whole has benefited from the consistently higher levels of growth that have been achieved primarily as a result. What's more, measures to actively reduce inequality such as highly progressive tax systems have the effect of reducing incentives. The opportunity for successful Americans to get extremely rich also has significant wider societal benefits—not just in the tax revenues wealthier Americans contribute but from effects such as extraordinary levels of philanthropy. From charities to artistic institutions to universities, hospitals, and many other institutions, the voluntary redistribution of American wealth has been a defining factor in the success of American capitalism.

But three factors in the last decade or so have significantly tilted the cost–benefit equation of extremes of wealth and poverty and exposed the damage to social trust done by extreme economic inequality.

The first is simply the scale of inequality today. As we discussed in the opening chapter, thanks in part to the combination of globalization, the decline of union power, deregulation, the growth of the financial sector, and tax changes in the last thirty years, basic measures of income and wealth inequality have reached the highest levels seen in more than a century. As Thomas Piketty showed in his 2015 book, *The Economics of Inequality*, the share of total income enjoyed by the top 10 percent of earners in America rose from 34 percent to 48 percent between 1980 and 2015. In only one other major country in the world—India—do the top earners take so much of the economic pie.[2]

Second, as inequality has grown, incomes of Americans in the middle have stagnated. For most of American history, even as inequality persisted, the American middle class kept enjoying rapid economic gains. But in the last fifty years, as the income of the wealthiest Americans grew and that of the poorest stayed the same in relative terms, the returns to the vast bulk of Americans in the middle class declined sharply—from 62 percent of aggregate US income in 1970 to 43 percent in 2018.[3]

Third, there is growing evidence that Americans no longer believe this widening inequality is fair or accounted for by merit, talent, or hard work. For inequality not to be a rapidly destabilizing force in society, people need to believe that it can be justified on the basis of opportunity for all. But polling now indicates a minority of Americans think that individual wealth and a high level of prosperity are out of reach for them. A YouGov poll in 2020 found that only 30 percent of the country believed in the "American Dream"—and that it was attainable for most Americans.[4]

As we have also noted, polling now shows consistently for the first time in history that Americans think their children will have fewer opportunities than they had themselves.

Social mobility in America—the ability to advance upward through the economic hierarchy so that a child born in poverty can enjoy a good living in middle age—has declined sharply.

An analysis for the World Economic Forum in 2018 found that a child born into the poorest 10 percent of American families in 1970 had a 90 percent chance of outmatching their parents' earnings by the age of thirty. But a child born in the same circumstances in 1980 had only a 79 percent chance. Even worse, a child born into a family at the median income levels saw its chances of out-earning its parents decline over the same period from 59 percent to 45 percent.[5]

Again, these are unprecedented in modern American history and offer some of the strongest clues to why trust in the system and its institutions has declined so much.

Proposals to reduce inequality have been a perennial topic in American public discourse for decades, but a new urgency is surely needed if the country is to rebuild the bonds that once united it. There are signs of widening support for just such an effort—intriguingly, not just on the left, for whom greater equality has long been a defining political cause, but increasingly by conservatives—concerned for the cohesion of the nation and increasingly aware that economic growth alone is not generating sufficient returns for everyone.

It will demand, in other words, a bipartisan effort. Part of the answer will be continued work to manage the retreat from globalization that is responsible for a significant part of the growth in inequality and the shrinking of opportunities for many middle-income Americans through the outsourcing and offshoring of jobs. Globalization has produced great economic benefits, but they have been unequally distributed—for the most advantaged in society the growth of global opportunities for employment and investment has dramatically improved their prosperity, but for many more Americans the gains have been negligible or nil.

Other changes could help reduce inequality—reining back the power of big corporations; improving the accountability of corporations to their shareholders; rebalancing the economy toward domestic manufacturing—once the source of the best-paying jobs for American workers—and away from a bloated financial sector.

One more point on inequality and trust. While more and more Americans believe the system is rigged against them, those who do succeed are convinced they have done so through merit—that America is a meritocracy that recognizes their talent and achievement.

But as Michael Sandel argued in *The Tyranny of Merit*, the idea that we live in a meritocracy is not only self-deluding—given the advantages we know that increasingly accrue to the children of the better-off in society—it may also be "corrosive of civic sensibilities."[6]

> The more we think of ourselves as self-made and self-sufficient, the harder it is to learn gratitude and humility. And without these sentiments, it is hard to care for the common good.

We not only need to advance toward a more meritocratic system; we need to build a society that values everyone—including those who, through no fault of their own, do not succeed.

GOING SMALL AND LOCAL

One striking feature of almost all the measures of declining trust in American institutions over the last thirty years is that the smaller and more local an institution is, the higher the level of trust.

This points the way to another potential solution to the trust deficit—shifting power away from the center to the periphery.

While trust in big business has declined, over the same period Americans' trust in local businesses has actually increased. In 1998 58 percent of Gallup respondents said they had high levels of confidence in small business. In 2022, 68 percent said the same thing.

The same is true of government. Polls consistently show low public trust in the federal government as an institution, but high levels of trust when people are asked about officials close to them. In 2020, according to Gallup, only 13 percent of the public had a great deal or some confidence in Congress to do its job.[7] Forty-five percent had very little or none. But in that same year, and according to the same poll, 60 percent of all Americans thought their local congressman deserved re-election; only 35 percent thought he did not.

In 2021, while only 39 percent expressed confidence in the federal government's handling of major domestic and international problems, 57 percent had confidence in their state government and 66 percent in their local government.[8] In other surveys, state and local governments rank consistently higher in voters' trust than central government.[9]

The same is true when it comes to trust in the media and education. Americans are much more likely to say they trust local news organizations than national news and to say they are satisfied with the education their children are receiving even as they express little trust in what they see and hear about education trends in the rest of the country.[10]

As Joel Kotkin, professor of urban studies at Chapman University in California, has written, the decline in trust in so much of American life may be in part at least a product of scale, and the solution may be in the rise of a new "community-based and self-governing model of localism." This trend "counteracts some of the worst aspects of globalism—homogeneity, deindustrialization, and ever-growing class-divides—while eschewing the authoritarian tendencies often associated with nationalistic fervor. It essentially seeks to replace, where possible, mass institutions and production with local entrepreneurship and competition."[11]

A number of factors are helping facilitate this shift toward local communities and away from the center. The COVID-19 pandemic led to a significant migration away from big cities toward suburbs and smaller towns as people discovered they could easily work from home and avoid the inconveniences of urban life. Technology reduces the need for concentration of resources in the center and helps achieve devolution—not just in enabling people to work remotely but in the advance of innovations such as 3-D printing, which is facilitating small-scale manufacturing capability.

The growth in the last decade or so of demand for local agricultural produce—the "locavore" phenomenon—and the support for small, craft-based businesses and local stores in the face of competition from remote, impersonal giant businesses all suggest that the more the most important activities in American life can be devolved to local communities, the more we can begin to restore trust.

Encouraging evidence suggests that Americans believe that devolving power and authority to local communities is indeed a way to build trust.[12] According to the Pew survey:

> Fully 86 percent believe it is possible to improve interpersonal confidence across the nation and a number of… answers focus on how local communities can be laboratories for trust-building to confront partisan tensions and overcome tribal divisions.

One respondent Pew interviewed offered an instructive take on the value of an increased emphasis on local matters.

> "Get to know your local community. Take small steps towards improving daily life, even if it's just a trash pick-up. If people feel engaged with their environment and with each other and they can work together even in a small way, I think that builds a foundation for working together on more weighty issues," said an anonymous 32-year-old woman.

All this may point to one other important reason for declining trust and a way to rebuild it. Local government, local news, the activities of local business are much less politicized than their counterparts at national level. Citizens depend on their local communities for the most practical needs in their lives—buying, selling, or renting a house; learning about crime or trash collection; discovering local recreational opportunities. These activities tend to be less susceptible to partisan political ideologies. A feature of national life in the last thirty years has been the politicization of everything—from movies to sports to children's educational curricula. This constant framing of every aspect of our lives as a dialectic between opposing political programs has fostered the polarization that is at the heart of so much of modern American pathology and helped diminished trust in one another and in the big institutions of national life. Anything—but especially a shift in focus away from national to local concerns and solutions—that turns Americans away from the endless political warfare that dominates their news will help restore some trust.

IMPROVING PERFORMANCE

It's been noted already that this is not the first time in American history that trust has been compromised—and then rebuilt. Are there lessons from past episodes?

It is an obvious point but one worth restating: a large part of the declining trust in America reflects the performance of America and its key institutions over the last thirty years. How do we go about turning around a long record of failures that have seen the economy stagnate and America's role in the world under increasing challenge?

The current crisis resembles in many ways the turmoil the country underwent in the 1960s and early 1970s. The distrust Americans felt then toward many of their institutions and each other was driven by a combustible combination of strife over the advances and disappointments of the civil rights movement, the escalating losses of the Vietnam War, and a series of political crises that culminated in Watergate. In 1968 the effects of the disintegrating social contract were manifested in multiple political assassinations, waves of terrorist attacks, vast public demonstrations against the war, and widespread civil unrest. An openly white supremacist candidate for the presidency got almost 14 percent of the vote in the election that year.

Yet over the next two decades the distrust that was splintering the nation steadily receded. In 1976 Gallup found that only 51 percent of Americans had a great deal or a fair amount of "trust and confidence" in the federal government to handle the nation's domestic problems. By 1998 that number was 64 percent. There was a similar rise in the proportion saying they trusted the government to handle international problems well. It's true that trust in many of the institutions covered in this book steadily declined over the period, but in the major bodies tracked by Gallup such as big business, the media, and schools, a substantial plurality of respondents had trust in those institutions.

The reasons for this restoration of trust in some key institutions over the last twenty years of the last century are varied. But it seems most likely that the main factor was simply the performance of the United States. As grim as the previous two decades were, the period between 1980 and 2000 saw an extraordinary renaissance in American self-confidence.

Between the late 1970s and the turn of the century, the United States conquered the debilitating economic disease of stagflation, enjoyed consistently strong growth and real wage increases, won the Cold War over the Soviet Union, and defeated communism as well as two hot wars—against Saddam Hussein's Iraq in 1991 and in the Balkans in 1998—and finished the period as the undisputed global superpower. As we have seen in various of the institutions analyzed here, it's performance more than anything else that drives trust. When Americans are experiencing prosperity at home and success overseas, it's hardly surprising they trust the institutions that helped deliver them.

Perhaps the most obvious way then to revive trust in America and its institutions is to give people a reason to trust them.

Sadly, there's no equally obvious solution—the reasons for a country's failures are varied and complex. But consider one factor: the quality of leadership.

In the last twenty years the caliber of the nation's political leadership especially has hardly inspired.

This is not simply a criticism of presidents and administrations of both political parties who have—through foreign and domestic policy blunders (Bush and Obama), or through their personal behavior and apparent eagerness to divide Americans rather than unite them (Trump)—badly let America down.

It is that the entire class of political leaders today seems diminished in comparison with previous generations.

Politics, in fact, seems less of a vehicle with which to advance positive change for the country and more a platform to vent about its vices and the irredeemable turpitude of our political opponents.

As polarization has increased, ambitious people no longer seem motivated to enter politics to achieve something. They seem focused instead on being someone.

The decline in the quality and performance of the US Congress is especially striking. The framers of the US Constitution made the legislative branch of the government the subject of the document's first article for a reason—it was expected to be the dominant branch—the one that, by creating law, would drive the nation's direction.

But as Yuval Levin, a writer and scholar at the American Enterprise Institute, argues, today's members of Congress seem to have chosen to largely surrender that leadership to the executive branch—which has hardly performed it with great skill—and have chosen for themselves instead a kind of cameo role of performance rather than practice.[13]

> Many members of Congress have come to see themselves as players
> in a larger political ecosystem the point of which is not legislating
> or governing but rather engaging in a kind of performative outrage
> for a partisan audience.

In the past, leading members of Congress wanted their name on important legislation that would change the country. Today they see more value in attaching their name to a tweet, trolling their opponents on social media, and constantly auditioning for the next opportunity on a friendly cable news network.

The currency of politics is now the denunciation of enemies and the parading of grievances—and it goes beyond Congress to the presidency. Rebuilding trust requires at minimum a revival in quality of political leadership—and it could start with the re-assertion of lawmaking and execution over performance as the primary objective of political activity.

TURNING BACK THE CULTURAL REVOLUTION

While all these changes can make a dent in America's trust deficit, it's hard to escape the basic conclusion that the overarching reason for the loss of trust in the nation's key institutions is the widening gulf between a highly educated, globalized elite, whose values are at odds with those of other Americans. The most pressing task in the effort to restore trust must lie in finding ways to close that gap.

Rising economic inequality, the overwhelming scale and remoteness of many of the nation's key institutions, and disappointment at their performance over recent decades must all be redressed if we are to start rebuilding. But the most important root of our trust deficit is this growing gap between our elites and the people and the disdain, resentment, and mutual mistrust it has bred.

These institutions have been captured over the last thirty years by a progressive ideology that disdains traditional American values and focuses instead on the concerns elevated by this ideology—racial and gender "equity," the centrality of identity as the defining characteristic of social and economic and civic relations, the elevation of global priorities over national identity and domestic obligations, and climate change. All this has been amplified by increasing intolerance for any diversity of views that might challenge this hegemony. It amounts to an American cultural revolution that has advanced further and faster than most Americans ever wanted.

How do we turn back the tide?

To some people the gulf is unbridgeable. Every survey taken, every poll conducted shows a nation sharply divided and mutually hostile. On the one hand we have an elite, highly educated class, geographically clustered on both coasts, major cities, and university towns, with values rooted in modern progressive thought that elevates racial, gender, or sexual identity, sees progress as a global opportunity, against climate change and for a virtually borderless world, and largely rejects the values and virtues of western and especially American-led civilization.

On the other, a large body of working- and middle-class Americans who continue to believe in traditional American values and ideals, put American domestic economic and social interests ahead of global concerns, and favor tough immigration restrictions and the reassertion of American sovereignty.

The constant dialectic between these two has created a vicious circle of eroding trust. As mutual distrust increases, each side ascribes the worst motivations to the other, believing they prove themselves to be morally inferior. So as new disputes emerge, the willingness to think only the worst of the other side increases. Since their motivations are deplorable, then every new point of tension only reduces trust further.

It ought to be clear by now where I stand in this intensifying dispute.

The march of the elites through the major political, economic, and cultural institutions of the country has been achieved without the consent of most people. They have pushed an ideological program—on race, gender, sexuality, crime and punishment, education, globalism, climate, even an understanding of what the United States stands for and how it was founded—on a populace in an extraordinary short period of time in a way that has only served to alienate large numbers of Americans.

Some of the resistance to the advance of this elite ideology surely comes from a dark place. Racism and prejudice and a desire to protect what some see as the proper privileges of the white male majority in America have always played a baleful role in American politics.

But it's hard to take a look at recent American history and the progress made in advancing social justice—the first black president and African-Americans, women, gays, and other minorities occupying more and more senior positions in government, business, the law, the military and culture—and not have confidence that the vast majority of Americans have shed most of their historical prejudices.

And polling data support the view that, while polarization has been a bipartisan phenomenon, the rapid movement toward more radical positions has been a feature of the left much more than the right.

A Gallup poll in 2022 measured how voters on both sides of the spectrum identified themselves. The proportion of Democratic voters describing themselves as liberal rose by almost thirty points between 2000 and 2022. The proportion of Republicans saying they were conservative rose by just thirteen points over the same period.[14]

This isn't dispositive, of course, but it supports the idea that it is progressive leadership that has moved farther away from the traditional center of American politics and culture than conservatives have.

And it is in any case a misrepresentation of the concerns of many ordinary Americans to ascribe their misgivings to bigotry, racism, and prejudice. It's not the product of prejudice to believe that America has a proud history and that the advances of its civilization have brought immeasurable benefits to the world. It's not racist to think that a nation has the right to control its own borders. It's not bigoted to believe that traditional virtues such as the nuclear family, the centrality of faith, or a local community are worth preserving and defending. Nor is it some result of prejudice or obscurantism to be suspicious of a ruling class that—from war to financial crisis to pandemic—has repeatedly failed the people. But in all these cases, populist sentiment is characterized by these same elites as something despicable.

In fact, sympathy for this populist sentiment is not necessarily right wing at all. Opinion polls show large majorities oppose many of the modern manifestations of cultural progressivism—and even significant numbers of minorities do too.

A number of Democrats—progressives who strongly support government activism to redress inequalities—argue that American elites have gone too far in advancing an ideological agenda over the wishes of most Americans.

Ruy Teixeira, a left-leaning author who co-wrote the seminal work in 2002 *The Emerging Democratic Majority*, which predicted that demographic and other changes were creating the conditions for structural Democratic advantage, has argued that the progressive advance has gone too far for too many Americans. The "woke" ideology, which encompasses all the modern nostrums of the regnant elites we have discussed, he says, will need to be dislodged.

> Wokeness is stubbornly entrenched in these institutions, and it is there that it will make its stand. Millions of people have jobs, money, positions that are now bound up with wokeness, and they will not give it up easily. The world they inhabit is more insulated from the views of ordinary people than those of social discourse and political competition.

Teixeira notes that many of the minorities who are deemed to be the beneficiaries of these elite "woke" programs and ideas are notably hostile to them. Majorities of Hispanics, for example, are strongly in favor of measures to curb illegal immigration; many blacks are alarmed at the soft-on-crime approach progressive extremists pursue in the name of racial justice.

He and other Democrats are converging with the views of many on the right in arguing that time is ripe for a new, multi-ethnic, democratic populism to seize the political high ground and begin to take back political and cultural direction of the country from these elites.

This may indeed be the best hope for restoring a sense of unity to the country and the trust that will surely follow, a movement that cuts across party lines and seeks to elevate the daily concerns of middle- and working-class Americans of all ethnic backgrounds, tackling the common challenges they face—of poverty, lack of opportunity, crime, drug abuse. Instead of endlessly focusing on issues that divide Americans, there is a need and an opportunity for leaders to focus on issues that will unite most of them.

*　　*　　*

It's become commonplace among writers and commentators to compare the current crisis to the one that precipitated the Civil War—when trust between the two sides had broken down to the point of armed conflict. Some argue that the divisions are so great today, as they were then, that either conflict or a national divorce is inevitable.

But this is much too bleak. For one thing, consider the stakes then: the mutual distrust among Americans revolved around the issue of whether or not states should be permitted to sanction nothing less than human bondage. The divide became existential for the republic because the underlying issue was itself central to human liberty.

The divisions in American society today are serious but not existential. Even for the most committed partisan, they should not come close to arousing serious talk of separation. What we have instead is another episode in American history where the zealots of a particular ideological camp have been able to exercise an influence way out of proportion to the weight of their argument. Reversing their dominance will require painstaking work, building coalitions across cultural and political lines, avoiding the temptations of extremist language and behavior, and eschewing demagogic narcissists willing to exploit genuine grievances for their own advantage.

As they have done in the past, Americans themselves will surely find a way to restore trust in their leaders, one another, and their nation.

ACKNOWLEDGMENTS

THIS BOOK WAS long in the making and, even before its actual gestation, benefited from many years of conversations, correspondence, and electronic exchanges with some of the sharpest minds ever to have pondered America's many virtues and vices.

Nothing of whatever I may have done of substance in the last twenty years would have been possible without the continuous support and encouragement of my colleagues and bosses at News Corp. Robert Thomson, the chief executive, has been my mentor, confessor, and friend for almost thirty years, and whether explaining the intricacies of Japanese baseball, dissecting the latest trends in global business, or exposing the structural flaws in American politics, his words have been an unmatched source of inspiration.

I am forever indebted to Rupert Murdoch for hiring me and presenting me with a succession of the best jobs in the world, and then letting me do them—in ways that perhaps didn't always succeed as he expected or deserved. I—along with a large share of the world's population—continue to benefit immeasurably from his extraordinary wisdom, energy, and generosity. Lachlan Murdoch has also been a benevolent and thoughtful leader under whose steady guidance I have been allowed to flourish. My longstanding colleague Anoushka Healy has been a dear friend and source of advice and ideas as the journalism we both love has evolved over the decades.

241

Acknowledgments

At the *Journal*, my deputy and subsequent successor, Matt Murray, has greatly enriched my understanding of American politics, history, and culture in a hundred different ways. Gerald Seib, the sage of American political journalists, expanded my understanding of Washington while, almost unique among the media these days, retaining a balance and objectivity that should stand as an object lesson in the nearly lost art of honest political journalism.

On the editorial pages, Paul Gigot, the editor for more than two decades, has generously shared his unrivaled understanding of US and geopolitics with me and continues to lead with rare intellectual rigor the daily production of the most influential conservative journalism in the world. My colleagues and fellow columnists, especially Kim Strassel and Bill McGurn, write with far greater depth on modern America than I, and I have learned much from their work and from our many lively conversations. James Taranto is that rare creature—a brilliant mind and creative writer of his own who edits without fanfare but with unerring attention and accuracy. Will Lewis, the *Journal*'s former publisher, and another journalist whose career has intersected at various points with mine, is the most dependable, brave, and fun colleague a newspaper editor could wish for. The same can be said for Les Hinton, former publisher, top media executive, and now accomplished writer on his own account.

Former *Journal* colleagues Alix Freedman, Michael Williams, and Nik Deogun have all helped refine and shape my views on America, journalism and culture, but most of all they provided great company and fellowship over the years.

From a previous life at the *Financial Times* I owe much to Richard Lambert, the first editor brave and probably unwise enough to hire me, whose love of news and America in equal measure have inspired me throughout. At the *Times* (London) Roland Watson has been a friend and colleague for more than twenty years and is now the sharp-eyed, wry, and knowledgeable editor of my columns, always weeding out with subtle diplomacy their many infelicities. I am also grateful to both John Witherow and Tony Gallagher, *Times* editors, for having tolerated my weekly columnar ranting with good grace, along with Emma Tucker, former deputy editor there and now editor of the *Journal.*

I have been fortunate to have the opportunity to discuss the themes of this book with some of the brightest stars in the intellectual firmament—and many have offered specific comments and helpful suggestions on various drafts: Nicolas Checa, Tim Montgomerie, Niall Ferguson, Larry Summers, Marc Lasry, Glenn Hutchins, Lally Weymouth, Mark Penn, Chris Wearing, and Walter Wilson, this last a world-leading physician and intellectual all-rounder whose range of knowledge and interests has me in its thrall.

My agent, David Vigliano, the first to put me on to the idea of writing what became this book, persisted against heavy odds through to its fulfillment. At Twelve Books, my editor Sean Desmond has demonstrated incomparable judgment, patience, diligence, and generosity, by turns cajoling and reassuring on the many occasions I doubted the book would ever surface. The fact that this book exists at all is truly owed primarily to him and his misplaced confidence in me. I owe my deepest thanks to him and his superb team of editors. My assistant, Deidra Redfeather Bennett, has tolerated way too many challenging demands of research and administration. I am also grateful to my many colleagues and friends at Fox News and Fox Business who have displayed way too much patience with my failing efforts at television.

As I said, the origins of this book go way back into my intellectual roots and were laid by those who first sparked an interest in American politics, history, and economics. Sir Brian Harrison, my history and politics tutor at Oxford, taught me how to write and think and always to be skeptical about conventional wisdom. Andrew Glyn, who sadly died way too young, taught me all the economics I have ever known, and always with an energy that has infected me with an enthusiasm I have never shaken. So many other fellows, students, and staff of my alma mater, Corpus Christi College, contributed to my intellectual formation—I suppose I should be apologetic for letting them down, but I have never been prouder than when I was elected to an honorary fellowship there.

I owe much also to Peter Jay, the polymath and former ambassador to Washington whom I met as my boss and economics editor of the BBC, for his brilliance in explaining the US and global economies to me, and to Martin Wolf at the *FT,* a dear friend and gifted mentor who probably disagrees with everything written in this but remains a model of intellectual rigor and honesty.

Above all, I am indebted to my family: my late mother, Della Baker, who first lit in me the fire of political passion, igniting flames that have burned brightly in her memory ever since; my dear father, a model of wise, selfless parenthood, who instilled in me my love of books, and who, as of this writing, is still going strong, well into his 104th year on this earth; along with my sisters and brother.

But I owe most of all of course to the family I helped create myself: Sally, unerring source of wisdom and strength, and model of virtue to our five daughters. Above all, to them: those peerless and brilliant young women, Kitty, Claudia, Eliza, Arabella, and Scarlett, who have taught me more about America, goodness, and the meaning of life itself than I ever deserved to know. Anything good I may ever have achieved is thanks to them. I'll happily take the credit for everything else.

1. The Great Distrust

1. https://www.newyorker.com/magazine/2021/07/26/are-americans -more-trusting-than-they-seem.

2. https://news.gallup.com/poll/394283/confidence-institutions-down -average-new-low.aspx.

3. https://www.npr.org/transcripts/1086732931.

4. Levi, M., and L. Stoker, "Political Trust and Trustworthiness." *Annual Review of Political Science* 3 (2000):475–507.

5. https://publications.iadb.org/en/trust-key-social-cohesion-and-growth -latin-america-and-caribbean-executive-summary.

6. https://www.sciencedirect.com/science/article/pii/S2352250X21000828.

7. https://www.pewresearch.org/politics/2019/07/22/trust-and-distrust -in-america/.

8. https://www.washingtonpost.com/outlook/2021/10/12/conservatives -have-long-stoked-distrust-government-now-were-paying-it/.

9. https://fivethirtyeight.com/features/what-happens-when-americans -dont-trust-institutions/.

10. https://www.minneapolisfed.org/article/2023/the-state-of-income -inequality.

11. https://www.wsj.com/articles/most-americans-doubt-their-children -will-be-better-off-wsj-norc-poll-finds-35500ba8.

12. https://www.inc.com/magazine/201505/leigh-buchanan/the-vanishing -startups-in-decline.html.

13. https://www.cbo.gov/publication/56945.

14. https://www.imf.org/external/pubs/ft/wp/2016/wp16176.pdf.

2. A Vote of No Confidence

1. https://www.pewresearch.org/politics/2022/06/06/public-trust-in
-government-1958-2022/.

2. https://www.pewresearch.org/politics/2022/06/06/public-trust-in
-government-2/.

3. https://news.gallup.com/poll/402044/supreme-court-trust-job-ap
proval-historical-lows.aspx.

4. https://theintercept.com/2017/07/22/donald-trump-and-the-coming
-fall-of-american-empire/.

5. https://www.jstor.org/stable/24027184; https://www.foreignaffairs.com
/articles/1990-01-01/unipolar-moment.

6. https://www.bls.gov/opub/mlr/2021/article/the-us-productivity-slow
down-the-economy-wide-and-industry-level-analysis.htm.

7. https://www.pnas.org/doi/10.1073/pnas.1518393112.

8. https://www.pewresearch.org/politics/2014/06/12/section-1-growing
-ideological-consistency/#interactive.

9. https://claremontreviewofbooks.com/digital/the-flight-93-election/.

3. Selling Out: How Corporate America Forfeited Trust

1. https://news.gallup.com/poll/5248/big-business.aspx.

2. https://news.gallup.com/poll/1597/confidence-institutions.aspx.

3. https://www.pgpf.org/blog/2022/12/Income-Inequality-Has-Been
-on-the-Rise-since-the-1980s-and-Continues-Its-Upward-Trajector. See
also https://www.pewresearch.org/social-trends/2020/01/09/trends-in-in
come-and-wealth-inequality/.

4. Bethany McLean and Peter Elkind, *The Smartest Guys in the Room*
(Portfolio, 2013).

5. https://www.wsj.com/articles/SB1023196847218251120.

6. https://www.wsj.com/articles/SB103222154024598075s.

7. https://www.aei.org/wp-content/uploads/2018/09/Public-Opinion-10
   -Years-After-the-Financial-Crash.pdf?x91208.

8. https://www.indexologyblog.com/2022/05/17/the-rebalancing-act-of
   -the-sp-500-esg-index/.

9. https://mendoza.nd.edu/wp-content/uploads/2019/01/2017_fall_semi
   nar_series_gustavo_grullon_paper.pdf.

4. BAD NEWS

1. https://reutersinstitute.politics.ox.ac.uk/digital-news-report/2022
   /united-states. See also https://news.gallup.com/poll/403166/americans
   -trust-media-remains-near-record-low.aspx.

2. https://www.maryellenmark.com/bibliography/magazines/article/the
   -new-yorker/the-howell-doctrine-637518015956665249/N.

3. https://www.vox.com/culture/2016/11/21/13682574/fake-news-facebook
   -fox-news-conservative-radio.

4. https://www.washingtonpost.com/wp-dyn/content/article/2010/11/12
   /AR2010111206508.html.

5. https://www.nytimes.com/2012/07/08/books/review/cronkite-a-biogra
   phy-by-douglas-brinkley.html.

6. https://www.poynter.org/archive/2003/journalists-are-more-likely-to
   -be-college-graduates/.

7. https://www.journalofexpertise.org/articles/volume1_issue1/JoE_2018
   _1_1_Wai_Perina.html.

8. https://whyevolutionistrue.com/2018/02/10/andrew-sullivan-on-the
   -spillover-of-campus-politics-into-society-at-large/.

9. https://www.washingtonpost.com/opinions/2022/10/27/new-york
   -times-tom-cotton-oped-james-bennet/.

10. https://www.washingtonpost.com/news/the-fix/wp/2014/05/06
    /just-7-percent-of-journalists-are-republicans-thats-far-less-than-even-a
    -decade-ago/.

11. https://www.science.org/doi/10.1126/sciadv.aay9344.

5. STRUGGLE SESSIONS

1. https://quillette.com/2020/07/08/a-declaration-of-independence-by-a-princeton-professor/.

2. http://knownandheard.princeton.edu/.

3. https://www.tabletmag.com/sections/news/articles/eisgruber-emails-princeton-katz.

4. https://www.pewresearch.org/social-trends/2019/08/19/the-growing-partisan-divide-in-views-of-higher-education-2/. See also https://www.pewresearch.org/fact-tank/2019/07/29/americans-have-become-much-less-positive-about-tech-companies-impact-on-the-u-s/.

5. https://www.insidehighered.com/news/2018/10/09/gallup-survey-finds-falling-confidence-higher-education.

6. https://www.chronicle.com/article/americans-confidence-in-higher-ed-drops-sharply.

7. https://www.thefire.org/research-learn/2021-college-free-speech-rankings.

8. https://www.aei.org/articles/are-colleges-and-universities-too-liberal-what-the-research-says-about-the-political-composition-of-campuses-and-campus-climate/.

9. https://www.nytimes.com/2021/02/02/magazine/classics-greece-rome-whiteness.html.

10. https://www.campusreform.org/article?id=10005.

11. https://www.forbes.com/sites/richardvedder/2020/08/03/who-is-ruining-our-universities—administrators/?sh=20f5736d14df.

12. https://www.jamesgmartin.center/2022/08/administrative-bloat-harms-teaching-and-learning/.

13. https://www.lendingtree.com/student/historical-faculty-pay-study/.

14. https://nces.ed.gov/programs/digest/d21/tables/dt21_330.10.asp.

15. https://educationdata.org/average-student-loan-debt-by-year.

16. https://theprint.in/pageturner/excerpt/high-family-income-not-sat-scores-ticket-to-harvard-yale-princeton/547180/.

17. https://www.wsj.com/articles/alumni-withhold-donations-demand-colleges-enforce-free-speech-11638280801.

18. https://www.newsweek.com/diversity-problem-campus-opinion
    -1618419.

6. Subscribe, Follow, Like, Distrust
1. https://arxiv.org/pdf/2203.16743.pdf.
2. https://www.edelman.com/sites/g/files/aatuss191/files/2022-10/2022%20
   Trust%20Barometer%20Special%20Report_Trust%20in%20Techno
   logy%20Final_10-19.pdf.
3. https://www.wsj.com/articles/chinas-new-tool-for-social-control-a
   -credit-rating-for-everything-1480351590.
4. https://www.pewresearch.org/internet/2019/11/15/americans-and-pri
   vacy-concerned-confused-and-feeling-lack-of-control-over-their-per
   sonal-information/.
5. https://www.reuters.com/article/us-yahoo-nsa-exclusive-idUSKCN
   1241YT.
6. https://www.nature.com/articles/d41586-020-00296-x.
7. https://docs.google.com/document/d/1diMvsMeRphUH7E6D
   1d_J7R6WbDdgnzFHDHPx9HXzR50/edit#.
8. https://www.wsj.com/articles/facebook-knows-instagram-is-toxic-for
   -teen-girls-company-documents-show-11631620739.
9. https://pubs.aeaweb.org/doi/pdfplus/10.1257/aer.20190658.
10. https://www.bloomberg.com/opinion/articles/2023-02-26/don-t-blame
    -social-media-covid-for-us-teen-mental-health-crisis.

7. Trust Me, I'm a Doctor
1. https://www.wsj.com/articles/how-diversity-policing-fails-science
   -equality-equity-education-texas-tech-job-candidates-interview-dei
   -pronouns-11675722169?mod=article_inline.
2. https://apnews.com/article/coronavirus-pandemic-science-health
   -covid-19-pandemic-4e99139d995581319dffab4107627a5e.
3. https://www.pewresearch.org/science/2022/02/15/americans-trust-in
   -scientists-other-groups-declines/.
4. https://gbdeclaration.org/.

5. https://www.aier.org/article/fauci-emails-and-some-alleged-science/.

6. https://www.cbsnews.com/news/transcript-dr-anthony-fauci-on-face
-the-nation-november-28-2021.

7. https://www.theatlantic.com/health/archive/2020/04/why-georgia-re
opening-coronavirus-pandemic/610882/.

8. https://www.cochranelibrary.com/cdsr/doi/10.1002/14651858.CD00
6207.pub6/full.

9. https://www.heritage.org/public-health/commentary/congress-must
-probe-biden-administrations-rationale-vaccine-mandates.

10. https://theintercept.com/2023/01/19/covid-origin-nih-emails/. See also
https://twitter.com/comfortablysmug/status/1629880685908447233?s
=46&t=DSHbNaNUS_HvDGDqFYsKD.

11. https://www.telegraph.co.uk/news/2022/01/12/duped-covid-lab-leak
-deniers/.

12. https://www.cnn.com/2020/06/05/health/health-care-open-letter-pro
tests-coronavirus-trnd/index.html.

13. http://www.psandman.com/col/Corona21.htm.

14. https://www.commentary.org/articles/tevi-troy/wokeness-threatens
-medicine/.

15. https://www.usatoday.com/story/news/politics/2022/07/13/josh-hawley
-called-transphobic-law-professor-hearing/10046037002/.

16. https://twitter.com/BjornLomborg/status/1424778121023262721
/photo/1.

17. https://www.nytimes.com/2021/07/28/us/the-end-of-summer.html.

18. https://www.wsj.com/articles/climate-change-natural-disasters-ahr
-river-flood-germany-wildfire-risks-11628177742.

8. Mutual Mistrust

1. https://www.pewresearch.org/fact-tank/2019/08/06/young-americans
-are-less-trusting-of-other-people-and-key-institutions-than-their
-elders/.

2. https://www.transparency.org/en/cpi/2021/index/usa.

3. https://www.icgg.org/corruption.cpi_olderindices_historical.html.

4. https://news.harvard.edu/gazette/story/2021/01/the-myth-of-merito cracy-according-to-michael-sandel/.

5. https://en.wikipedia.org/wiki/Income_inequality_in_the_United _States#/media/File:Income_inequality_panel_-_vi.png.

6. https://www.pewresearch.org/social-trends/2020/01/09/trends-in-in come-and-wealth-inequality/.

7. "Growing Apart, Losing Trust? The Impact of Inequality on Social Capital," by Eric Gould and Alexander Hijzen. https://www.imf.org /external/pubs/ft/wp/2016/wp16176.pdf.

8. https://news.gallup.com/poll/354638/approval-interracial-marriage-new -high.aspx.

9. https://news.gallup.com/poll/1687/race-relations.aspx.

10. https://edition.cnn.com/election/2022/exit-polls/national-results/house /0. See also https://www.nytimes.com/interactive/2016/11/08/us/politics /election-exit-polls.html.

11. https://www.wsj.com/articles/why-are-americans-so-distrustful-of -each-other-11608217988.

12. https://www.pewtrusts.org/en/trust/archive/winter-2020/how-amer icans-view-trust-facts-and-democracy-today.

13. https://www.pewresearch.org/politics/2019/10/10/how-partisans-view -each-other/.

14. https://www.nytimes.com/2017/01/31/upshot/are-you-married-to-your -party.html.

15. https://www.nytimes.com/interactive/2016/11/10/us/politics/red-blue -divide-grew-stronger-in-2016.html.

16. https://link.springer.com/article/10.1007/s11205-009-9471-4.

17. "Does the Nuclear Family Affect Social Trust? Morten Bleksaune, 2021. https://www.tandfonline.com/doi/full/10.1080/14616696.2021.1974511.

18. https://news.gallup.com/poll/341963/church-membership-falls-below -majority-first-time.aspx#:~:text=Story%20Highlights&text=WASH INGTON%2C%20D.C.%20%2D%2D%20Americans'%20member ship,2018%20and%2070%25%20in%201999.

9. Conclusions: Rebuilding Trust

1. https://www.youtube.com/watch?v=jQKTAMiaFT8. And https://www
   .amazon.com/Next-Civil-War-Dispatches-American/dp/1982123214/ref
   =pd_lpo_1?pd_rd_w=d7pca&content-id=amzn1.sym.116f529c-aa4d-47
   63-b2b6-4d614ec7dc00&pf_rd_p=116f529c-aa4d-4763-b2b6-4d614ec7d
   c00&pf_rd_r=X946BXVJS2C3SNSCPG27&pd_rd_wg=Z5utK&pd
   _rd_r=c4cc59e2-4e0a-4258-9ef9-fc7f0584e7b0&pd_rd_i=1982
   123214&psc=1.

2. https://news.harvard.edu/gazette/story/2020/03/pikettys-new-book-ex
   plores-how-economic-inequality-is-perpetuated/#:~:text=Q%26A
   -,Thomas%20Piketty,rooted%20in%20ideology%20and%20politics.

3. https://www.pewresearch.org/fact-tank/2020/02/07/6-facts-about-eco
   nomic-inequality-in-the-u-s/.

4. https://today.yougov.com/topics/politics/articles-reports/2022/07/14/do
   -americans-believe-american-dream.

5. https://www.weforum.org/agenda/2020/09/social-mobility-upwards
   -decline-usa-us-america-economics.

6. https://news.harvard.edu/gazette/story/2021/01/the-myth-of-meritoc
   racy-according-to-michael-sandel/.

7. https://news.gallup.com/poll/1600/congress-public.aspx.

8. https://news.gallup.com/poll/355124/americans-trust-government-re
   mains-low.aspx.

9. https://morningconsult.com/tracking-trust-in-institutions/.

10. https://knightfoundation.org/articles/local-news-most-trusted-in-keep
    ing-americans-informed-about-their-communities/.

11. https://www.spiked-online.com/2023/02/12/the-retreat-from-globalism.

12. https://www.pewresearch.org/politics/2019/07/22/trust-and
    -distrust-in-america/.

13. https://www.commentary.org/articles/yuval-levin/congress-weak
    -members-want-weak/.

14. https://news.gallup.com/poll/467888/democrats-identification-liberal
    -new-high.aspx.

1619 Project, 120

Abbot, Dorian, 137
Adams, John, 29
Ailes, Roger, 100
airplane analogy, 1–2, 8
al Qaeda's terrorists, 93
Alina Chan, 175
Allcott, Hunt, 161
alumni rebellion, 136
Amazon, 145
America. *See also* modern technology;
    mutual mistrust; rebuilding
    trust; struggle sessions
  2004 election, 32
  acknowledge basic legitimacy
    election results, 32–33
  anti-racism, 128
  attempt at academic censorship,
    117
  authoritarian progressivism on
    campus, 136
  became a bete noire, 116
  broadband prices are double in, 85
  cancellation battle defending, 128
  capacity for mutual association,
    193

capitalism in, 57–58, 63
Cold Civil War in, 11
collapse in trust, 98
compensation for jobs in, 131
condemned the speech, 115
conspiracy theories, 12
cost of college, 134
COVID pandemic, 168
culture of "anti-Blackness", 117
decline in higher education, 132
decline of trust in institutions,
    8–10, 12
decline of trust in media, 101, 112
deterioration in Americans' mental
    health, 162
disputes about federalism, 29
distrust between Soviet Union
    and, 10
distrust in government, 30
diverse country, 11–12
domestic tension in, 10–11
domination of student bodies, 130
economic considerations, 134
education in, 121–125
educational divide between, 168
elite level universities, access to, 132
emphasis on identity, 126

Index

America (*Cont.*)
emphasis on praxis, 128
end of Cold War, 10
erosion of trust, 5–7
events of 2021 elections, 11
factors for mistrust, 37
FBI and CIA in, 33
financial crisis 2008 and 2010,
64–66
first slave ship to, 120
formal dinner to Xi Jinping, 53–55
free speech at Princeton, 119
Gallup survey, 122
hegemony in, 121–126
history of companies in, 57–58
hostility from faculty, 116
ideological repression, climate of,
115
ideological totalitarianism, slide
into, 116
in K– 12 education, 123
ineffective institutions, 12
institutions and social
relationships, 15
institutions of American learning,
115–139
killing by police officer, 117
lack of trustworthiness in, 8
leading businesses with distrust, 56
lecture at Vassar College, 115
levels of student debt, 134
lingering effect of Wall Street, 67
loss of trust in government, 13, 17
lost faith in scientists, 167
means to be American, 193
minorities, injustice to, 128
mistrust in intelligence agencies, 33

mistrust to distrust, 8
modern extremism in, 126
mutual mistrust, 192–213
nation's public schools, Faith in,
122
Nobel Prize winners, 137
own Apple product, 146
Pew Research Center survey, 121
pinnacle of the education process,
138–139
political and judicial battles over
the New Deal, 29
preferential treatments on black,
117
presidential election in 2000, 32
problem of "presentism", 120
public high schools, case of,
122–123
race on campus, 117
racism persists in, 128
racist places in, 119
radical teaching curricula, removal
of, 123
rebuilding trust in, 139
rebuilding trust, 214–240
Republican winning, 32
riot on Capitol Hill, 31, 35
riots in 2022, 80
rise of political violence, 35–36
safe spaces, 115
scandals and abuse of power by
federal law enforcement, 33
self-reflection media type, 94
skepticism of, 168
social trust, 6
summer of 2020, 117
Supreme Court's legitimacy, 33

Survey conducted each year, 167
teaching at institutions, 137
technology Americans interact
    with, 152
Texas Tech University, 164
trust in 1950s and 1960s, 30
trust in big business, 59
university salaries of, 131
vicious circle of cronyism, 85
weakened confidence in agency
    during COVID-19, 34
world-beating American
    innovation, 121
American National Election Studies,
    6
American Revolution in 1776, 120
Andersen, Arthur, 62
anti-government agenda, 17
Anti-discrimination policies, 128
anti-racist commitments, 118
Anti-Wall Street sentiment, 66–67
The Apprentice, 17
Arab Spring, 149

Bankman-Fried, Sam, 68–69
Barrett, Amy Coney, 112
Barry Goldwater's agenda, 46
Bennet, James, 108
Bergstresser, Charles, 105
Bernstein, Carl, 106
Biden, Hunter, 143
Biden, Joe, 151
Biden, Joe, 31, 44, 46, 81, 151, 175,
    184
birthing people, 184
Bishop, Bill, 208
Black Justice League, 118

Black Lives Matter (BLM)
    movement, 80, 107
Black Lives Matter protests, 117
BlackRock, 78
Boies, David, 68
Braghieri, Luca, 161
Brecht, Bertolt, 18
Brinkley, Douglas, 102–103
Brooks, Arthur, 205
Buffett, Warren, 58
Bush, George W., 32, 38–39, 45,
    47–48, 62, 103

campaign emails, 140
Campus Reform, 127
Carnegie, Andrew, 58
Carreyrou, John, 68
Case, Anne, 41–42
Cayne, Jimmy, 65
Center for Education Statistics,
    134
Centers for Disease Control and
    Prevention, 34
Central Intelligence Agency, 33
ChatGPT, 152
China, 18, 53–56, 74, 120, 130, 149,
    175, 188, 221
China's Cultural Revolution, 130
Christakis, Erika, 130
Christakis, Nicholas, 130, 161
Citigroup, 145
climate change, 187–190
Clinton, Bill, 31, 41, 46, 62, 125, 151,
    217
Clinton, Hillary, 151
Clinton, Hillary, 32, 74, 95, 151
Coca Cola Company, 81

The Coddling of the American Mind,
129
Cold War, 128
College Pulse, 124
Collins, Francis, 173
Columbia Journalism Review, 95
Commentary magazine, 182
Common Sense, 28
Communist rule, 18
Congressional Budget Office, 24
Cook, Tim, 54
corporate, distrust in
   capital and labor after Cold War,
     86
   China and US business, 53
   culture wars, 61
   dot.com crash 2000, 67
   economic inequality, 60–61
   economy in 1980s and 1990s, 53
   ESG fund, 78–80
   factors leading to loss in faith, 60
   globalization and elevation of
     foreign opportunity, 56–57
   globalization, 75–76
   labor share, 86
   labor unions, 87–88
   leaders forfeit trust, 59
   lobbying expenditures, 86
   merger mania, 84
   pension plans or 401k, 87
   profitability, 87
   scandals, 61
   sense of injustice of political
     leaders, 87
   theology, 76–77
   WEF, 70–73
Cotton, Senator Tom, 108

COVID pandemic, 154–191
   antilockdown protests, 180
   Biden's declaration, 175
   challenge the authorities, 171
   coverage by news organizations,
     170
   early days of the pandemic,
     169–170
   headline in magazine, 174
   lockdowns in, 171
   mortal threat, 170
   non-pharmaceutical interventions,
     170
   preferential treatment to patients,
     182
   scientific leadership, faith in, 174
   social and economic costs of, 171
   start of, 176
   Trump, political damage, 170
   vaccines were launched, 174
   zoonotic origins, 175
*Crashed, How a Decade of Financial
   Crises Changed the World*, 43
Crenshaw, Kimberlé Williams, 126
critical national security decisions, 13
critical race theory, 123, 126
Cronkite, Walter, 102–103
Crow, Jim, 198
Cuban Missile Crisis, 10
cyberhacking, 156

Davos, 20, 71–76, 88
*Deaths of Despair and the Future of
   Capitalism*, 41
Deaton, Angus, 41–42
deep state, 34
Democrats. *See also* Republicans

anti-government rhetoric strategy,
  17
hyperpartisanship, 30
in 2000 elections, 32–33
questioning legitimacy of court, 33
legitimization of huge inflows of
  migrants, 44
ideological gap between
  Republicans and, 44
New Democrat centrism, 46
liberal or progressive, 111
Ginges study of, 205
Hispanics favor, 202
on Hillary Clinton 2016 election,
  151
support government activism, 238
voters increased from, 167
Deng Xiaoping, 53
DeSantis, Ron, 123
digital revolution, 100. *See also* social
  media
direct trust, 4–5
distrust
  effect on economic performance,
    14
  impact on health of society, 15
  inefficiency in system multiply, 14
  meaning of, 14–15
  negative effect on civic
    engagement, 13
  of big business, 13
  of government, 28
  of news media, 13
  of science and medicine, 13
  of technology, 13
  undermined prosperity, 14
Dow, Charles, 105

Downie Jr., Leonard, 113
Draper, Robert, 39
drive-by media, 100
Dukakis, Michael, 46, 103
Dungy, Tony, 183

Ebbers, Bernard, 64
Eichmeyer, Sarah, 161
Eisgruber, Christopher, 118
Elisha, Ety, 178
Elkind, Peter, 62
The End of Gender, 185
Enron, 62–63
environmental, social and governance
  goals (ESG investing principles),
  61, 79
European Management Forum, 70
extreme ideological movements, 36
Exxon Mobil, 145

Facebook Revolutions, 150
Facebook, 55, 94, 100, 109, 143,
  145–146, 150–151, 155, 158–159,
  161, 177, 206–207
fair and balanced slogan,100
fake news, 26, 92, 100, 150
Fauci, Anthony, 173–176
Faustian pact, 83
Federal Bureau of Investigation, 33
Fink, Lawrence, 78
Flight 93 election, 45
Floyd, George, 80, 107, 117, 126, 179,
  199, 201
Ford, Henry, 58, 146
Foundation for Individual, 124
The Fourth Industrial Revolution, 72
Fowler, James H., 161

Fox News, 94, 100, 102–104, 111, 243, 265
Freud, Sigmund, 178
Fried, Amy, 17
Fukuyama, Francis, 4

Gallup organization, 5–6, 33, 59, 98, 122, 200, 212, 229, 233, 238
Gates, Bill, 147
gender-transition surgery, 185
General Electric, 145
General Social Survey, 6
Gentzkow, Matthew, 161
Germany. *See* Weimar Republic
Gerth, Jeff, 96
Giordano, Joseph, 192–193
Glenn Youngkin, 123
Google, 140
    case of algorithmic discrimination, 141
    email system, 142
    fears about privacy, 143
    Gmail biased, 141
    no political choices, 142
    spam, campaign emails, 140
government, distrust in
    9/11 attacks, 38–39
    Afghanistan war, 38
    chronic economic debility, 41
    demographics, 41
    financial crisis, 42
    Great Recession, 42
    hyperpartisanship, 44–46
    Iraq conflict, 40
    landslides in election, 46
    polarization, 45
    political leadership failure, 37–44
    technocratic failure, 47–52
    to produce consistent and efficient rule, 28
    untrustworthy, 28
Gore, Al, 18, 32, 148
graveyard of empires, 39
The Great Reset, 72
The Great Reversal, How America Gave up on Free Markets, 84
greenhouse gases, 76
Greenspan, Alan, 48–50
Gresham's Law, 99
Greta Thunberg of Sweden, 188
Grullon, Gustavo, 84
Guetzkow, Jiosh, 178
Gutierrez, Rochelle, 127

Haidt, Jonathan, 129–130, 157–158
Harris, Douglas, 17
Harvard *Crimson*, 124
Hassan Ali Khan, 141
Hassan Iqbal, 141
Hemingway, Ernest, 125
HERI. See Higher Education Research Institute (HERI)
Higher Education Research Institute (HERI), 124
high-trust societies, 14
Hill, Jason, 128
Hilton, Steve, 25
Holmes, Elizabeth, 68
Huntington, Samuel, 70–71
Hussein, Saddam, 39
hyperpartisanship, 30, 37, 151, 217

The Idea of a University, 138
ideological homogeneity, 123

Iger, Bob, 55
infection fatality rate (IFR), 171
Inter-American Development Bank
    paper, 14
interpersonal trust, 4–5
intersectionality, defined as, 126–127
Ioannidis, John, 171

J. P. Morgan Chase, 65, 67
Jackson, Judge Ketanji Brown, 184
Jacobson, William, 115–116
Jefferson, Thomas, 98
Jim Crow 2.0, 81
Jobs, Steve, 58
Johnson, Lyndon B., 46
Jones, Edward, 105
Jordan, Michael, 82
Journal of Expertise, 105
Journal, 68, 89–92, 96, 105, 156, 158,
    242–243
journalism. *See also* journalists
    advertisement, 108–109
    audience find news to suit own
        interests and ideology, 110
    collapse of American, 92
    combat propaganda with facts, 91
    conservative media, 111
    conservative-leaning outlets, 112
    contrast to objective reporting, 100
    declining trust in, 108–109
    demographic and economic
        factors, 104
    demographic trend in, 106–107
    digital age, 109–110
    diligent reporting, 92
    erosion of trust, 92
    Fox News in 1990s, 104

free press, 98
    fundamental problem of, 92
    in 1950s, 104–105
    left-leaning staffs, 107, 110
    mainstream media, 111
    new generation domination in, 107
    objective reporting, 92–93
    partisan nature of news, 100
    partisanship, 110
    polarized news, 110
    principles guiding to success, 105
    reporting bias, 112
    revenue decline in, 109
    role of, 90
    subscriber-based model, 109–110
journalists, 92–93
    gatekeepers of news, 101
    graduated from nation's top
        universities, 105
    importance in society, 93
    left-leaning across all news outlets,
        111
    liberal or progressive, 111
    moral clarity vs. problematic idea
        of objectivity, 113–114
    registered Republican or
        Democrats, 111
    reporters from past vs. modern
        journalists, 106
    reporting bias vs. editorial bias, 112
    some become partisan players in
        political contest, 96

Kafka, Franz, 118
Katz, Joshua, 116–119
Kauffman Foundation, 24
Kavanaugh, Brett, 36, 112

Keefer, Philip, 14
Keeley, Terence, 78–79
Kendi, Ibram X., 128
Kennedy, John F., 151
Kennedy, John F., 46
Khan, Abraar, 180
Klainerman, Sergiu, 119
Koonin, Steven, 189
Koppel, Ted, 102
Kozlowski, Dennis, 63
Kroc, Ray, 58
Krugman, Paul, 95
Kulldorf, Martin, 179

Larkin, Yelena, 84
Lawrence Summers, 41
Lay, Kenneth, 62
legacy admissions policies, 133
Lehman Brothers, 65
Levi, Margaret, 13
liberal democratic capitalism, 10
liberal-leaning outlets, 111
Limbaugh, Rush, 100
LinkedIn, 154
Lippmann, Walter, 104–105
Lomborg, Bjorn, 189
Los Angeles Times, 110
low-trust societies, 14–15. *See also* tax
    evasion
Lukianoff, Greg, 129–130

The Magic Mountain, 75
Mann, Thomas, 75
Mao Zedong, 53, 149
Mao Zedong's Cultural Revolution,
    120
Martin, Brian, 178

Marx, Karl, 106
Massachusetts Institute of
    Technology, 137
McCain, John, 46
McCoy, Alfred W., 35
McGovern, George, 46
McLean, Bethany, 62
Mendoza Business School, 84
Meta Platforms, 145
Michaely, Roni, 84
Microsoft, 145
misinformation, 99
mistrust, 6–7
Mittell, Jason, 101
modern technology, 140–163
    alarm about privacy, 153
    annual trust survey, 144
    apps track users, 155
    behind health care, 144
    big tech companies, 158
    Bipartisan distrust of media, 152
    central monitoring, 149
    dependency on devices, 153
    exposure to smartphones, 157
    fears about privacy, 143
    feeds conspiracy theories, 142
    government agencies, 155
    history of *Homo sapiens*, 157
    in China, 149
    instant access to books, 147
    instant availability of information,
        147
    internet emerged in, 146
    loss in confidence, 140–144
    Marriott International, 155
    medical researchers, 157
    Pew survey in 2019, 154

promises of internet revolution, 144

punishment for offenses, 149

reasonable suspicions of political bias, 142

system of "social credit", 149

totalitarian governments, 148

wave of mistrust, 142

world of politics, 147

Worries about security, 155

Mondale, Walter, 46

More Human, 25

Moynihan, Senator Daniel Patrick, 12

Mueller, Robert, 95

Muhammad Shahzad, 141

Murdoch, Rupert, 100, 102

Musk, Elon, 110

mutual mistrust, 192–213

    corruption is, 195

    COVID pandemic isolation, 206

    debate among sociologists, 210

    economic inequality, 196–197

    growing isolation, 209

    more politically homogeneous, 208

    race, 198–205

    religious observance, 211–212

    social and cultural changes, 213

    trust in nuclear family, 211

    wealth inequality, 197–198

mutual trust, 194

National Basketball Association (NBA), 81–82

Nazi analogy, 138

neologisms, 125

net zero carbon emissions, 76

Netanyahu, Benjamin, 128

New Democrat centrism, 46

New York Post, 151

New York Times, 93, 95–97, 102, 105, 107–108, 110–111, 120, 154, 188, 205, 209

New Yorker, 93, 112

Newman, John Henry, 138

Nike, sportswear company, 82

Nixon, Richard, 46, 48, 217

NORC (formerly the National Opinion Research Center), 6

Nvidia, 145

Obama, Barack, 20, 31–32, 40, 45–46, 51, 53, 55, 55, 189, 217

Occupy Wall Street, 66

OpenAI, 152

Paine, Thomas, 28

Peng Liyuan, 54

Pentagon Papers, 98

Peralta, Dan-el Perilla, 127

Pew Research Center survey, 6, 15, 30, 44–45, 121

Pfizer, 145

Philippon, Thomas, 84–86

Pichai, Sundar, 140–141

Political Trust and Trustworthiness *paper*, 13

Ponzi scheme, 69

Porush, David, 146

post-truth era, 12

Public Opinion book, 104

Pulitzer Prize, 89

Putin, Vladimir, 95

Putnam, Robert, 8, 18–19, 194, 207

Quillette, 117–118
Quincey, James, 81

radical intellectual movement, 126
Ramaswamy, Vivek, 78, 83
Rasmussen Reports, 92
Rather, Dan, 103
Reagan, Ronald, 18, 29, 46, 48,
    192–194
Real Clear Education, 124
rebuilding trust, 214–240
    by big business, 220–221
    changes on both fronts, 216
    contemporary United States, 214
    cultural revolution, 235–240
    by education, 223–224
    going small and local, 229–232
    by government, 216–218
    improving performances, 232–235
    by media, 219–220
    modern pathology of American
        society, 214
    reducing inequality over, 225–229
    science and medicine, 224–225
    by technology, 222–223
    trust is like, 214
Republicans
    agree media is enemy of people, 92
    anti-government agenda, 17
    anti-Republican screeds, 35
    Capitol Hill riot, 31
    comprehensive immigration
        reform, 44
    decline in trust, 167
    for costing Trump election, 151
    fraudulent claims on Obama, 32
    Ginges study of, 205

ideological cap between
    Democrats and, 44
justices on the Court nominated
    by presidents of, 33
mistrust among, 34
Pew survey on, 45
proportion of, 238
pushing for removal of radical
    teaching curricula, 123
responsibility of politicians and
    supporters, 36
trust in government, 30–31
Reuters Institute for the Study of
    Journalism, 92
Ridley, Matt, 175–177
Rights in Education, 124
Roe v. Wade decision, 33, 102
Ronel, Natti, 178
Rowling, J. K., 186
Russian campaign, 151

Sachs, Goldman, 67
Safetyism, 129
Sailer, John, 164
Sandel, Michael, 135, 197
Sandman, Peter, 181
Scalise, Steve, 35–36
Scartascini, Carlos, 14
Schumer, Chuck, 34–35
Schwab, Klaus, 70, 72
Schyns, Peggy, 209
Scientific American, 182
Second Coming, 82
Self-selection, 132
Shir-Raz, Yaffa, 178
Shrier, Abigail, 161
Siberian Candidate, 95

Silicon Valley giants, 140
The Smartest Guys in the Room, 62
Smith, Adam, 3
Smith, Sam, 82
social capital, 4, 194
Social Indicators Research, 209
social media, 100, 161
Social Security and Medicare, 51
social trust, 194
Soh, Debra, 185–186
Spadaro, Giuliana, 15
Spam filtering algorithms, 141
Stearns, Bear, 65
Steube, Greg, 140–141
Stoker, Laura, 13
Strauss, Levi, 58
struggle sessions, 115–139. *See also* America
successive government programs. *See* Social Security and Medicare
Sullivan, Andrew, 107
Summers, Lawrence, 125
Super Bowl ads, 69
Sweet, James, 120
systemic racism, 119
systemic, 179

Talk radio, 100
tax evasion, 15
Tea Party, 65
Texas Tech University, 164–167
  breakthroughs in treatment of, 164
  cell biology candidate, 164–165
  confidence in work of scientists, 166
  faculty or research posts in, 164

submit a "diversity statement", 164
Theranos scandal, 67–68
TikTok, 159
To Start a War, 39
Tolstoy, Leo, 16
too big to fail phenomenon, 66–67
Tooze, Adam, 43
transgender, 185–186
Trump, Donald
  2016 election, 65, 89, 125, 151
  36 percent trust number reported for, 31
  a shock to American politics, 16
  articulated and exploited mistrust and discontent, 17
  character and behavior, 97
  claims of collusion with Russia, 34, 111
  confrontation between White House Corps and, 94–95
  conspiracy theories, 34–35
  crystallized a process, 97
  dominated political scene, 36
  election of, 125
  erosion of trust during presidency of, 92
  factors that characterized his campaign, 91
  false claims on elected Biden, 31
  full-frontal assault on cultural and political institutions in America, 16
  Hillary defeat to, 32
  inauguration crowd in 2017
  judges refused to uphold bogus claims of, 11
  loss of trust in, 37

Trump, Donald (*Cont.*)
  news organization deception and
    dishonesty of, 96
  outright advocacy journalism,
    96–97
  response to COVID pandemic, 44
  stolen election, 11
  stormed a session of Congress, 31
  threat from virus, 170
trust, 2. *See also* distrust; mistrust
  in Asia, 4
  efficacy of relationships, 4
  evolution of, 3–4
  network of, 4
  significance of, 4
  system on, 5
  in United States, 4
*Trust: The Social Virtues and the
  Creation of Prosperity,* 4
Tryon, Chuck, 101
Tyco, 63–64
The Tyranny of Merit, 197

UN environment program, 188
US National Survey, 157
Usman Mahmood Khan, 141

Vallier, Kevin, 195
van Prooijen, Jan-Willem, 15
Vedder, Richard, 129

Vietnam War, 36
Viral, 175

Walensky, Rochelle, 174
Wall Street Journal, 23, 68, 89, 96,
  105, 108–109, 156, 158, 164, 189,
  220, 265
Walt Disney Company, 81
Wang, Haiyan, 15
Warta, Ashlynn, 129
Washington Post, 17, 95, 97, 110–111, 113
Watergate, 98–99, 106, 217, 233
The Wealth of Nations, 3
Wired 25. *See* Ebbers, Bernard, 64
Wokenomics, 83
Women, definition of, 184–185
Woodward, Bob, 106
World Economic Forum (WEF), 70
World Trade Center, 93
Worldcom, 64
Wuhan, 175

Xi Jinping, 53

Yahoo, 154
Yale University, 133–134
yellow journalism, 104

Zoom videoconferencing, 154
Zuckerberg, Mark, 55, 150

GERARD BAKER WAS Editor in Chief of the *Wall Street Journal* between 2013 and 2018. He is now the *Journal*'s Editor at Large, writing the weekly "Free Expression" column for the paper and hosting a podcast of the same name. He also writes a weekly column for the *Times of London*, is a regular commentator on Fox News, and appears on a range of national and international media.

In a career in journalism that spans more than three decades he has also worked for the BBC and the *Financial Times*.